Thank you!

Thank you so much for choosing this book!

Preface

Hi! Are you interested in designing, simulating and manufacturing three-dimensional objects using Autodesk's Fusion 360?

This book is for you! I am an engineer and would like to introduce you to Fusion 360 in a simple and easy to understand way. By the way, you can use Fusion 360 as a private user with a hobby license for FREE!

Use this link for downloading:

https://www.autodesk.de/products/fusion-360/free-trial

This comprehensive and detailed course is specifically for beginners/intermediates and shows from the very beginning how CAD designs, animations, simulations and production planning, succeed. In addition to theoretical explanations on the use of the software and design methodology, you will learn in this course on the basis of practical and exciting design projects!

In this course you will learn everything you need to know about Fusion 360 as a beginner or intermediate! Get started with Fusion 360 with this book today! Let's go!

Table of Contents

1 Introduction: Scope and Software

1.1 What to expect and what you will learn in this course

Hi there and welcome to the Fusion 360 course for beginners and intermediates!

In this course you will find an introduction to the basics of the multifunctional program Fusion 360 from Autodesk and will learn in particular CAD design, animation, simulation and manufacturing of components and much more in detail. I will share with you my knowledge as an engineer from study and professional practice, so that you will get an optimal learning experience with theoretical basics on the one hand, and practical examples on the other hand. Therefore, after a theoretical introduction, this course includes many practical design examples to make the learning process as easy and efficient as possible for you.

And with Fusion 360 from Autodesk, as with other CAD programs, you can not only design. Rather, this program combines and integrates several engineering disciplines such as CAD ("Computer Aided Design"), CAM ("Computer Aided Manufacturing") and FEM ("Finite Element Method"), summarized as CAE ("Computer Aided Engineering"), in one platform. Thus, Fusion 360 can be used not only to create parts or assemblies, but also to perform simulations and animations, as well as to create programming for a CNC machine. The main focus of this course is on how to design with Fusion 360, i.e. the CAD part of the program. However, the other features of Fusion 360 will not be neglected, so don't worry!

As mentioned earlier, the abbreviation CAD stands for "Computer Aided Design". CAD software is used to create or edit three-dimensional objects. Starting with simple individual parts, to complex parts, up to entire assemblies that can be virtually assembled.

In this course, especially designed for beginners, you'll learn how the environment of Fusion 360 is structured and how to make the most of each feature for creating three-dimensional objects. You'll be able to follow each design, animation and simulation project step-by-step and one-by-one, in order to get an easy start and become more familiar with the program's multiple functions with each project.

If you are also interested in 3D printing, you can even materialize the objects afterwards by simply printing them out. Check out my book 3D Printing 101 for this.
In short, this course will teach you the following in detail:

- quickly and confidently finding your way in Fusion 360
- mastering all important functions of Fusion 360 quickly and with confidence

- learning the basics of CAD design and the different ways of working
- creating 2D sketches and 3D objects in Fusion`s Design area
- creating parts and assemblies in Fusion`s Design area
- Rendering and animating parts and assemblies
- simulating single parts and assemblies, i.e. apply loads and display stresses and strains (FEM simulations)
- learn about the computer-aided manufacturing process in Fusion 360 (CAM) and prepare a simple part for milling operations
- get to know the drawing environment in Fusion 360 and create engineering drawings, also using a practical example

It is best to stay in the order that the course provides, as the lessons build on each other. If you do not understand functions or commands right away or miss the explanation for a function, just stay tuned. The course is structured in such a way that all important and basic functions are sufficiently explained. However, sometimes this is done in another chapter in order to make the course as clear and practical as possible and to be able to convey a very intuitive approach to Fusion 360 as well as to design itself.

1.2 Fusion 360 and software download

Fusion 360 from Autodesk offers a clear and simple user interface and is also available free of charge for non-commercial/hobby users as a so-called personal license! This version has a somewhat limited range of functions, but is perfectly adequate for private and hobby users. For all users who want to use Fusion 360 commercially, there is a paid full version starting at currently 60 $ per month.

After creating a user account with Autodesk, you can choose one of the two versions after comparing the range of functions. But as I said, if you are a private or hobby user, you can definitely choose the free version! Here you have to cut back in the area of "Generative Design" and "Simulation", because for the use of these two functions you need a paid license, but for hobby and private users these functions are often not necessary at all. You will learn later what you can do with these two functions. However, as a home user, you can also just start with the free version and still upgrade later if you need to. You can download Fusion 360 directly online at:
https://www.autodesk.de/products/fusion-360/free-trial
after creating a user account.

The structure of the design features is relatively identical for all common CAD programs used by engineers and technicians in their daily work. Mostly other professional CAD program licenses like SolidWorks, Catia, SolidEdge or AutoCAD and Autodesk Inventor are used, which cost one to several thousand dollars and are therefore usually only worthwhile for professional users and freelancers. With these programs, however, you can at least usually download a trial version for 30 days or even more. As a student you could get a free student license for the duration of your studies.

And now let's get started! Before we get to the basics of CAD design, we will make general program settings and familiarize ourselves with the program interface and functions.

2 Preparation: Getting started with Fusion 360

2.1 General Settings

When we first start the program, we are asked to create or join a team. This is necessary and useful because Fusion 360 is very good for working on files and projects across users. Click on "Create Team" or join a team you belong to. When you create a new team, you can assign any name for the team. Optionally, you can then invite people to join the team to work together on projects, if you want to.

Figure 1: After the first start of the program a team must be created

We then enter the Fusion 360 program environment.

Let's first check a few general program settings to create a same starting situation. To do this, click on your user account icon in the upper right corner and then select "Preferences".

Figure 2: Open the general program settings "Preferences"

A window for the general settings opens.

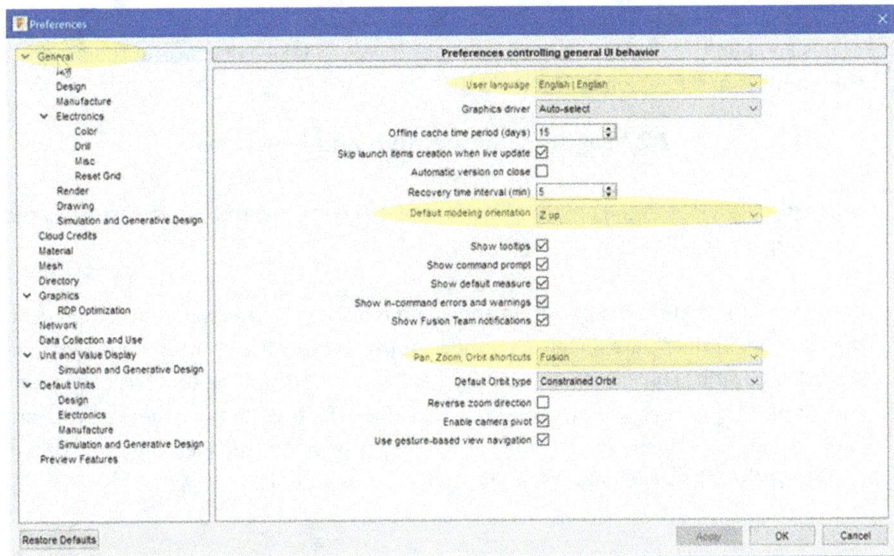

Figure 3: General settings in the "General" section

In the "General" section, you can set the program language. We of course stay in English. First of all, check whether "z up" is selected in the "Default modeling orientation" field and whether "Fusion 360" is selected in the "Pan, Zoom, Orbit Shortcuts" field.

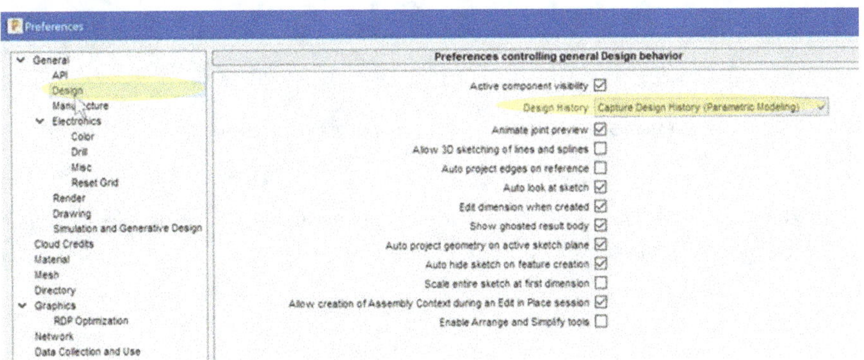

Figure 4: General settings in the "General" → "Design" section

In addition, we want to make sure that "Capture Design History (Parametric Modeling)" is selected in the "Design" section. Other important settings can be found under "Default units". Here you can set the default units for each part of the software. In our case we want to use the metric system, so we check that in "Design", "Electronics", "Manufacture" and "Simulation and Generative Design" the unit "mm" is selected in each case. All other settings are optional, and can be changed to your liking. If you wish, simply click your way through the individual sections. Otherwise we accept the set values and quit the settings. In the next chapter we will take a first look at the program environment and functions of Fusion 360.

2.2 Program Environment and Functions

Let's first take a look at the program environment and the menu bars, which are located in the upper and side areas.

At the top left, there is the option to show and hide the "Data Panel", which opens on the left side. In this "Data Panel" all projects for the respective team can be managed, as well as libraries and examples can be called up. In the bar at the top, basic functions and notifications can also be accessed. The "Job Status" shows whether you are currently working online in the cloud or offline, i.e. whether the files you are working on are synchronized with your team, if you have one, or not.

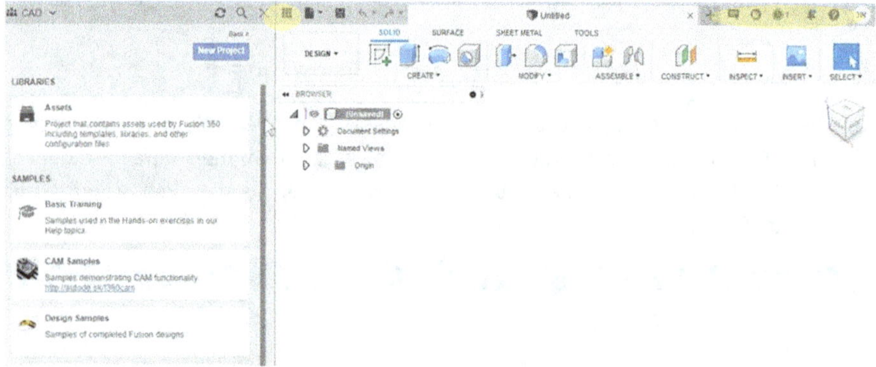

Figure 5: Execution of basic commands in the bar at the top

With the highlighted selection tab of the main menu bar, it is possible to switch between the individual sub-functions of Fusion 360.

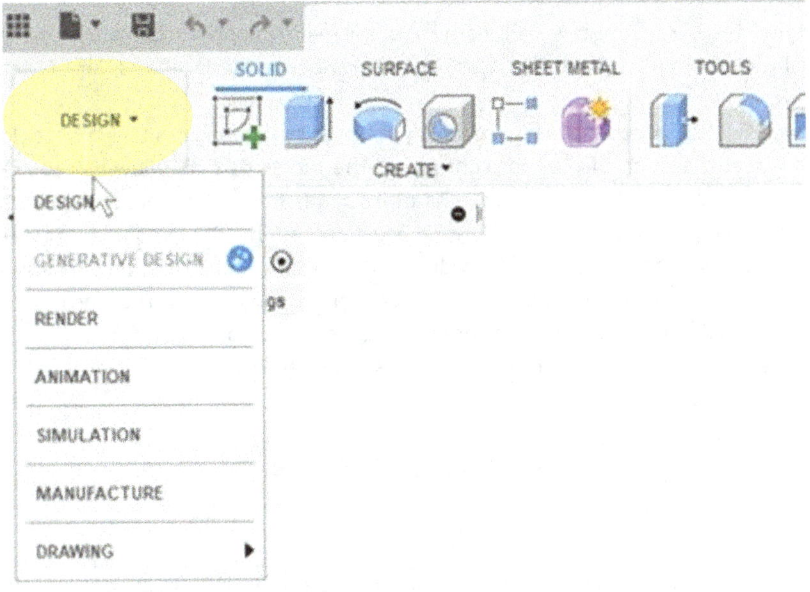

Figure 6: The choice between the individual sections of Fusion 360

In this first section we will deal with the "Design" sub-function, i.e. CAD.

There are five different menu tabs in the Design section. "Solid", "Surface", "Mesh", "Sheet metal" and "Tools". Apart from "Tools", these menu tabs have an identical structure. They contain the sections "Create", "Modify", "Assemble", "Construct", "Inspect", "Insert" and "Select", respectively.

Figure 7: The different tabs in the Design section

Depending on what you want to design, you have to choose one of the three sections. If you want to create a solid, you remain in the "Solid" section, if you only want to create a surface, you use the "Surface" section and if you want to create a sheet metal part, you switch to the "Sheet metal" tab. In this course we will mainly deal with the "Solid" section, which covers all the important design features of a basic course. We will leave out the "Tools" section, as we will learn about the features of this tab in other positions. Finally, we will discuss the differences and peculiarities of "Surface" and "Sheet Metal".

As we said, the three tabs have a relatively identical structure. Let's take a closer look. The "Create" section of the tabs contains all the functions that, allow you to create something. In the "Modify" area, on the other hand, are all the functions with which you can change an object that has already been created. The "Assemble" area contains all the functions for assembling individual parts and the "Construct" area contains all the tools for construction, such as planes, axes or auxiliary points. The "Inspect" area contains tools for analyzing curves or the mass properties of a part, for example. The last areas "Insert" and "Select" are relatively self-explanatory.

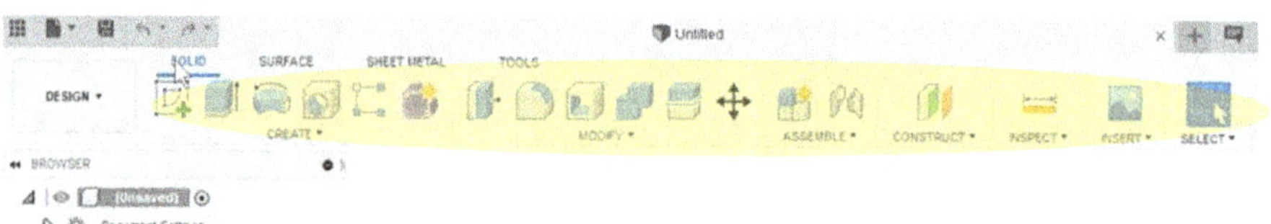

Figure 8: Commands of the individual menu sections in the "Design" area

Don't be afraid of the multitude of elements and features, in the progress of the course we will get to know the individual elements step by step and in detail by means of a practical way of working. Therefore, only this short summary.

If we look at the drawing area, we can find the browser of the design project in the left area. Here we find specific settings for the document unit, which we can edit by clicking on the small pencil icon. Furthermore, all views, as well as the origin, the layers and the axes are provided here. However, the main function of this structure tree is to list the created components, bodies, construction elements, etc. in order to be able to activate / deactivate or edit them. We will get to know how this works later on.

It is also very good if you get used to name the individual components, joints and perhaps even sketches and layers right from the start, in order to find your way around more easily later. Simply double-click on the element and enter a new name.

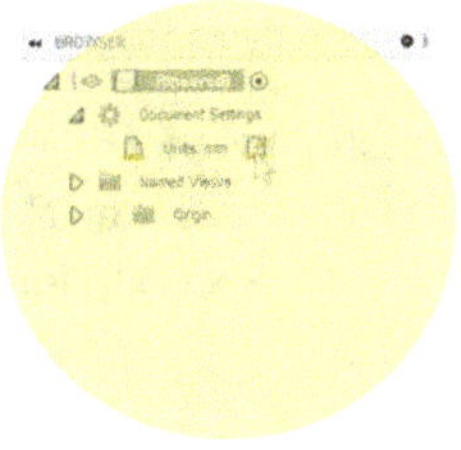

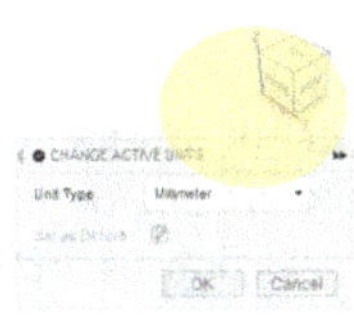

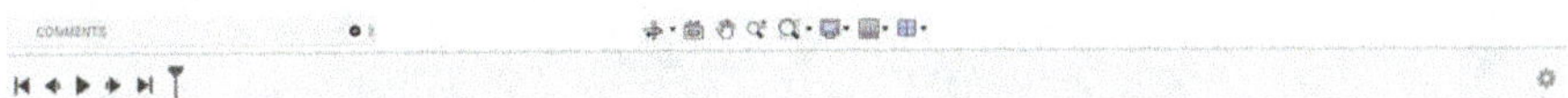

Figure 9: The "Browser" of the file with individual folders

In the upper right area there is the orbit cube. Here you can select views of the current design and rotate the drawing environment including the object.

Rotation of the drawing environment is also possible by holding down the SHIFT key and moving the mouse at the same time. Moving is possible with the mouse wheel pressed and a mouse movement. Zooming is done as usual by turning the mouse wheel.

With a right click with the mouse, we can call up the quick selection menu, with which a variety of commands can be executed quickly. Move back and forth between the menus without clicking.

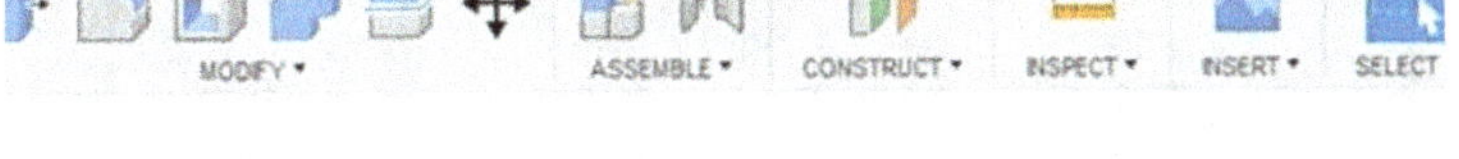

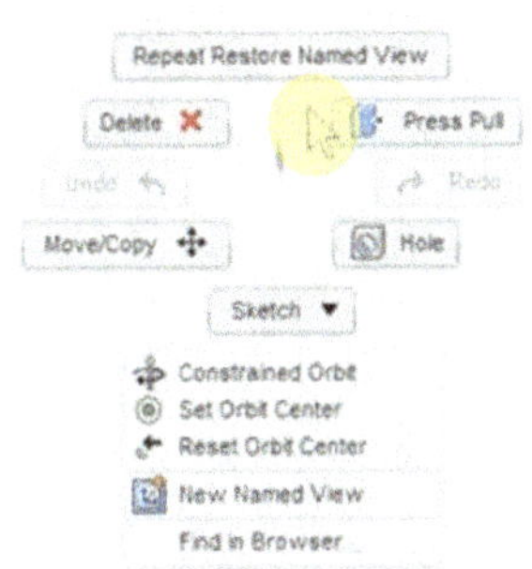

Figure 10: Quick selection menu (open with a right-click on the drawing layer)

In the lower area of the drawing environment, there is the possibility of noting comments on the design at the bottom left, and in the middle area there is a quick selection bar that can also be used to make a few basic operations, especially for visualization.

Finally, the bar at the very bottom is the timeline, in which the individual processing steps are listed and can be easily followed chronologically. We will see what this means later on.

Figure 11: Lower area of the drawing environment

Very good, now we can easily navigate in the program environment and can start with the next chapter.

As already mentioned, common CAD programs work in a very identical way. Let us now take a look at this way of working.

Section I: CAD Construction / Design

3 Basics of CAD: Function and Methodology

3.1 2D sketching environment

Each 3D component must first be started as a 2D sketch. This is where we define the blueprint of the object. Imagine that you are taking a look at the top of a simple three-dimensional object. For example, what do you see when you look at a cylinder from above, at a perfect right angle to the axis?

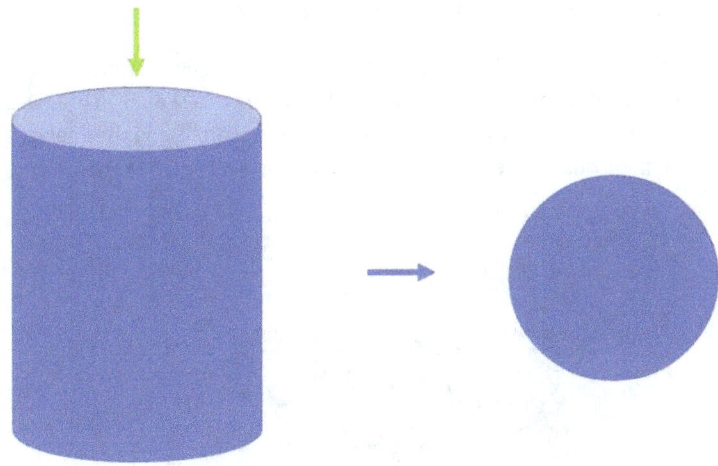

Figure 12: A three-dimensional cylinder has a 2D circle as its basic shape

Correct, a two-dimensional circle, nothing else. And it is exactly from this 2D shape that the cylinder, analogous to all other elements, is created in the program. In the first step, we have to draw this circle for creating the object. The three-dimensional shape is then obtained by further command steps. For the 2D sketch, e.g. the top surface of an object, a side surface, or the section of the part can be used . This requires somewhat spatial imagination.

Before we make the first 2D sketch, you can, if you want to, uncheck "Layout Grid", i.e. "Design Grid" for the 3D environment in the lower menu bar. Then the grid is suppressed and you get a gridless layout, which in my opinion displays the designed object in a more puristic way. However, this setting is a matter of taste and does not necessarily have to be made.

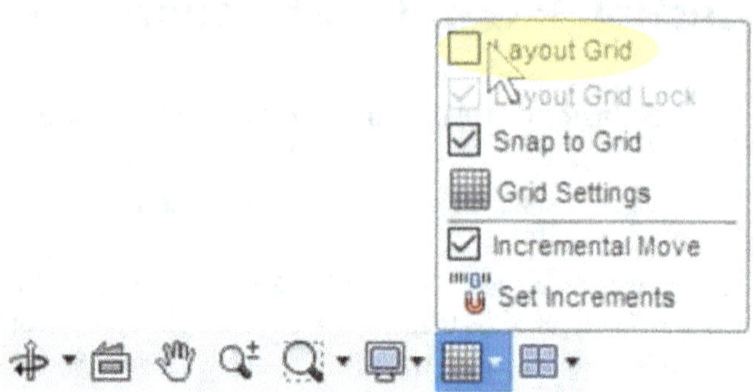

Figure 13: Deactivate "Layout Grid" in the lower area of the drawing environment if required

Let us now try to design our first component. To do this, as already mentioned, we must first create a two-dimensional sketch. At the beginning of a sketch, in the "Design" area and in the "Create" drop-down menu, select "Create Sketch" and then select a plane of the three-dimensional space on which we want to draw the 2D sketch.

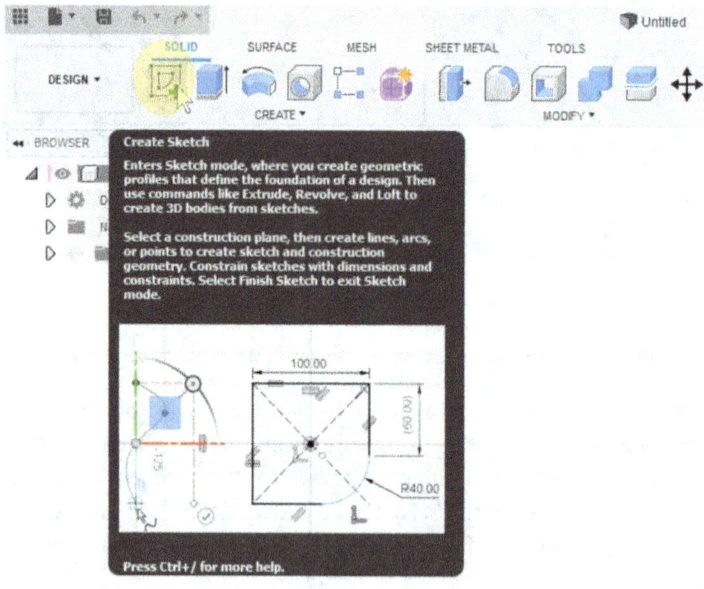

Figure 14: Select "Create Sketch"

Alternatively, you can also select the sketching plane in the browser on the left side. In our example with the cylinder, we want to look at the circular surface or top surface from above, so we should select the x-y plane, i.e. the plane that is formed by the x and y axes.

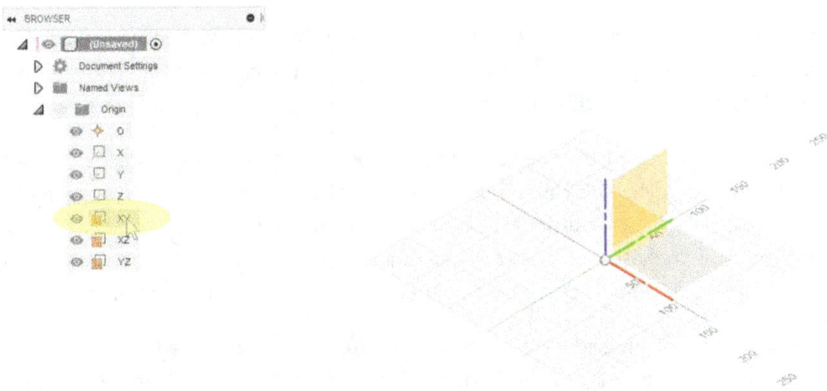

Figure 15: Select a sketching plane, e.g. the x-y plane

Which plane you choose is basically only important for the alignment of the views. The program then opens the selected sketching layer. As you will notice, the menu bar "Sketch" automatically opens in the upper area, with which you can create 2D geometry elements and modify them, as well as create the so-called "constraints" or dependencies, which are also called: connections, links or conditions in other programs.

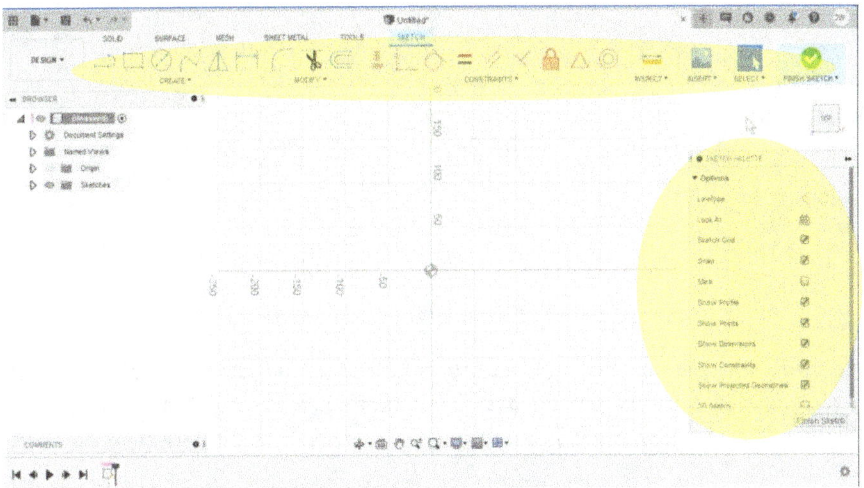

Figure 16: 2D sketching environment in Fusion 360

In addition, the familiar menu items "Inspect", "Insert" and "Select", as well as the option to exit the 2D sketching plane. Furthermore the "Sketch Palette" on the right side with helpful options for the view and with settings for the sketching environment.

For creating the geometry of a 2D sketch, a variety of basic drawing elements are available. By selecting a "line", for example, a geometry can be formed from line-shaped elements. Let's try this out.

Just click on any point, e.g. on the center of the coordinate system and start a drawing by clicking and dragging with your mouse. The drawing should correspond, for example, to the cross-section of the desired 3D object, or, in the case of simple objects, to the upper surface or cross-sectional area of the object. Enter the desired dimensions using your keyboard. You can switch between dimension and angle using the tab key.

You can also draw freely and use the displayed values as a guide, or add or change the dimensions and angles later. If the options "Sketch Grid" and "Snap" are activated in the "Sketch Palette", you can select the grid points of the drawing environment using your mouse as if it they were magnetic. The small icons that appear are the "constraints" for each element. We'll take a closer look at these in a moment.

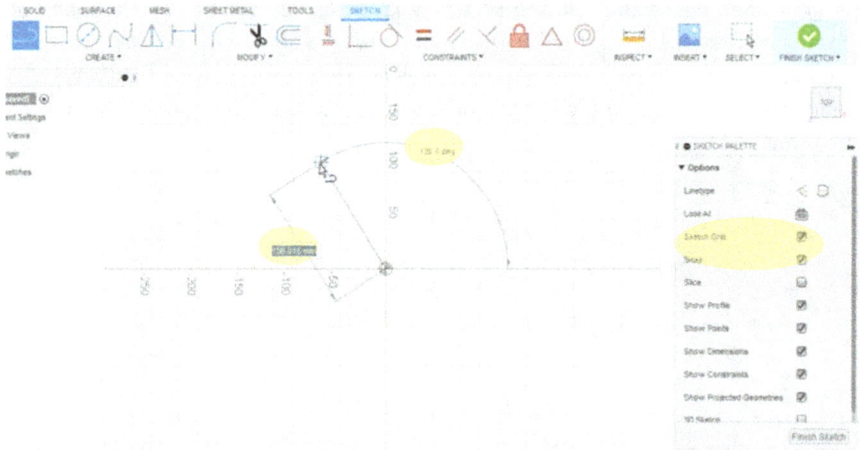

Figure 17: The first line of a 2D sketch

Besides a line, you can also create a circle, an ellipse, a spline, an arc, an oblong hole or a rectangle. Let's just try that too, one after another. In the "Create" menu you will also find: a point, various arcs and other elements, as well as the possibility to create dimensions.

It is best to try out all the elements at least once. To do this, simply pause briefly and start by yourself in the sketching environment of the CAD program. It is best to use this approach throughout the course. This is the most effective way to learn.

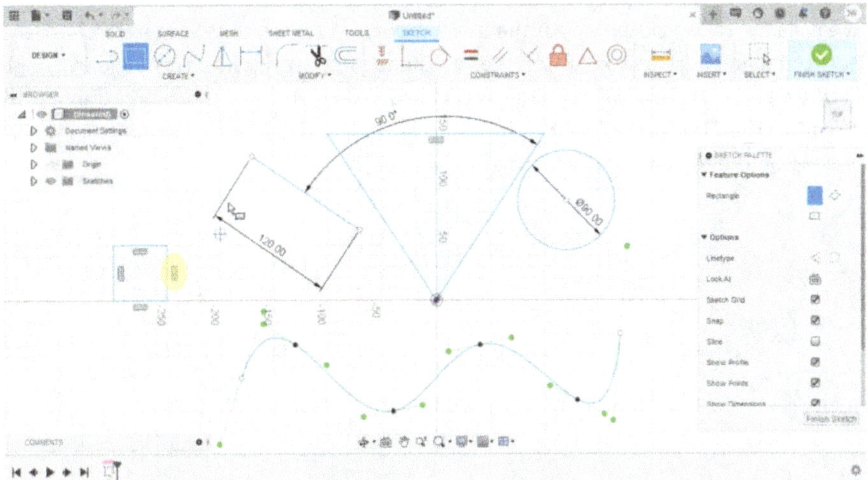

Figure 18: First sketching exercises in the 2D sketching area

One more tip for geometry elements such as rectangle or circle: When drawing, you will notice that the rectangle, for example, always starts from a corner. However, if you want the rectangle to start from the center, you can make the often very helpful setting "Center Rectangle" or "3-point rectangle" in the "Sketch Palette" under "Feature Options". This setting option is also available for other elements, such as the circle, where you can - if desired - also create a tangential circle. Take a look at the "Sketch Palette" from time to time when using the other elements as well. For each element there are different functions.

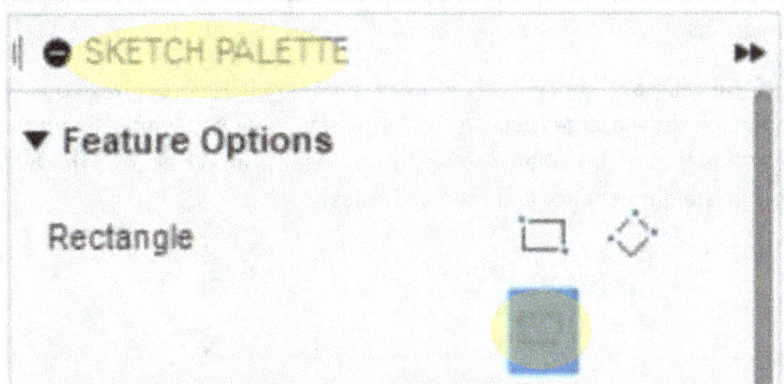

Figure 19: Draw a rectangle starting from a center point

Before we conclude this chapter, let's get acquainted with the world of "constraints" as promised. You can use these in the 2D sketching environment and use them to create constraints between individual geometric elements. This is sometimes, but not always, necessary or helpful.

We will now take a closer look at the most important "constraints". Let's start with the horizontal and vertical constraints. Let's assume we try to draw a rectangle freehand and we get a polygon whose lines unfortunately do not represent a rectangle. By selecting the "horizontal" constraint, we can get two perfectly horizontal lines by clicking on the top and bottom lines.

Figure 20: Use of "constraints"

In an identical way, we apply the "vertical" condition to the lateral lines and end up with a rectangle. As we can see, these conditions are displayed as small symbols next to the respective line and are also already suggested when creating a sketch. However, in the "Sketch Palette" you can hide these conditions, as well as areas, points and dimensions.

With the relation "concentric" you can set two circle structures concentric to each other. Let's draw a large circle and a slightly smaller one. We want to get two concentric circles, i.e. two circles where the centers are identical. We achieve this by selecting the appropriate dependency and the two circles.

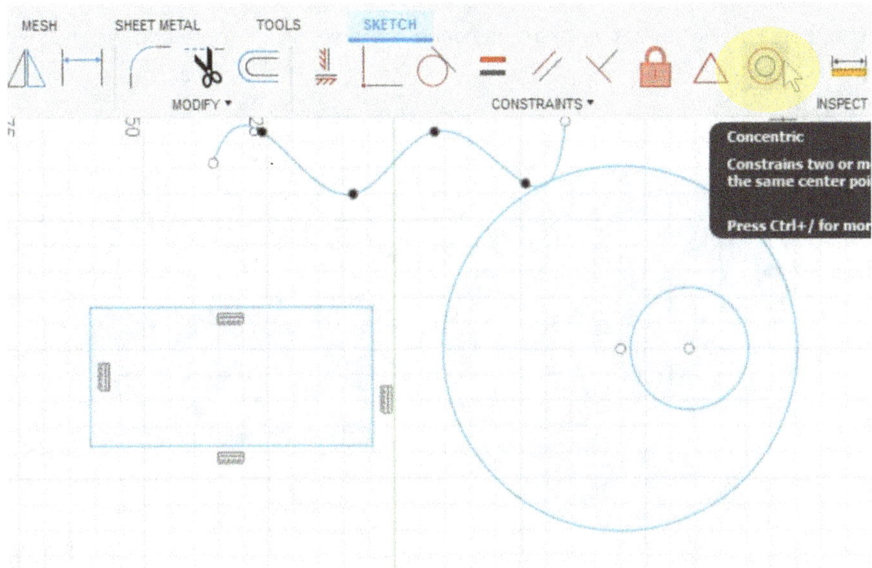

Figure 21: "Concentric"

The two "constraints": "Perpendicular" and "Parallel" are relatively self-explanatory. Nevertheless, let's look at a small example with two lines each. For the function "Perpendicular" we draw the following two lines. By selecting the condition and selecting the lines, we get two lines that are perpendicular to each other.

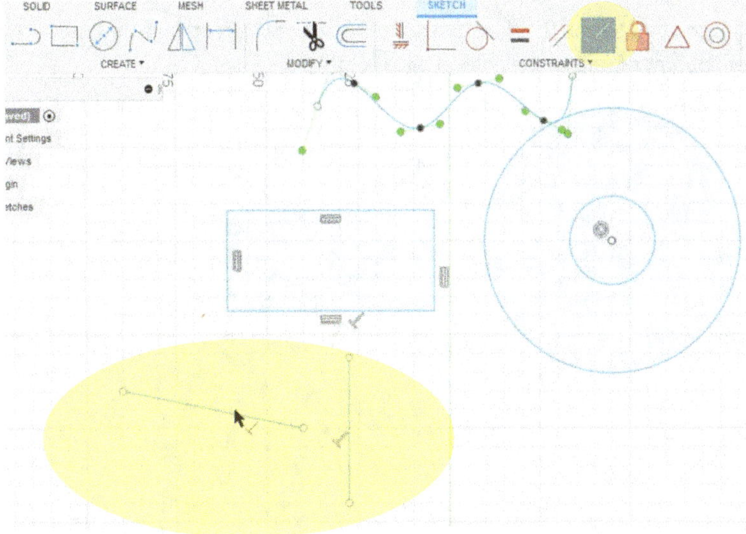

Figure 22: The "Perpendicular" constraint

For "Parallel" we draw two more lines and by selecting the condition we get two perfectly parallel lines.

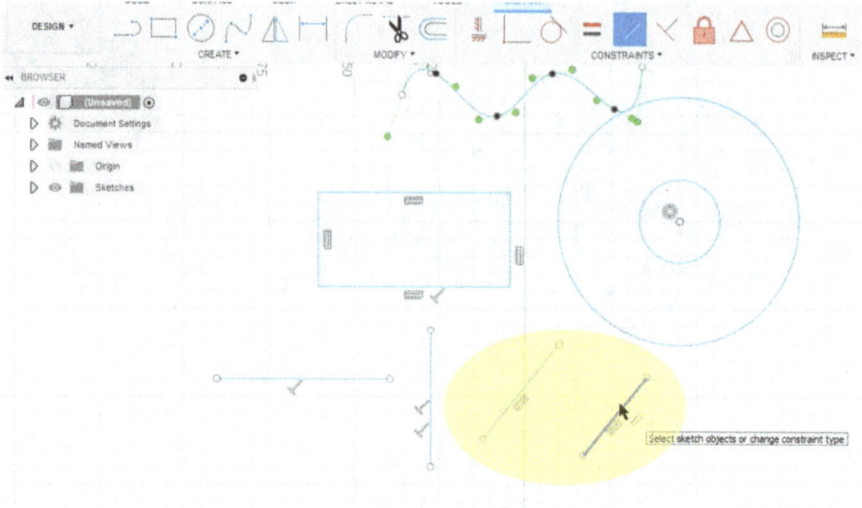

Figure 23: The constraint "Parallel"

We use the "constraints": "Coincident", i.e. congruent, and "Midpoint", whenever we want to connect two points or connect a point of one element with the midpoint of another element. To illustrate, let's draw a rectangle and two lines.

We want to connect the first line to a corner point of the rectangle and the second line to the midpoint of one of the lines of the rectangle.

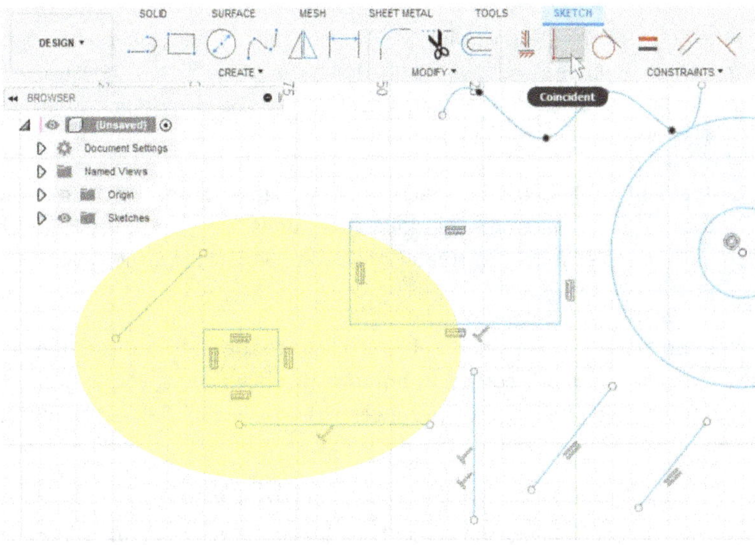

Figure 24: Constraints "Coincident" and "Midpoint"

By the way: You can also apply several "constraints". For example, we could also apply the condition horizontally to a line.

Let's have a look at the condition "Tangent". As the name and the small picture already indicate, we can use it to set a line tangential to a circle, for example. Let's try it out. First draw the circle, then a line and then apply the condition.

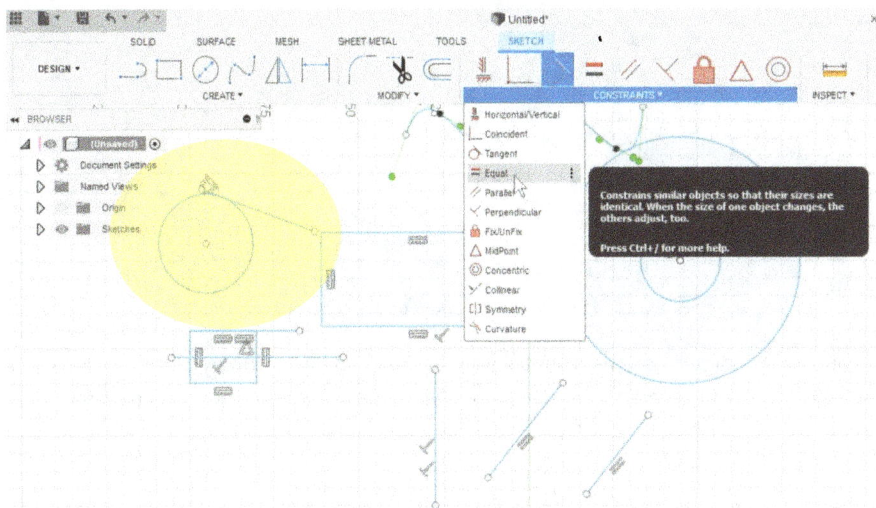

Figure 25: Constraint "Tangent" and other available constraints

Just try the two remaining "Constraints": "Fix/Unfix" and "Equal" for yourself. You can't go wrong and the name is relatively self-explanatory. The "Fixed" constraint simply fixes an element in place and "Equal" ensures that the same dimensioning exists between elements.

To finish these first 2D sketching exercises, please draw another circle in a new file, which you can then provide with fictitious dimensions using the "Sketch Dimension" function. For example, select a diameter of 50 mm. Simply draw the circle and select the "Sketch Dimension" tool.

There are two ways to do this, both of which lead to the goal: You can draw a circle with the dimensions already correct by entering the values using your keyboard while drawing. Use the Tab key to switch between the individual fields for entering the dimensions.

Alternatively, you can draw any circle and then change the dimensions. You do this with the function "Sketch Dimension" / "Sketch Dimension" and a double click on the dimension. Then enter the desired value and confirm with Enter.

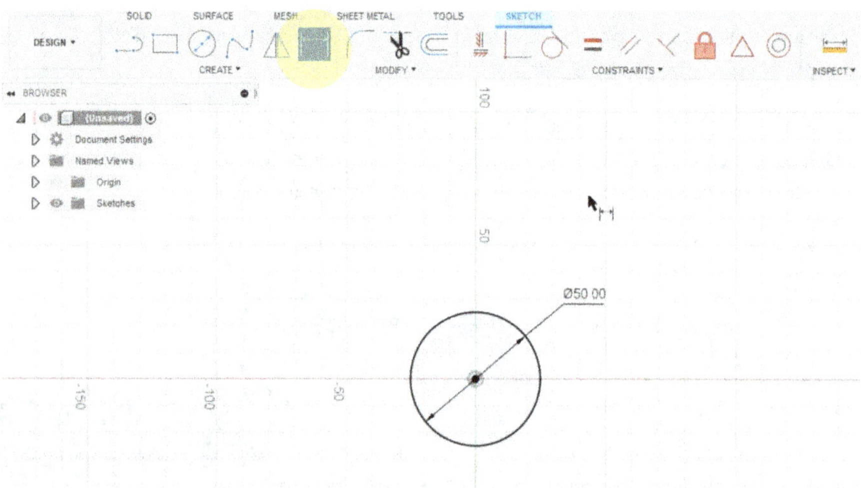

Figure 26: A simple circle, started on the center of coordinates

You can also dimension the distance between two lines. To do this, simply click first on the first line and then on the second line whose distance you want to dimension.

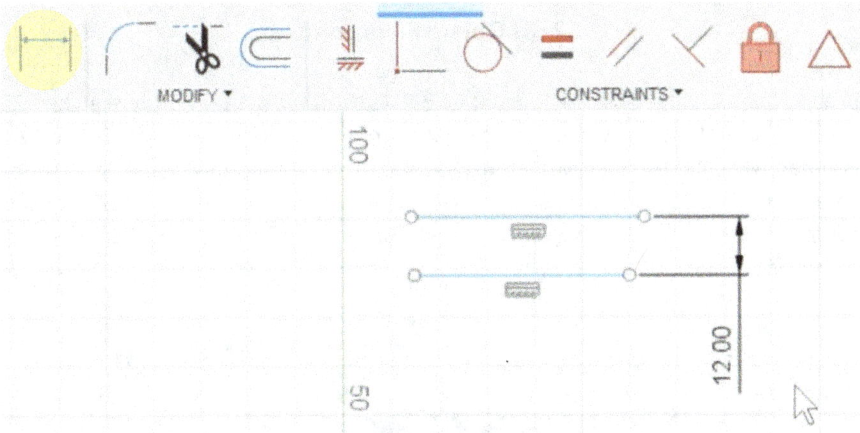

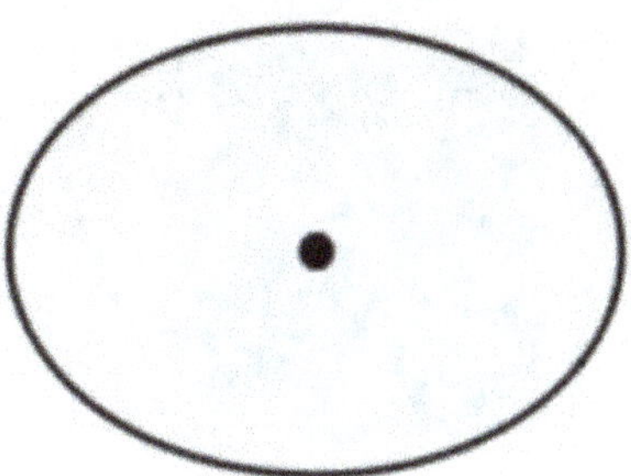

Figure 27: Dimension the distance between two lines

You can then exit sketch mode with the green check mark in the top menu bar.

To create a three-dimensional object, it is important that the sketch is completely enclosed and has no gaps. This is indicated by the light blue area that fills the surface of the sketch in 3D mode. It means that the sketch has continuous boundary lines without gaps and thus represents an enclosed surface.

Figure 28: Sketched circular area in 3D mode with blue background

After finishing the sketch, move the design environment with your mouse or by using the coordinate cube in the upper right corner. By the way, you can double-click your mouse wheel to fit an object into the current view, which is very helpful if you ever find yourself very far away in virtual space and can't see any object.

In the next chapter we will create a three-dimensional object from the 2D sketch we made. Very good, you are making good progress!

Soon we will already get to the first real design project!

3.2 3D Object Environment

In this chapter, we would like to create a 3D object from the previously sketched 2D surface. To do this, we will use the functions from the "Create" section. To create a cylinder, we will use probably the most needed function from this menu. We use the command "Extrude" / "Extrusion". This function represents a so-called extrusion command. In other CAD programs you will therefore often find the name "Linear Extrusion" or similar.

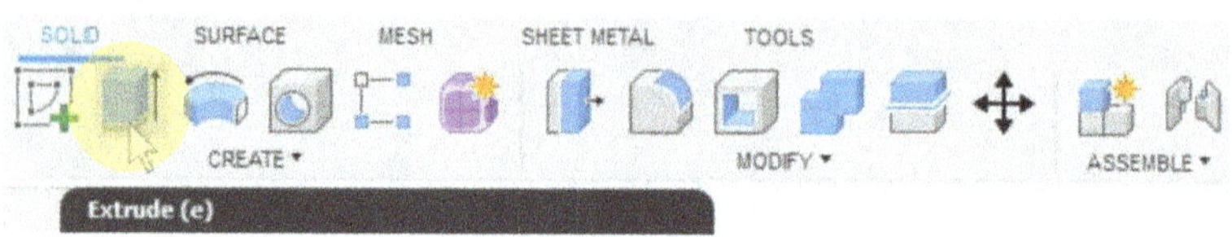

Figure 29: The "Extrude" command in the Create area

Now simply select the function and the surface and, after selecting the blue arrow that appears, move your mouse within the possible range of motion and create a 3D object in this way. Alternatively, you can also enter the desired dimension and confirm with Enter.

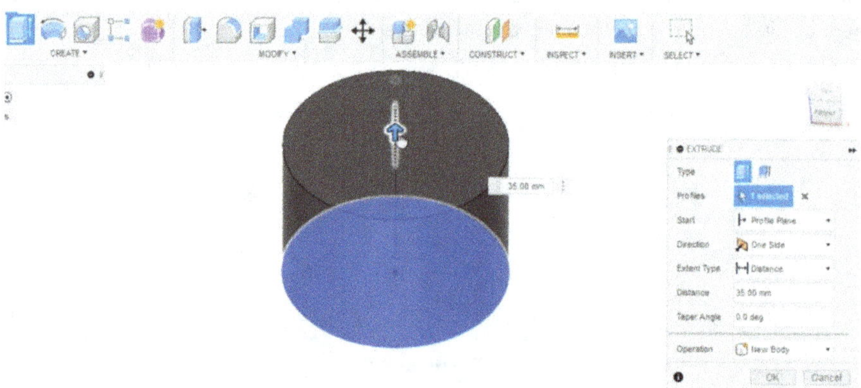

Figure 30: Use the "Extrude" command to create a 3D body from the 2D surface

Before we take a look at the other commands from "Create", we will use the cylinder to first get to know the most important commands from the "Modify" section. We use this section whenever we want to modify an object. For example, we can use the function "Fillet" to round one or more edges. Simply select the function and select one or more edges. Again, an arrow appears, which we use in the same way as for the "Extrude" command. In the additional window that appears, we can change other options if necessary.

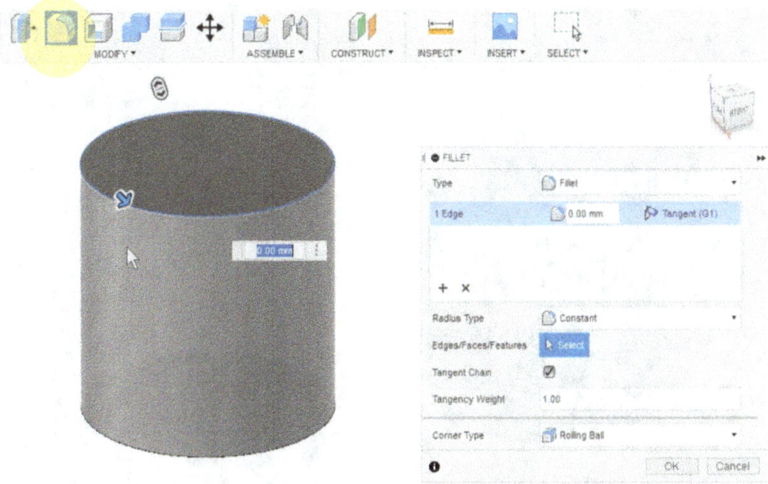

Figure 31: Use the "Fillet" command to make edge fillets

In an analogous way to this, we can create a chamfer with "Chamfer".

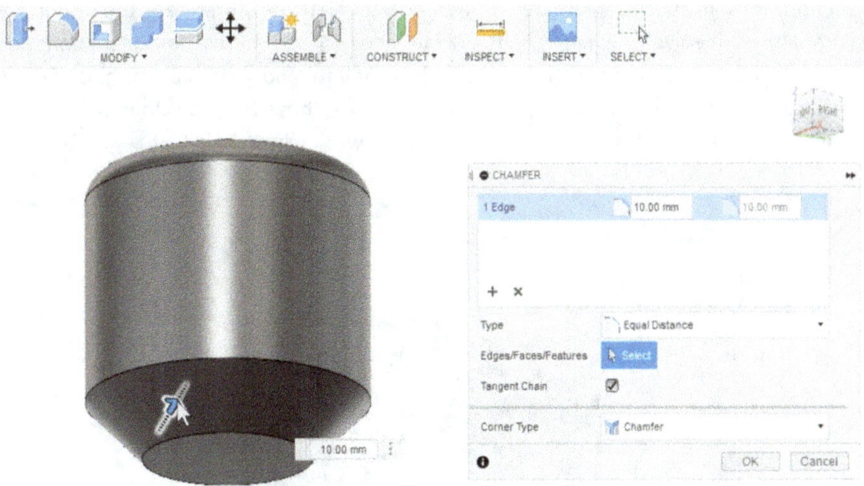

Figure 32: Create a chamfer using the "Chamfer" command from "Modify"

With the very versatile "Press Pull" command, we can make a variety of changes to an object in a very quick way. For example, depending on the selected face or edge, we can make a fillet or simply change the diameter or dimension of the object. Another important command is "Shell". With the help of this command you can easily hollow out an object, i.e. create a thin-walled 3D object. Select the command and the top surface of the cylinder and enter a wall thickness or use the arrow.

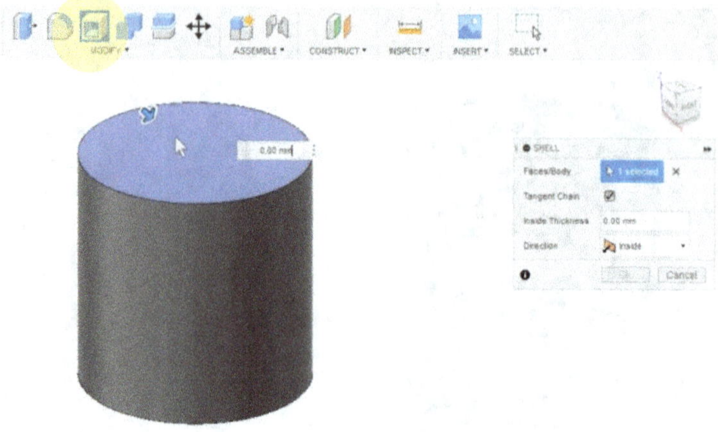

Figure 33: Use "Shell" to hollow out an object

Pretty simple, isn't it? Now that we know the most important commands from this section, let's get back to "Create". In addition to "Extrude", there are the important commands "Revolve", "Sweep", "Loft", "Hole" and "Thread" here. The explanations and example images of the software are very clear, helpful and give us a first hint of what these commands can do. We will look at how to use these functions in more detail in the next chapter, as this is related to the way we work when designing.

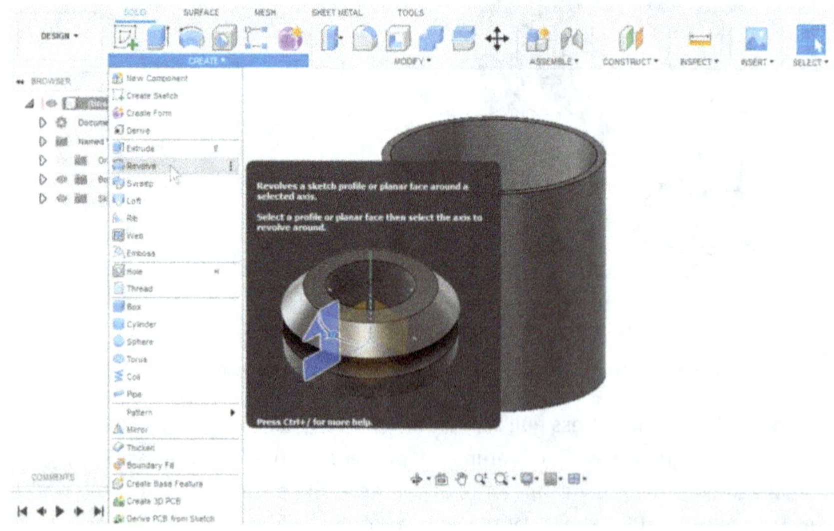

Figure 34: All functions from the "Create" menu

By the way, in Fusion 360 it is also possible to shorten the process from 2D sketch to 3D object by combining both steps for some elements. For example, we can directly build a cuboid, a cylinder, a sphere and other elements with the respective command. Just select the command, sketch the base profile on a plane in the 3D environment, and extrude the element. And now, on to the next chapter!

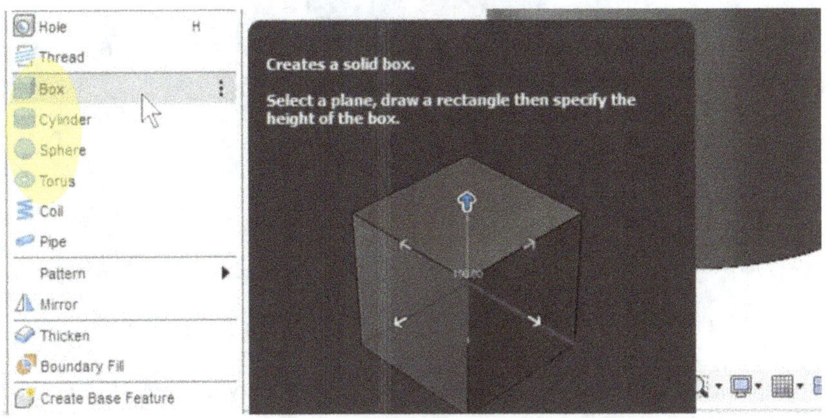

Figure 35: Commands from "Create" to quickly create solids

3.3 Design Methodology

As already briefly mentioned in the previous chapter, there are different approaches to the design of 3D objects. One possible approach to the design is, for example, to design as the actual machining - e.g. a milling or turning of a starting material, the so-called semi-finished product - would proceed. In the CAD program, you first create the raw material, in this case, for example, a cuboid material, and then work on it successively in further steps - using cutouts, holes, fillets and other design features, so that you get the final element. That is why this method of design is called subtractive. You reduce the initial material through individual processing steps until you get the desired object. But there are also other approaches, such as the additive method. With this approach, the CAD model or even the real object - as is the case with 3D printing, for example - is built up element by element instead of by removing material. We will take a look at how this works in detail in a moment.

We'll first start with the classic subtractive approach. In the next steps, we want to add a hole and a cutout in rectangular form to a simple cube. I have already prepared the cube. For example, the dimension is 50 mm in all directions. To create the hole we can use the function "Hole" from the section "Create". Simply select the command and the surface on which you would actually place the drill in reality.

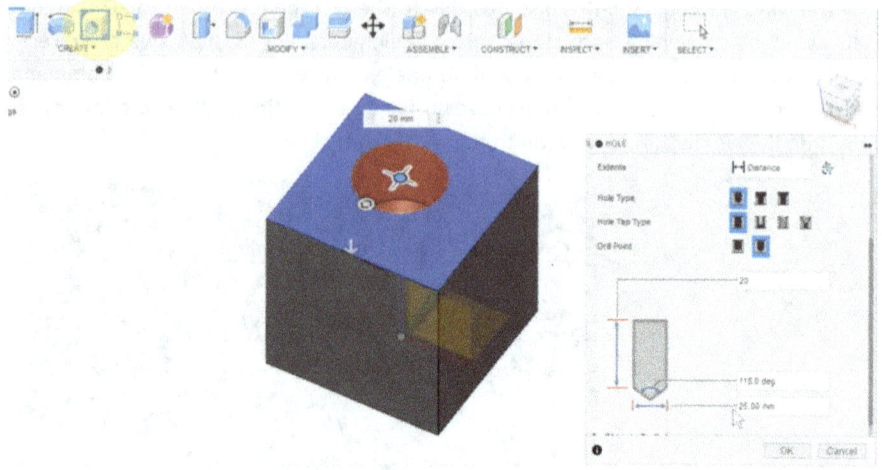

Figure 36: Creating a simple hole in a cube

In the options window that appears, you can then select the type of hole, the dimension of the hole and the specific hole parameters. For example, we select a simple, so-called blind hole with a diameter of 10 mm and a length of 20 mm. We could also create threads here, but more about that later.

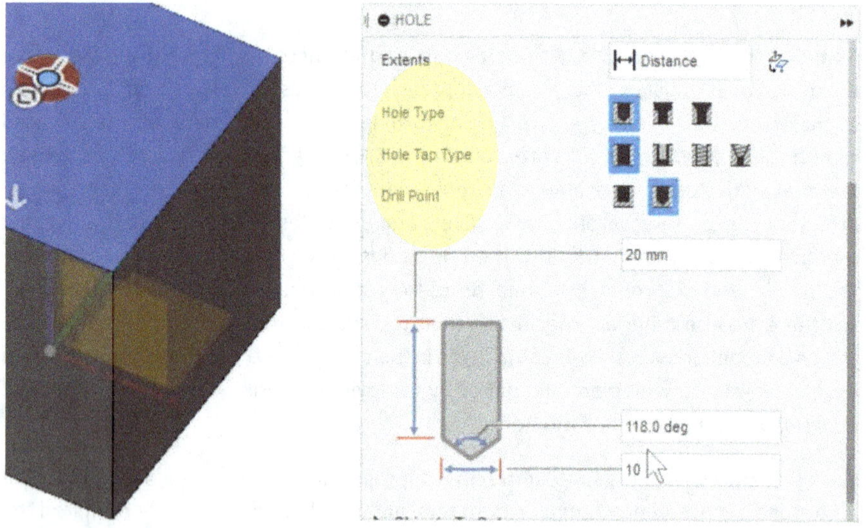

Figure 37: Selection of parameters in the "Hole" option window

For the cutout, we first need to create a 2D sketch of the geometry. To do this, click on "Create Sketch" and select, for example, the upper surface of the cuboid, since we want to bring the cutout into the cuboid from top to bottom.

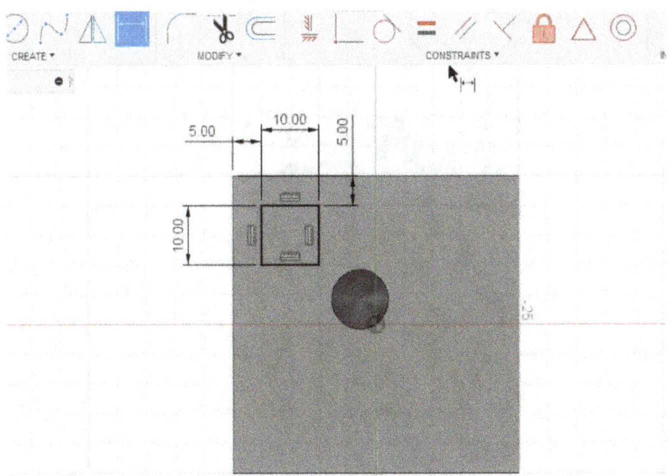

Figure 38: Make the 2D sketch on the upper surface for the cutout

Place a rectangle on the surface in the area of the cube with a click and enter a dimension of 10 mm each. Confirm with "Enter". Then we define the position of the rectangle on the surface using the "Sketch Dimension" function.

Since we are in two-dimensional space, i.e. sketching on a parallel of the x-y plane, we need an x and a y dimension to finally define the sketch, i.e. the rectangle's position and geometry completely. Enter the desired dimensions, e.g. 5 mm each from the left and upper edge of the rectangle. Now the rectangle is completely defined.

As you may have noticed, the profile has turned black. This indicates that all degrees of freedom are fully constrained, i.e. the position of the profile in the plane is fully defined by dimensions and/or constraints, and cannot move by itself in later editing steps. A complete dimensioning and a fully defined sketch is very important for good results, always pay attention to it.

After we have finished the sketch, we can create the cutout using the "Extrude" function. For example, the cutout should go completely through the part.

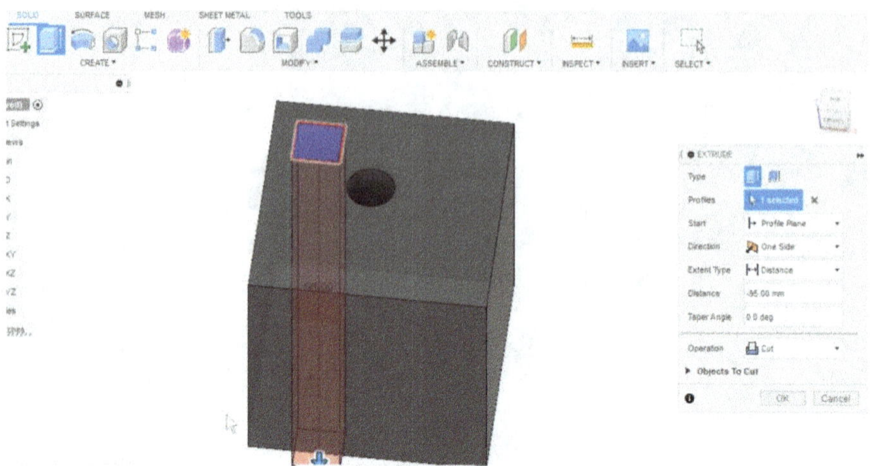

Figure 39: Create the section with "Extrude"

However, material can also be added with the "Extrude" command instead of removing it. So you can use "Extrude" for both subtractive and additive approaches of working. To illustrate the difference between the two ways of working, let's design our first very simple useful part: a coat hook to hang on a door. First with an additive working method and then with

a subtractive working method. By the way, which working method you choose doesn't matter in the end, both lead to the same result. The only difference here is in terms of effort and time required.

For the additive working method, we simply draw the cross-section of the part. In this case, we can even do it in one step. Of course, we could also divide the hook into its five rectangular bodies and line them up body by body, which would be more like the actual additive way. But that would be very cumbersome. So, in 2D mode, we first draw the cross-section of the hook on a plane of the coordinate system. Start by selecting a new sketch and the plane. By the way, you can also right-click on the desired plane in the browser and then select "Create Sketch". We then draw the first line as shown:

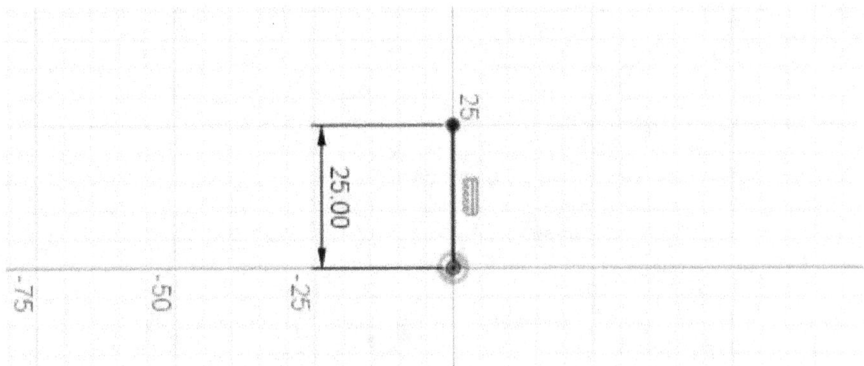

Figure 40: The first line of the 2D sketch of the cross-section for the simple coat hook

Complete the profile with the following lines and dimensions. Just draw along!

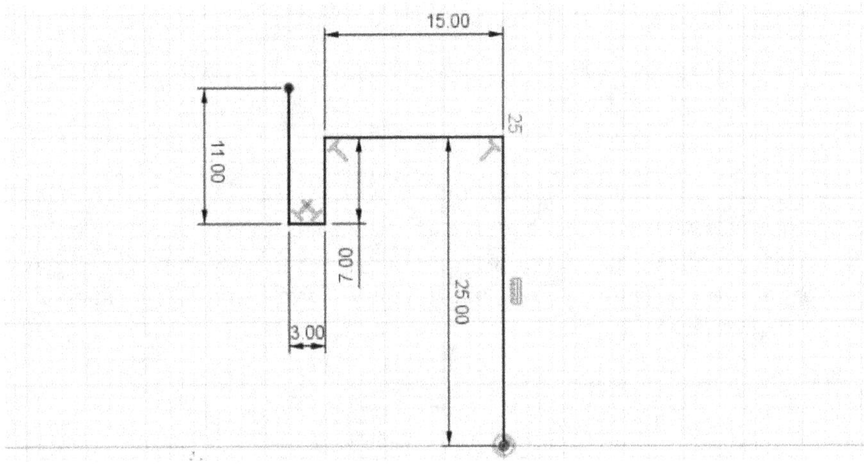

Figure 41: Continuing lines for the cross section profile

Then complete the cross-section profile with more lines as follows:

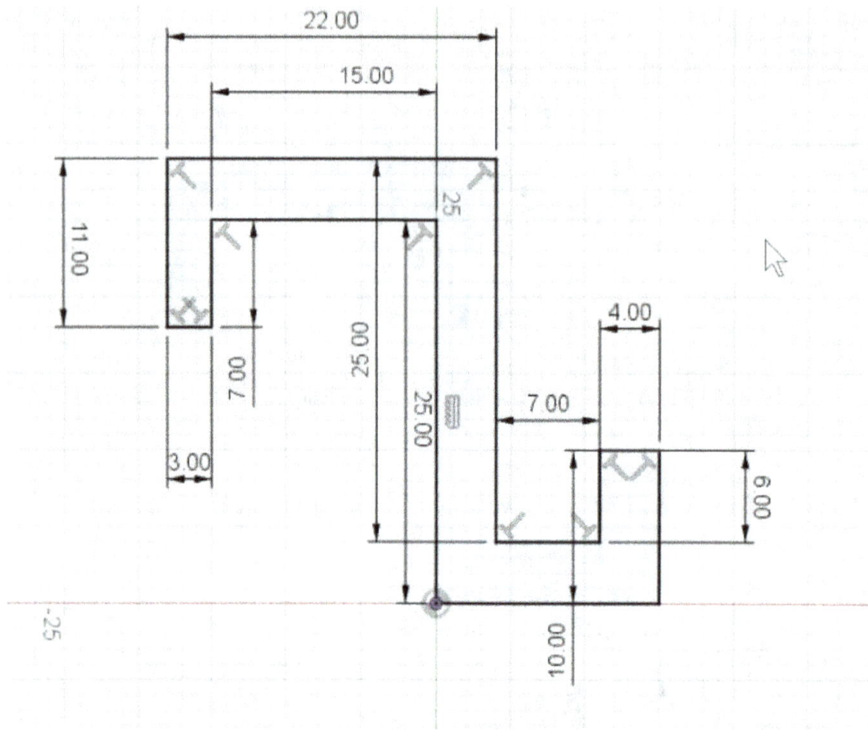

Figure 42: Complete cross section of the hook in the 2D sketching environment

Then you can leave the 2D sketching environment and thus switch to 3D mode. Select the "Extrude" command and create a three-dimensional body from the 2D cross-section, by dragging in the direction of the displayed arrow. Enter a dimension of 15 mm with your keyboard.

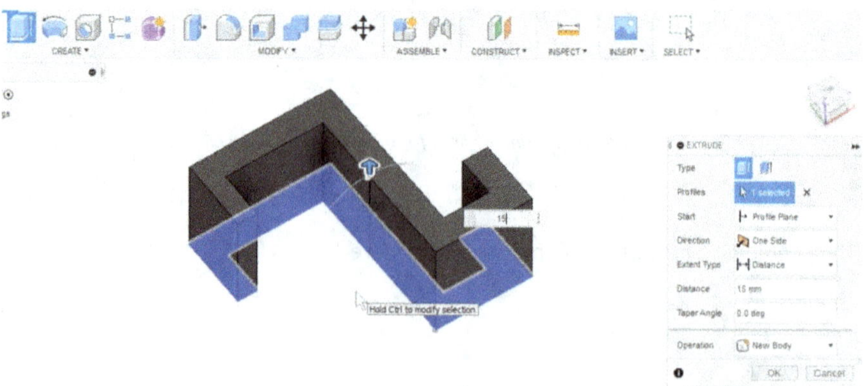

Figure 43: Creating the hook with the "Extrude" command in the 3D environment

That's it! Now we would like to use the subtractive construction method for the same hook for understanding the difference.

To do this, we draw a rectangle with the dimensions 33mm and 29mm in 2D sketch mode in a new document and create a cuboid with a thickness of 15mm using the "Extrude" command. We thus virtually first create the starting material, the so-called semi-finished product, from which the hook would be stamped out in reality, for example, or cut out by laser or waterjet. In this case, however, the hook would probably be cut out of a sheet metal part and created with the help of a bending machine, which would make more sense.

Figure 44: Initial material for the subtractive design methodology

Then we draw the cutouts into the solid material. To do this, we first create a 2D sketch on the upper - alternatively, of course, the lower - surface. First sketch the left half of the cutout for the geometry of the hook.

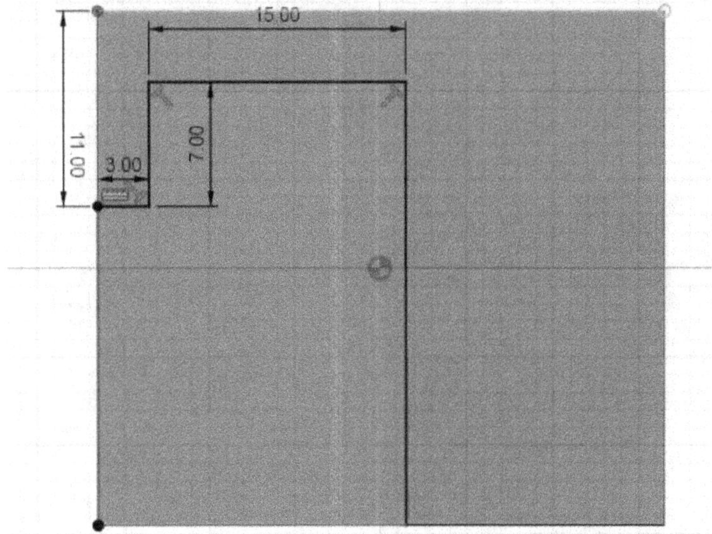

Figure 45: The left half of the cutout for the coat hook

And then draw the right half. We need to draw a negative of the hook in the solid material. Make sure that surfaces are created by closing the profiles on the edges of the rectangle with lines.

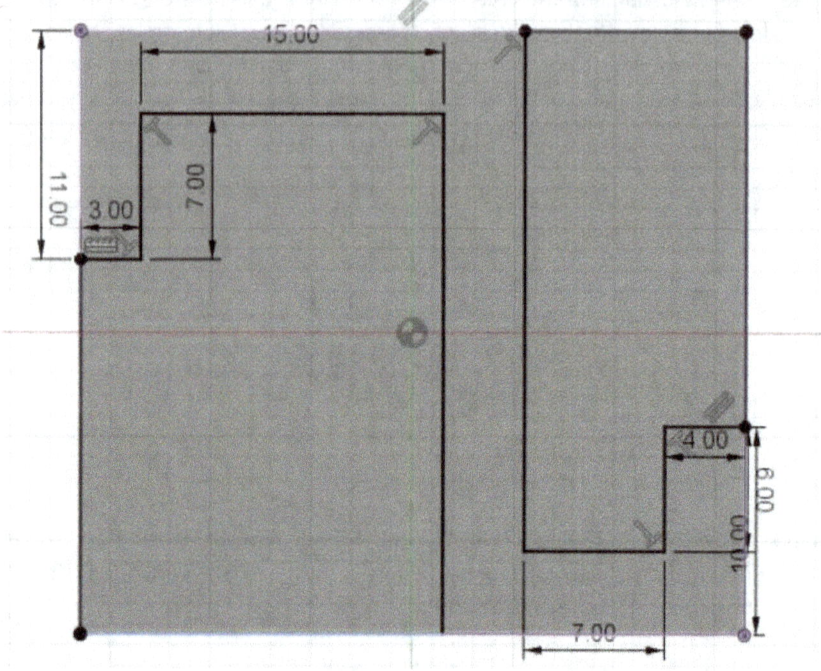

Figure 46: The right half of the cutout for the hook

Then you can again use the Extrude function to cut out the two drawn faces from the solid.

Figure 47: Cut out the drawn surfaces in 3D mode

Two approaches for an identical solution. One quite simple, the other a bit more complex. Now let's look at a few more possible ways of working.

In addition to "Hole" and "Extrude", there are a few more functions in the "Create" section that we would like to look at briefly in this chapter. First, there is the command "Revolve". You can use this whenever you want to design a part with a rotation axis, e.g. a part that would be machined mechanically by turning. To do this, simply draw a cross-section on one of the planes, e.g. the x-z or y-z plane.

Why these planes? Because we want "z" to be our axis of rotation. Or you could also use the x-y plane and then use y as the axis of rotation. Let's take a closer look. Feel free to draw along. For example, we'll create the following basic profile of a bolt in the 2D environment. We have to draw one half of the cross section of the 3D body.

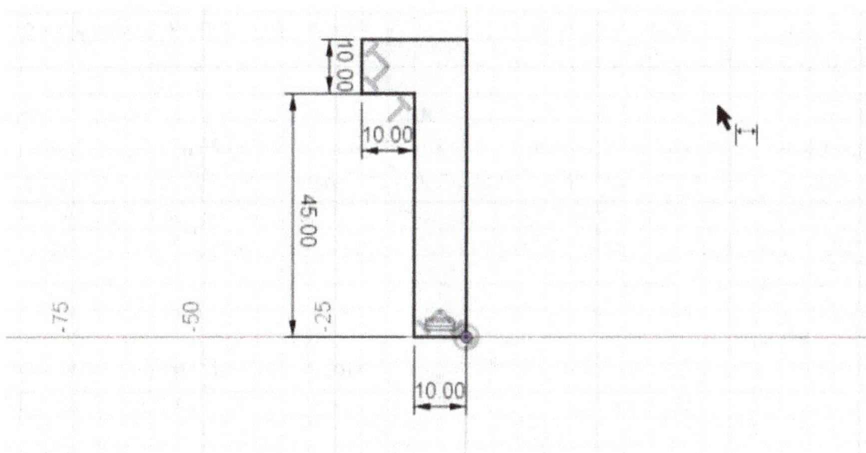

Figure 48: Half the cross section of a bolt in 2D sketch mode

After finishing the sketch and selecting the command "Revolve", we first have to define our rotation axis, in our case the z-axis.

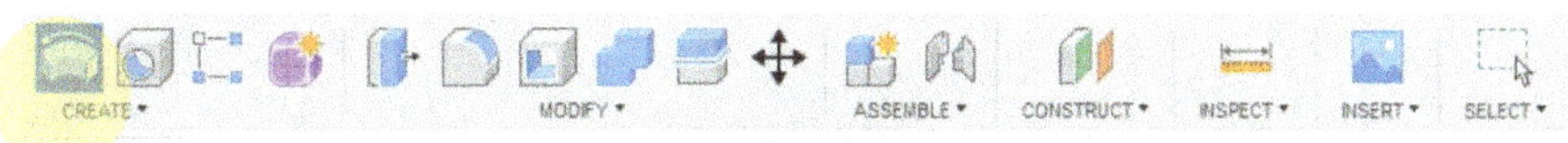

Figure 49: Selecting the "Revolve" command in the "Create" menu

As you can see, the program creates a solid. With the help of entering a number of degrees you can define the range of rotation.

Figure 50: Rotation after selection of axis and profile (360° rotation)

Of course, such a bolt could also be created using the "Extrude" command, in an additive manner, with multiple sketches. Just think for a moment how that would work in this case. Do you see the solution?

However, the rotational way is usually a lot faster and more elegant for a rotational part like this. This is what I meant when I mentioned that there are several ways of working - even for the same part. Depending on the part, there are fast, slow / simple or cumbersome ways, but usually all lead to the desired result. In reality, by the way, bolts are not produced by turning but rolled in mass production. The thread is produced by rolling between two cylindric matrices.

The "Sweep" command is always useful when you want to create a part that follows a slightly more complex path. Let's take a look at how to understand this. For the "Sweep" command, you always need a 2D sketched cross-section profile and a path. This simply means drawing a line or arc or spline.

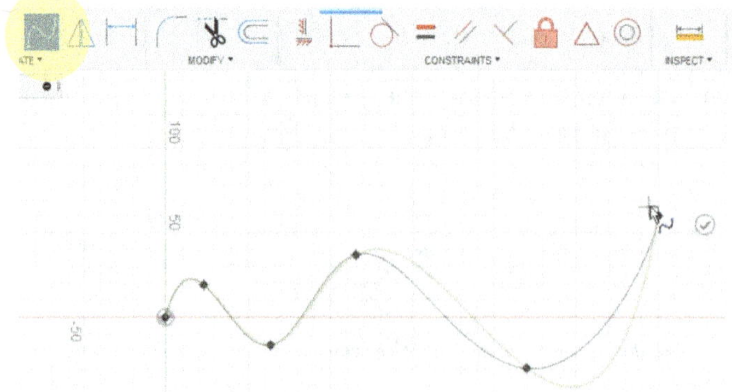

Figure 51: A "spline" or freeform curve (choose form and dimensions on your own)

For example, let's create a spline by selecting the command in a 2D sketch and draw several points at will. But make sure that the end point or start point is the coordinate center.

The more points, the more detailed the contour will be. For the cross-section profile, we now need to change the plane. To do this, we close the sketch and start a new sketch on the y-z plane. For example, we draw a circle or a rectangle and select the end point of the previously drawn profile from the x-y plane (coordinate center).

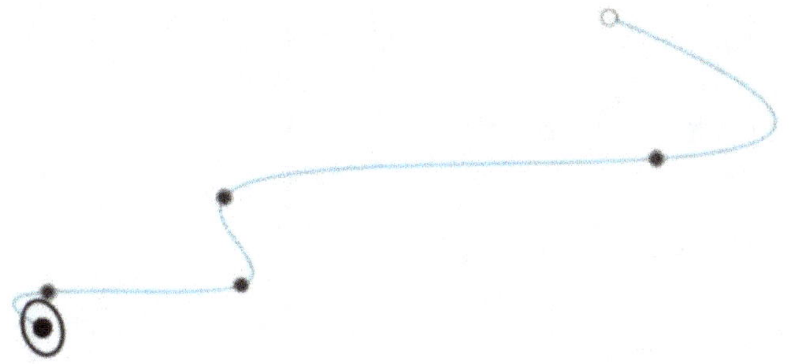

Figure 52: Finished profile: circle in the y-z plane already drawn and sketch finished

Then, when we finish the sketch, we can run the "Sweep" command in 3D mode and must first select the profile and then the path.

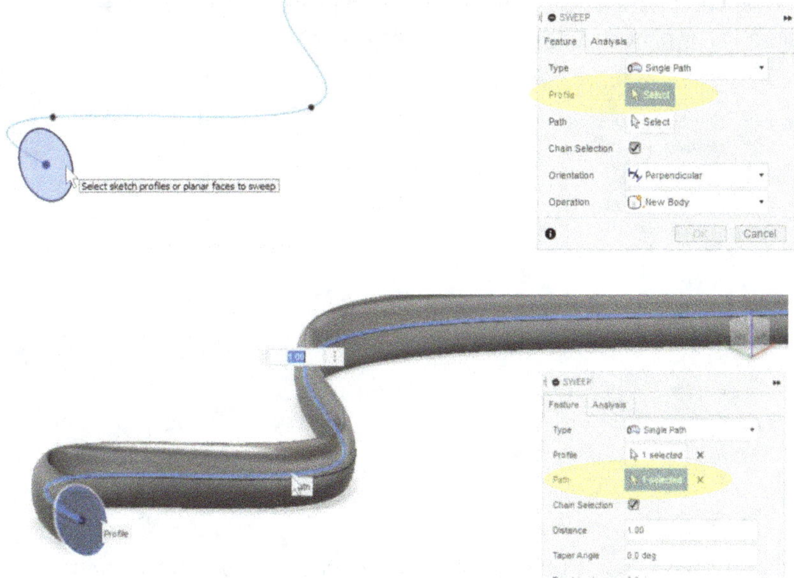

Figure 53: First select the profile (circle; upper image), then the path ("Spline"; lower image).
In the menu bar on the right, switch between the two selection options

Then the program creates the solid. In the bar on the right side we could make various settings, e.g. change the orientation.

The last important command from this section and for this chapter is "Loft". With "Loft", you can have two surfaces connected to each other in 3D space. Let's try it out! We draw a profile in the x-y plane, e.g. a rectangle or any other shape.

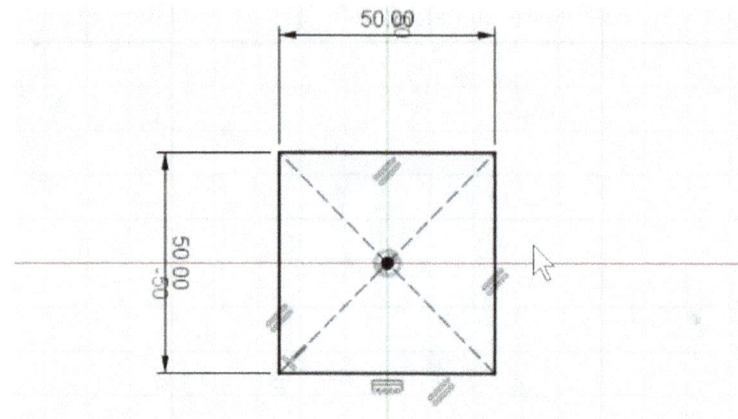

Figure 54: First sketch of a rectangle on the x-y plane (each side 50 mm)

Then we first create a new plane parallel to the x-y plane with an offset to it. This is easily done by right-clicking on the x-y plane and selecting "Offset Plane".

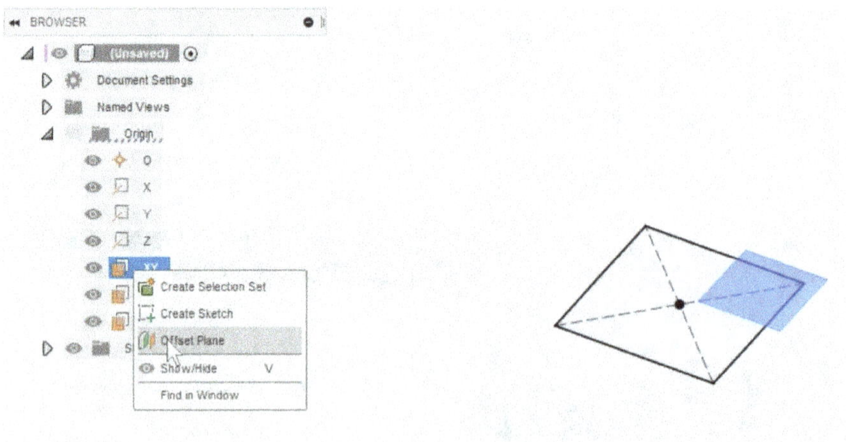

Figure 55: Create an offset plane (also possible in the menu above at "Construct")

We then drag the blue arrow or enter a dimension with the keyboard.

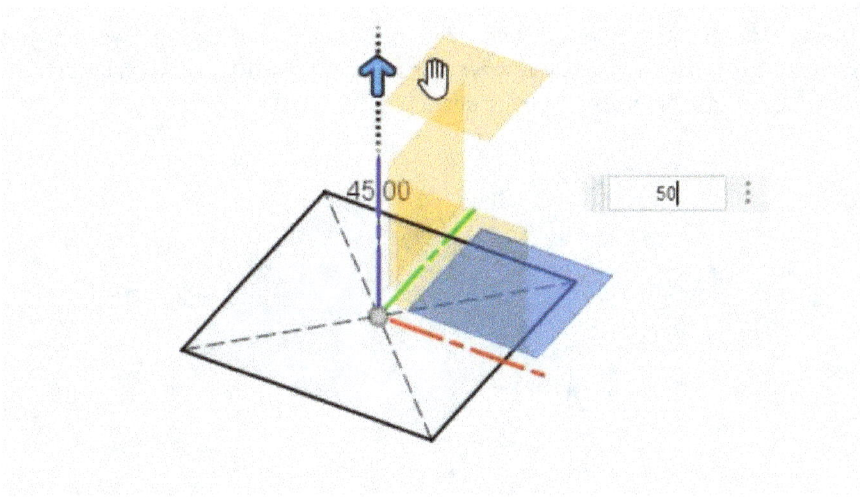

Figure 56: Creating the 50 mm offset plane to the x-y plane

On this new plane we draw the second surface for our project in the next step. For example, a slightly larger rectangle. The centers should be congruent.

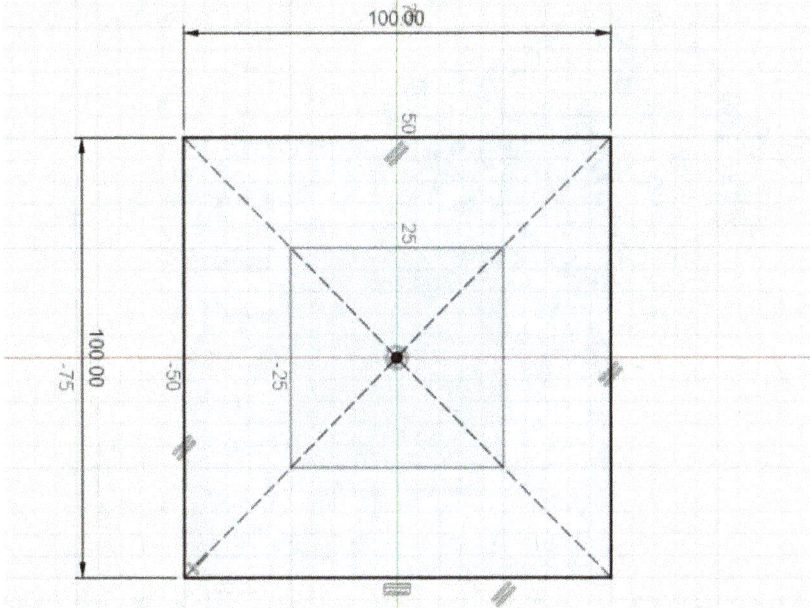

Figure 57: Draw second rectangle on the offset plane (first rectangle is also slightly visible)

Then we finish the sketch and select the "Loft" command and the two sketched surfaces. The program then joins the two surfaces to form a 3D solid. With the settings we could control this process in more detail.

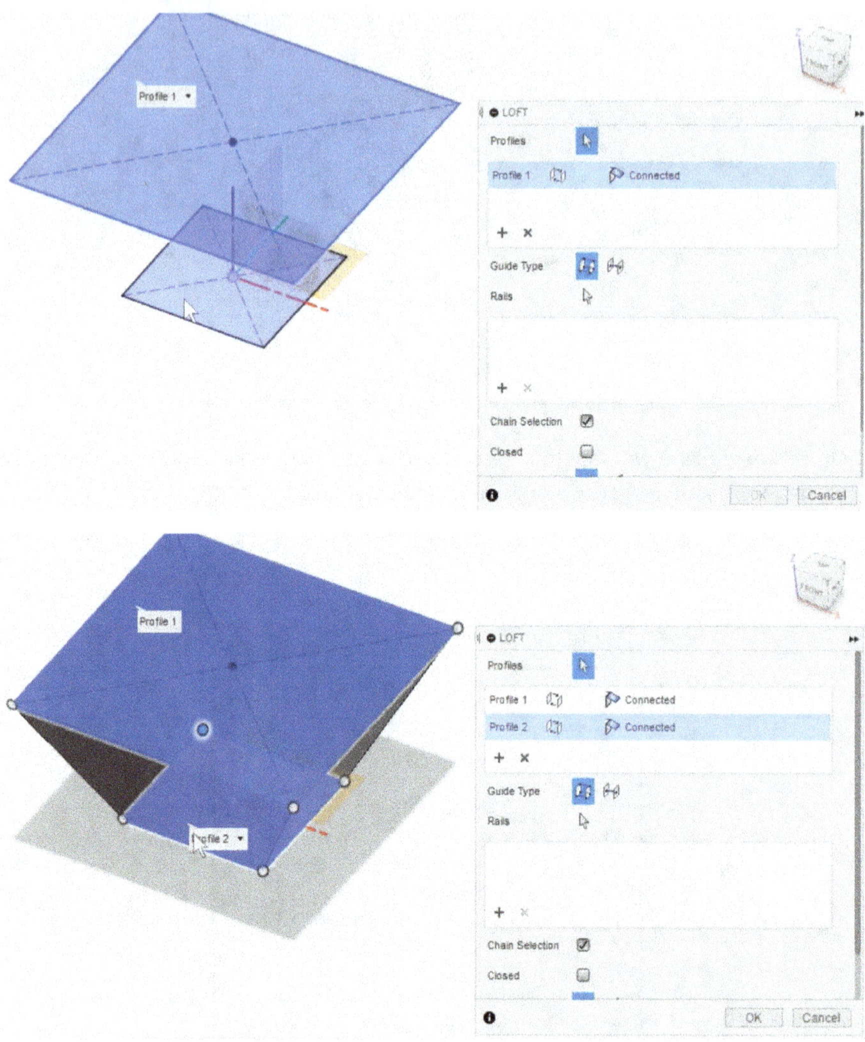

Figure 58: Use the "Loft" command to create the 3D body

Very good! So much for the approach and methodology in CAD design. We can check off this chapter and move on to the next one. In the following, we will take a closer look at the difference between a single part and an assembly.

3.4 Single Parts vs. Assemblies

As in the real world, you can also assemble several components in the CAD environment to get an assembly. To design a complex machine or other complex part, you first design the individual components of this complex item and then assemble these individual parts virtually in Fusion. To do this, you use links, connections or relationships. In Fusion 360, you use "joints". But more about that later.

In Fusion 360, you create all components directly in one environment and then connect them in the same document to form an assembly. Each part has its own origin and its own folder an will appear separately in the browser. Other CAD programs are a bit different and there are extra file formats for assemblies and parts and you create each part in its own file.

When you have finished designing the first part, e.g. such a simple turned part, you simply create a new component with the button "New Component" from the menu bar or a right click on the folder of the part and the selection of "New component" and select the "Parent" body, i.e. the already existing part as reference.

Figure 59: A simple rotating part (dimensions freely selectable) and "New Component"

This part then becomes transparent and you can start creating the new component. The new component then appears in the browser and can be named. By the way, each component has its own coordinate system.

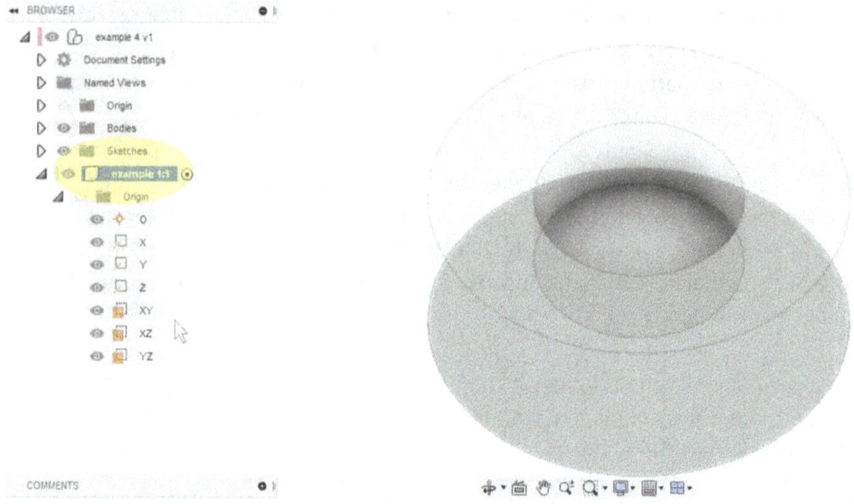

Figure 60: Transparent parent component and new component in the browser (left)

For example, we start a sketch on the x-z plane of the new component, and use the first component as a reference for our new part. We could, for example, draw such a profile for a new turned part, which we then create using the "Revolve" command.

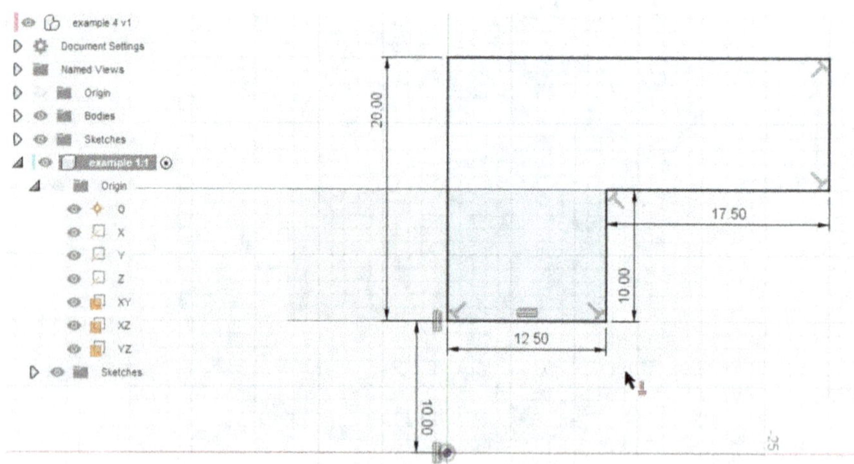

Figure 61: A sketch on the x-z plane of the new component

It is quite convenient that we can take a look at the first component (transparent) for reference and can thus draw the dimensions for the new part relatively easily with an exact fit. By the way, the sketch for the new part is now also placed in the folder of the new component, of course.

Now let's take a look at the assembly of these two individual parts. We have drawn the second component in such a way that it would already be an exact fit with the first component, but a linkage has not taken place yet. We can move the second component freely, so we have to link the two individual parts in the next step.

Figure 62: The component was created from the sketch with a 360° rotation and was then moved

Here we need the menu "Assemble" and the command "Joints". In other CAD programs, the assembly of individual parts is usually structured somewhat differently. Constraints are usually created, e.g. with a distance condition or e.g. a concentric condition between two parts, to get an assembly. In Fusion 360, a slightly different approach is taken. Here you create joints that - instead - define the desired range of motion. However, you can also rigidly link a single part. Let's look at how to do it in our simple example. In the "Assemble" menu, we first select the "Joint" command.

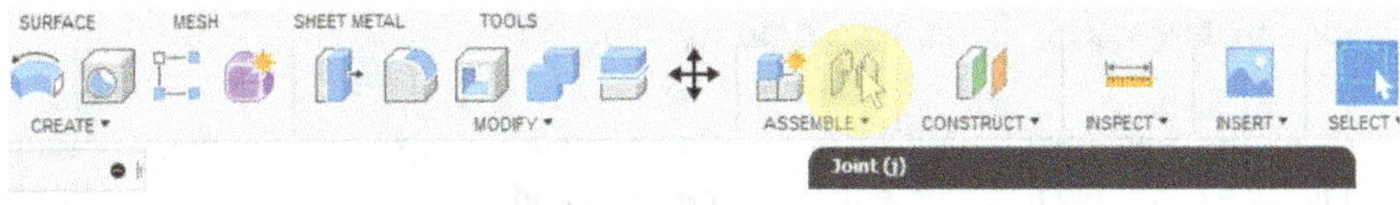

Figure 63: The "Joint" command from the "Assemble" menu

Then we have to perform two steps. On the one hand, we have to define the positions of the joint origins. For example, select the points on the surfaces that we want to link. And on the other hand, we have to define the range of motion or the joint type. Let's try a few possibilities. For example, we could select these two joint origin points on these surfaces and create a rigid link with "Rigid".

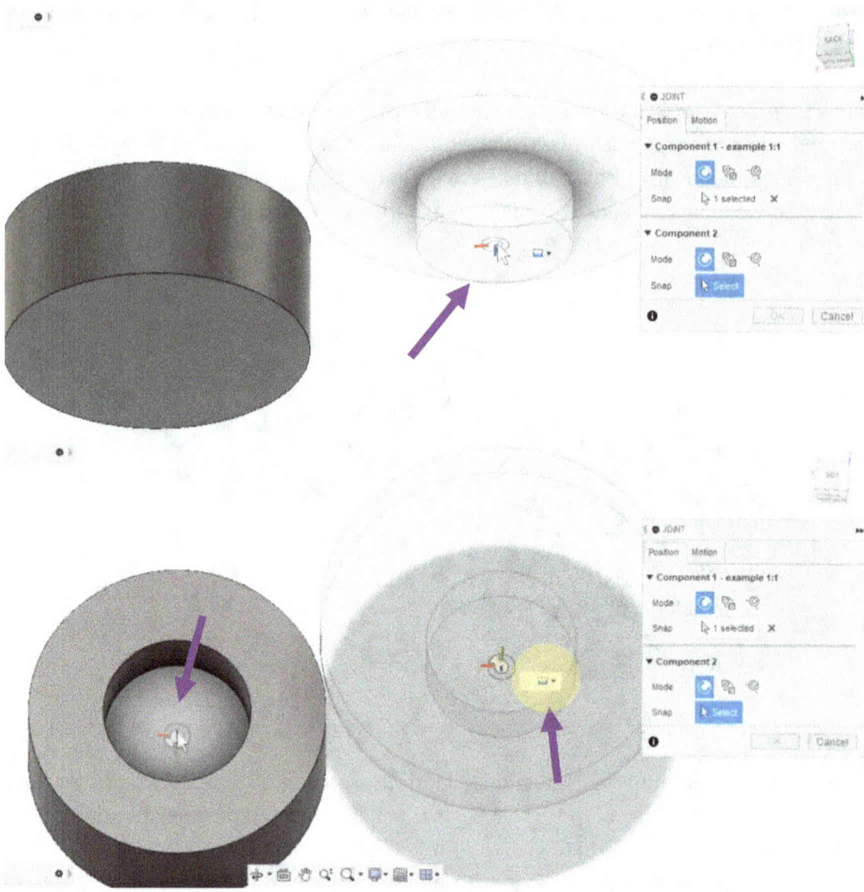

Figure 64: Select a joint origin on each of the components and select "Rigid"

By the way, when selecting the joint type, a short animation of the possible range of motion is played, which I personally find very useful and beneficial. A really great feature that makes this program so sophisticated.

On the other hand, we could allow a rotation around the z-axis with "Revolute". With "Slider" we can allow a movement along the z-axis and with "Cylindrical" we can allow a movement along the z-axis as well as a rotation around this axis. With "Pin" we can allow a rotation around one axis and a linear movement along another axis, but as you will see, this does not make much sense in this example. The same is true for "Planar". With "Planar" the component can move linearly in a plane and rotate around an axis. Very interesting is "Ball", which creates a spherical joint.

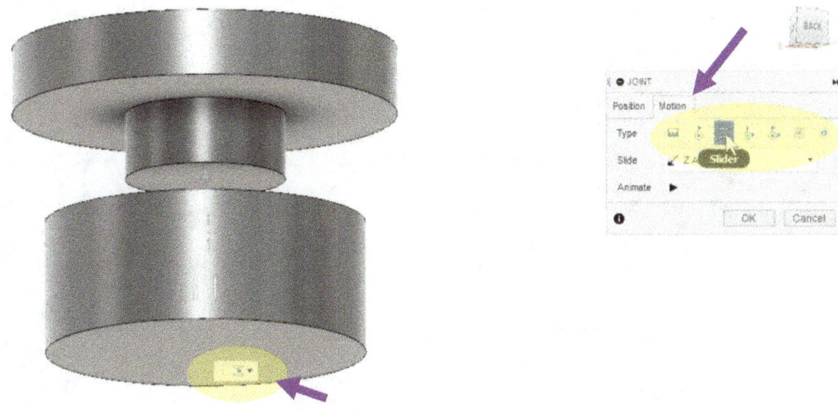

Figure 65: Select the different joint types in the "Motion" tab

In the "Rotate" field, the respective axis or surface can be selected for the movement, and if we jump back to the "Position" tab, further settings can be made, such as an offset, or mirroring the orientation of the component with "Flip".

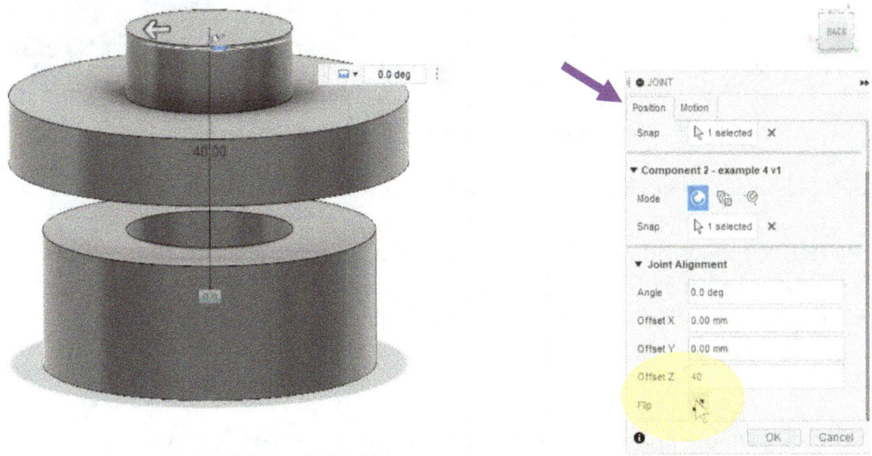

Figure 66: Add an offset and reverse the joint orientation

If we now select, for example, the movement type "Cylindrical", we see that we can only move the component in the defined degrees of freedom. The relationship also appears in the "Joints" folder in the browser and can be deleted, suppressed or otherwise edited by right-clicking on it.

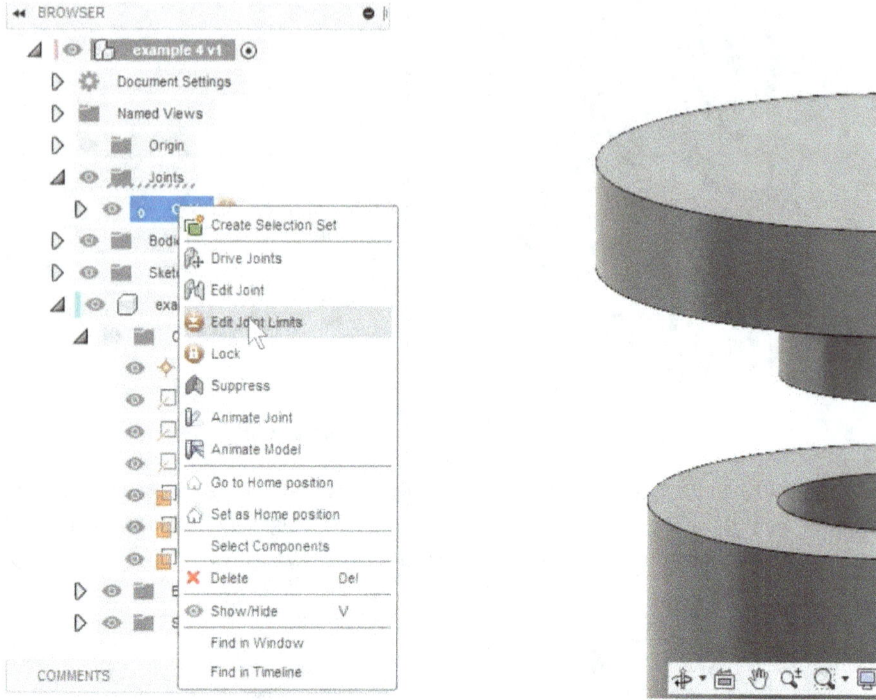

Figure 67: Right-click on the joint in the "Joints" folder in the browser (left)

By the way, if absolutely no motion is desired, just select the joint type "Rigid".

Perfect! In this lesson we learned how to create multiple parts in Fusion 360 and link them together or assemble them virtually. In the next lesson, we'll take a look at different views and visualizations. Then we will finally get to more advanced and great design projects!

3.5 Views and Visualizations (Basic views, Sectional view, etc.)

In this lesson we will briefly look at the possible views and displays in Fusion 360, which can often be very helpful. The basic views can be found on the left in the browser at "Named Views". In this folder we can choose between "Top", "Front", "Right" and "Home".

Figure 68: Select "Named Views" in the browser

If we want to look at a specific surface, we can select one in the menu bar in the lower area with the function "Look at". This surface will then be displayed vertically from above. With the function "Zoom Window", also from this bar, we can enlarge a defined area. To do this, we simply extend a small window in the desired area.

Figure 69: "Look At" and "Zoom Window" in the bar in the lower area

The selection menu "Display Setting" is also located in this bar, with which we can change the visualization of our components. This can be done with "Visual Style" for the component or "Environment" for the design environment. With "Object Visibility" we can generally define which elements, such as planes and axes, should be displayed or not.

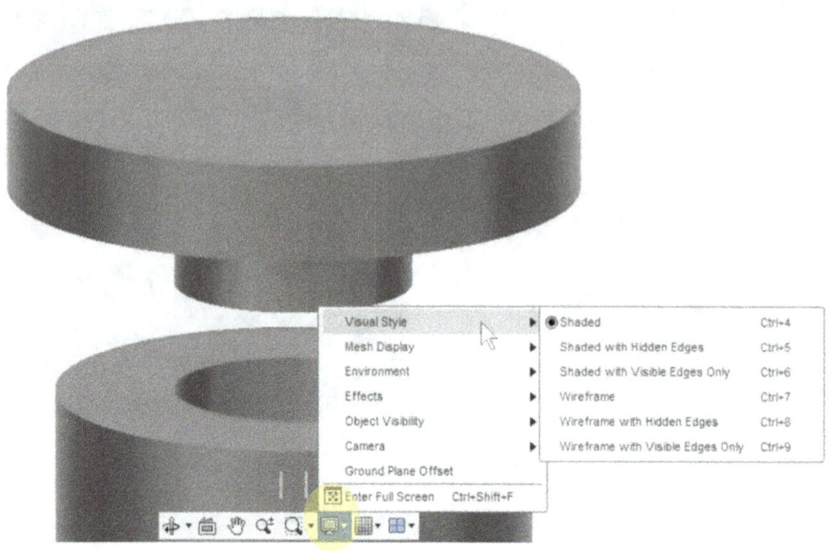

Figure 70: "Visual Style" selection menu in the "Display Setting" tab in the bottom bar

With "Multiple Views" you can display several views in parallel, which can sometimes also be very helpful.

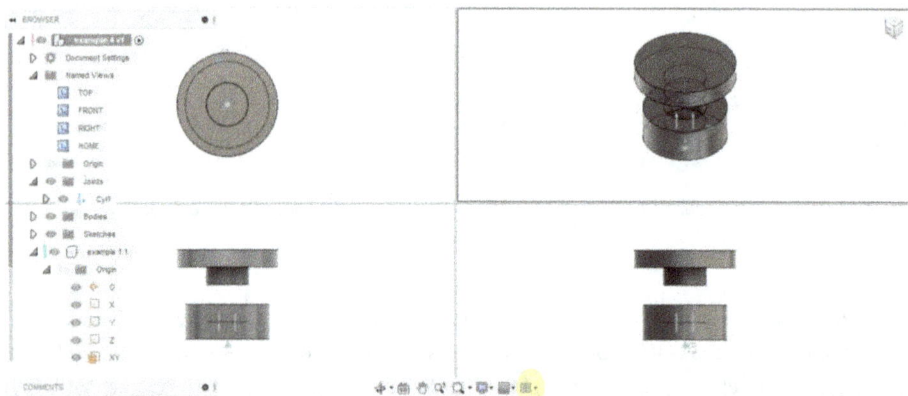

Figure 71: Display after selecting "Multiple Views" in the bottom bar

Finally, we will get to know a few useful visualizations from the "Inspect" menu. First of all, the most important one is the section view. Using the "Section Analysis" command, we can view the cross-section of a component or assembly. Just think of it as cutting a cake and looking inside. After selecting the function, we need to select the plane in which we want to cut the part. Alternatively, we can select a surface. For example, we select the y-z plane. The part will then be cut in this plane. We can now either confirm, or move the cut surface using the blue arrow or by entering a dimension.

After confirming, the section view appears in the menu folder "Analysis" on the left in the browser, where we can edit, hide or delete it with a right click.

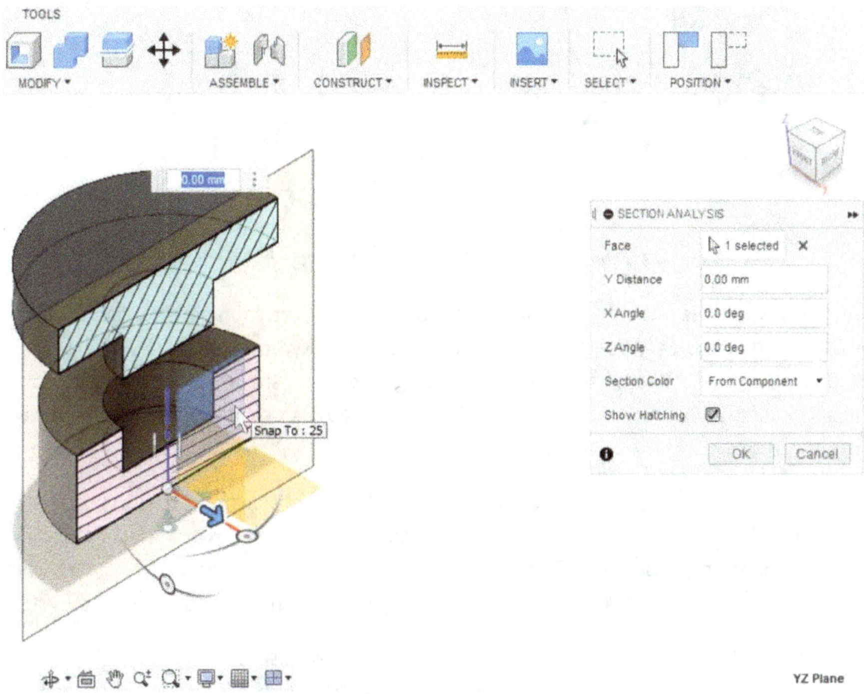

Figure 72: Sectional view of the 3D environment (menu tab "Inspect" ->"Sectional view")

At "Inspect" you will also find analysis functions, such as the "zebra analysis". With the help of this command you can check transitions between surfaces by means of black and white stripes projected onto the surface and, for example, examine the surface of an aircraft wing for its surface continuity or smoothness. When designing a plane, this is of importance for the flow resistance, for example.

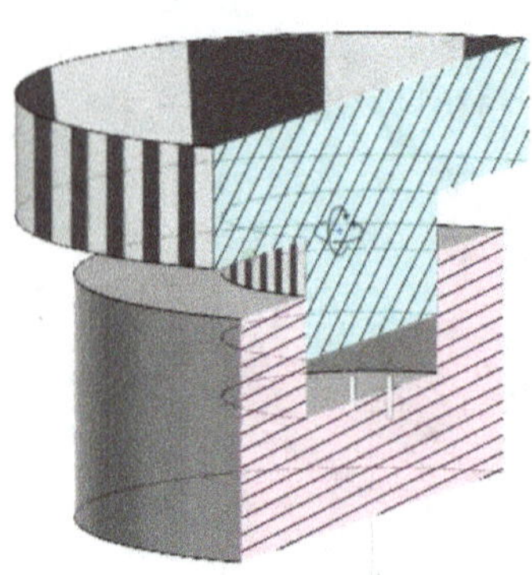
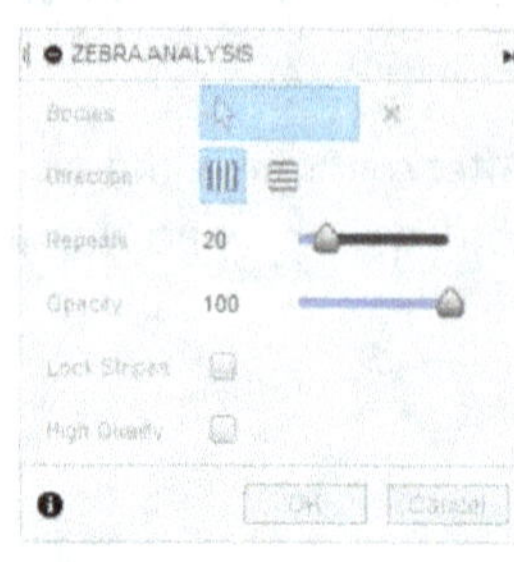

Figure 73: Zebra analysis applied to the part displayed in section view

At the end of this chapter we will take a closer look at the "timeline" of the program mentioned at the very beginning. It is located at the very bottom of the window. Here a chronological order of the individual design steps is shown and we can find all executed features such as "Sketch", "Extrusion" etc., depending on the respective design.

The great thing about this is, that with this timeline, the design process can be easily retraced. The individual steps can even be displayed with the help of a short animation. To do this, simply place the cursor at the start of the construction and/or simply click on Play. You can also click between the steps to jump to an earlier stage of the design.

By right-clicking on the individual design steps, you can also edit the respective steps, e.g. change a 2D profile or a joint. This bar is also very helpful in order not to lose the overall view, especially with more complex designs.

Figure 74: The timeline of Fusion with the commands performed so far

If you click on the small gearwheel symbol at the bottom right, you can also activate the "Component Color Swatch" option, which provides us with even more clarity for more complex design objects by giving the individual components a colored marker and thus assigning the design steps in the timeline.

Figure 75: Activate "Component Color Swatch" to get the colored markers displayed

Awesome! Now that we have learned all the relevant and important basics and the general handling of the CAD section of Fusion 360, we will move on to design some components and assemblies.

In the first project, we'll dive into design by learning how to make a very simple carabiner hook. This is followed by a cup, which is a bit more difficult to realize, then a simplified model of a truck with a passenger compartment and finally a simplified model of a four-cylinder car engine, which is a bit more complex. But don't worry, we will approach it step by step.

By working in this hands-on way, we will get to know more new functions and commands and reinforce the understanding of the basics.

Learning by doing! Stay with me, it will get exciting!

4 Practical CAD Application: Design Projects

4.1 Design project I: Simple snap hook

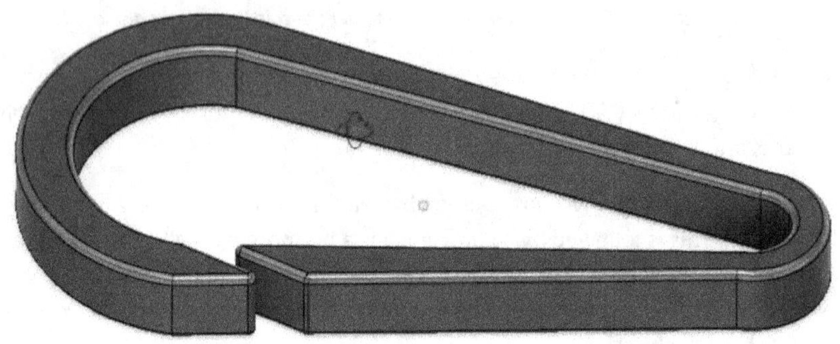

Figure 76: A simple snap hook is the first design project

For the carabiner we start in a new "Design" project with "Create Sketch" and the selection of a plane, e.g. the x-y-plane. Let's first consider how the carabiner is best designed. If we look at the snap hook a little more closely, we notice that we can place a circular shape in each of the left and right areas, and that the struts of the snap hook represent tangential connections between these circles.

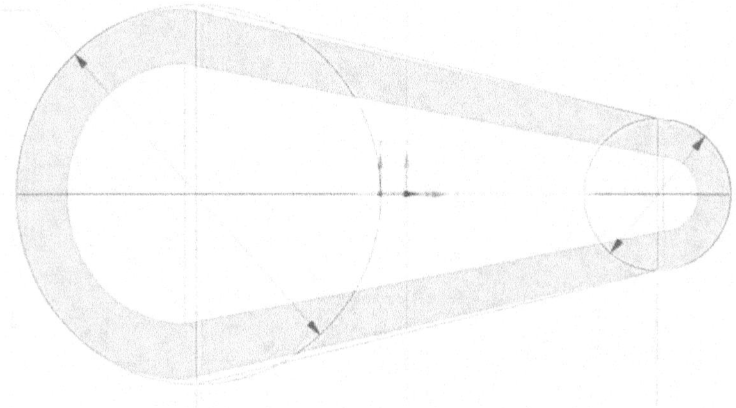

Figure 77: Design approach using circles and tangential connecting lines

Let's design the carabiner in this way. First of all, we will draw the initial circle with a starting point on the horizontal red line, which in this case, is the x-axis. For example, we choose a diameter of 50 mm. Then create another circle with a diameter of 20 mm a little further to the right. We then dimension the distance between the two circles as 70 mm. To completely define the previous sketch, which you will see by the black coloring, we need a reference in the direction of the x-axis and y-axis relative to the origin. We define the position of our sketch in x-direction for example by another dimension of 35 mm from the center of the first circle to the origin. The y-position is simply set with a horizontally constraint.

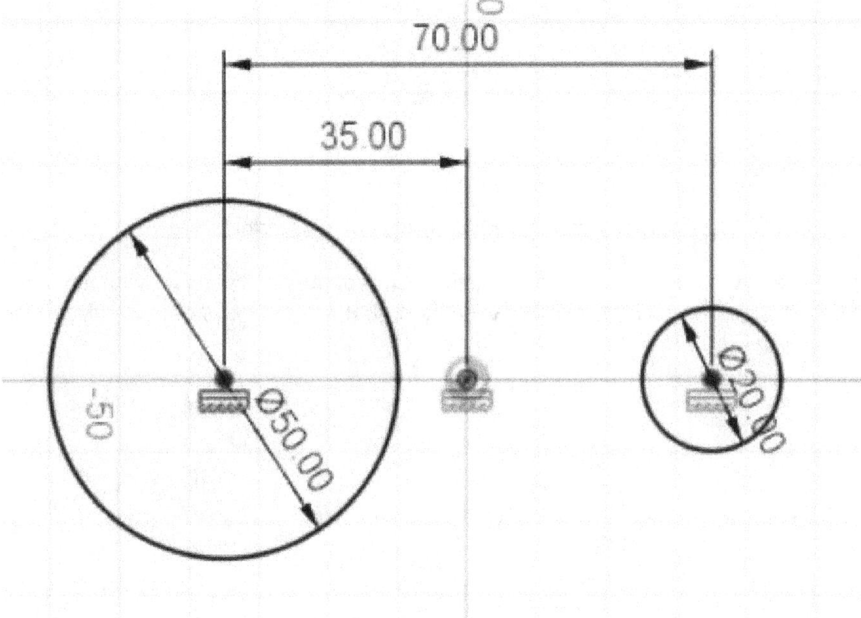

Figure 78: The two circles for the basic geometry, already dimensioned and horizontally constrained

You can either define a sketch by dimensions only, or choose a combination of dimensions and constraints, as we did in this example. For the constraint we choose the center of each of the two circles and then the origin. Now the sketch got black and is fully defined, i.e. it cannot be moved within the plane.

Then we draw horizontal and vertical auxiliary lines through the centers of the two circles to make it easier to apply the dimensions and the tangent lines. Draw the lines and right-click on them to select "Normal/Construction Line".

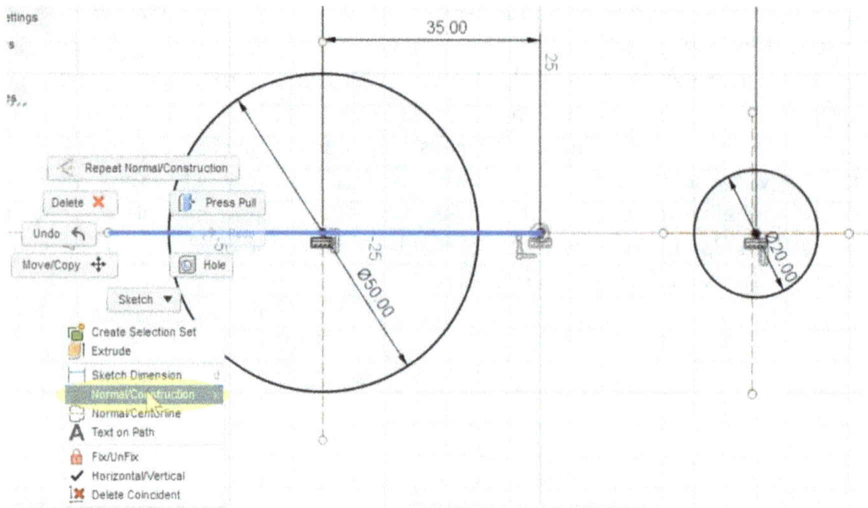

Figure 79: Turn a normal line into an auxiliary / construction line

In the next step we connect the intersection points of the vertical guides with the circles by two lines. To get a closed shape, we only need the outer contour, therefore we use the "Trim" tool.

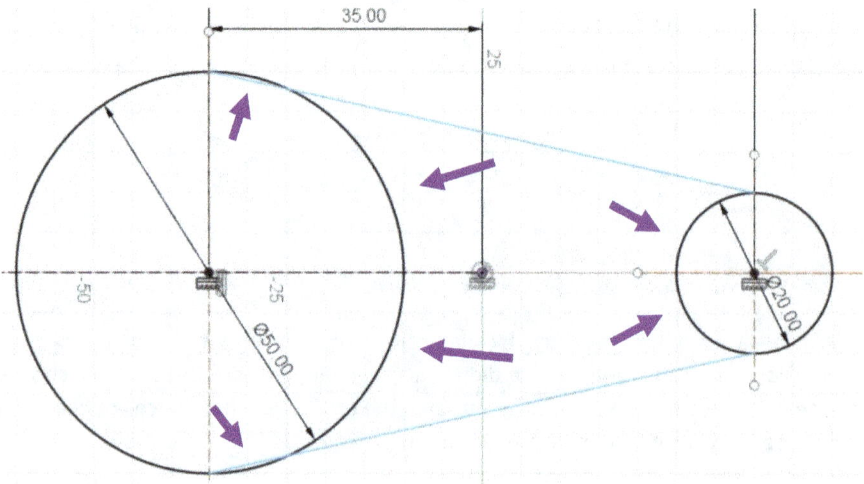

Figure 80: The two tangential connecting lines (light blue) have been drawn;
excess lines/arcs are marked with arrows

Use the tool to remove all superfluous line segments as follows:

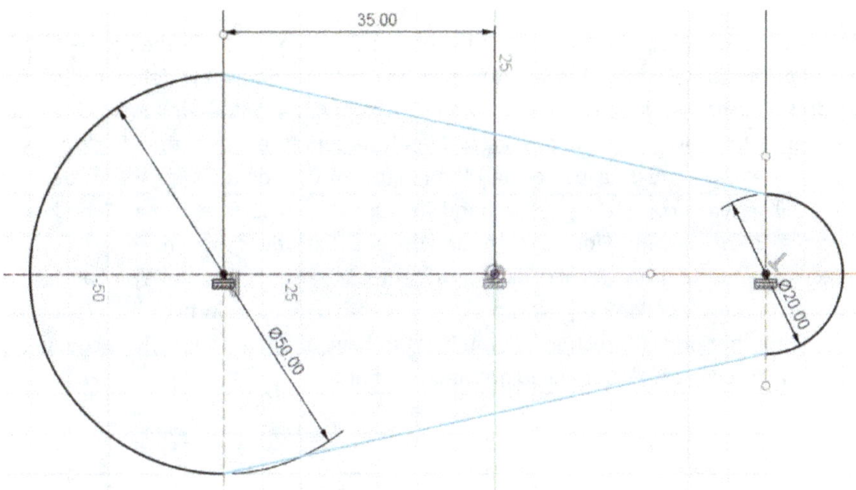

Figure 81: Used "Trim away" to remove the excess lines/arcs

Now we could extrude the surface. But then we would have to make another cutout to get to the final shape of the carabiner. But we can also apply a faster solution right away and draw the cross-section of the snap hook in one step. To do this, add two additional circles of 35 and 10 mm diameter to the inner area of the carabiner and, analogous to the previous steps, draw two lines from the intersections of the circles with the auxiliary lines once more and then, by using the "Trim" feature a second time, remove all superfluous line segments.

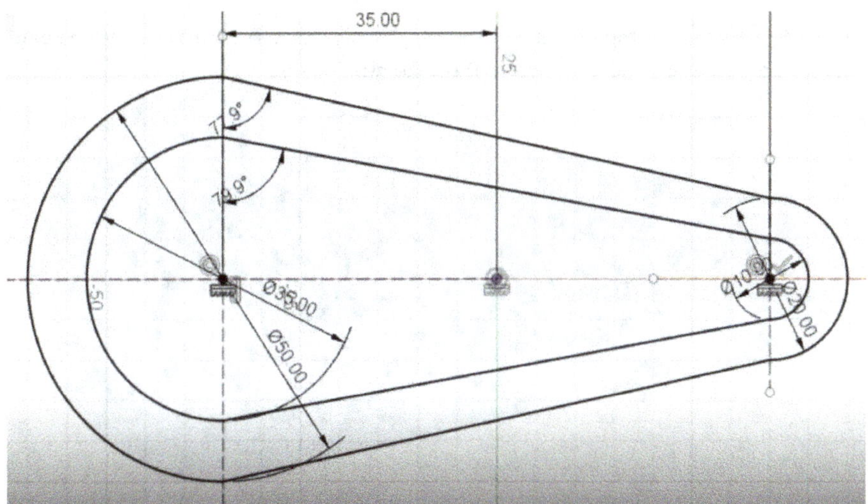

Figure 82: Completed 2D sketch; the angles for the complete definition are specified

As you can see, we eliminated one editing step and can now extrude the finished basic shape of the carabiner right away. However, in order to completely define the sketch beforehand, we simply specify the angles between the tangential connecting lines and the vertical auxiliary line in this case. Simply accept the value that is displayed. Alternatively, we could have specified the lengths of the connecting lines, or defined the auxiliary lines completely beforehand. To turn the 2D surface into a 3D body, we switch to 3D mode with "Finish Sketch" and use the "Extrude" function. To do this, only select the outer surface for extrusion, and enter a value of 10 mm. You can either extrude in one direction only, symmetrically or independently in two directions. You choose this option at "Direction". If you want to have a tapered shape, you could also specify a "Taper Angle". But we do not need that here.

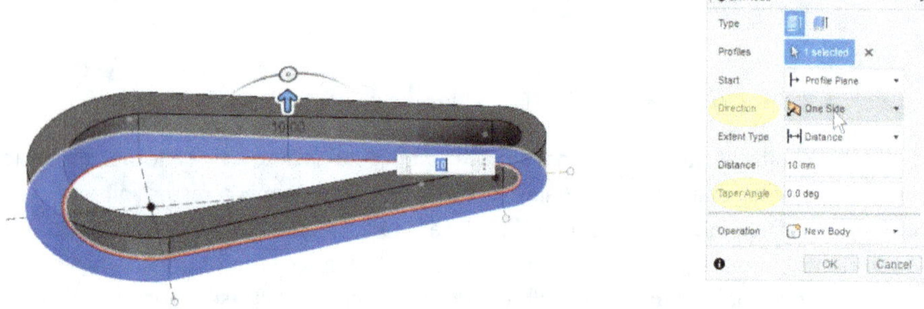

Figure 83: Extrusion of the carabiner by 10 mm in one direction

To create a cutout for the opening of the snap hook, we start a 2D sketch once again, this time on the top or bottom side of the snap hook.

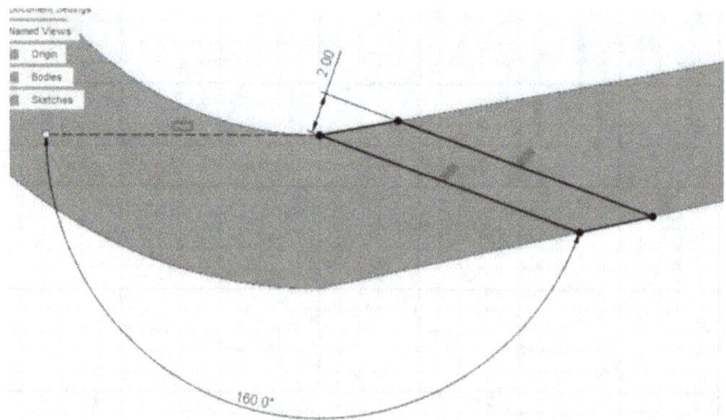

Figure 84: The 2D sketch for the cutout

We draw a line at 160° from the base of the inner tangential connection line to the outer connection line of the carabiner. The dimension results from the specification of the angle and the end points. You can switch between dimension and angle input with the tab key. Then draw a second parallel line and dimension a 2 mm distance. If the parallelism is not created automatically - pay attention to the small constraint characters - you have to create it yourself. Then connect the two parallel lines with further lines to create a parallelogram and finish the sketch. With "Extrude" the cutout is created. Simply drag the arrow until there is no more material or alternatively specify the thickness of the carabiner as the cutout dimension. Of course, we could have already integrated this step into the first sketch, as you may have just noticed.

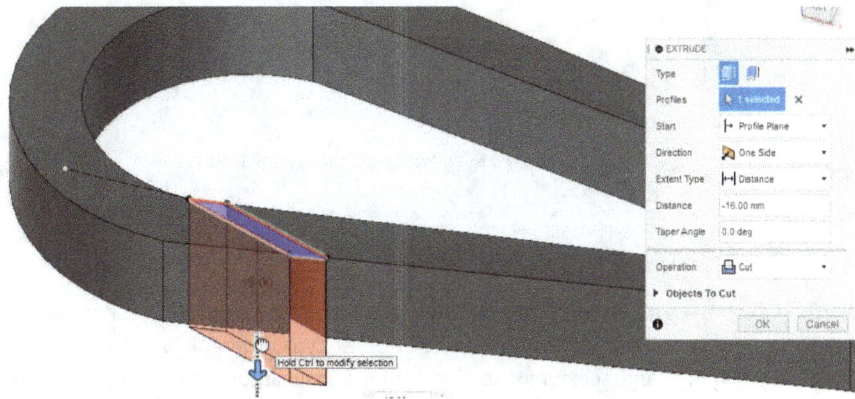

Figure 85: Cutting out the drawn 2D geometry with "Extrusion"

Finally, we round a few edges using the "Fillet" command from the "Modify" section. 20 mm for the back top edge.

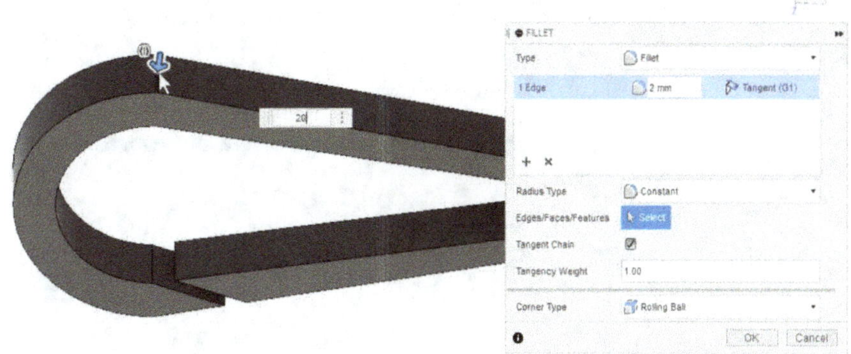

Figure 86: Rounding of the rear upper edge with 20 mm

And 1 mm for the edges of the opening as well as the sides. Select multiple edges by holding down the CTRL or SHIFT key. For the side edges, you can simply select the two side faces.

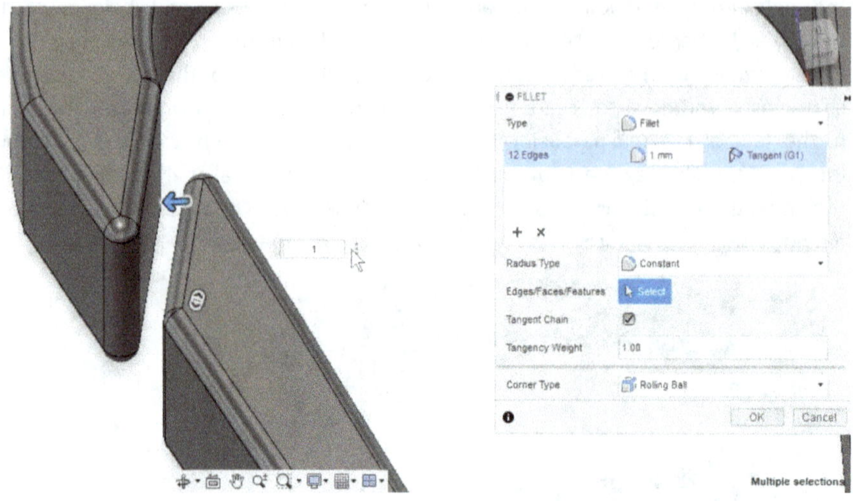

Figure 87: Rounding of the edges of the opening as well as the sides with 1 mm

Perfect! Before we move on to the next design project, let's save the file. If we want a different file format, e.g. for 3D printing or another CAD program, we can create this file using "Export" and selecting the file format and location. For example, we can choose the "Fusion" and "Inventor" formats, as well as commonly known "stl" and "step" file formats.

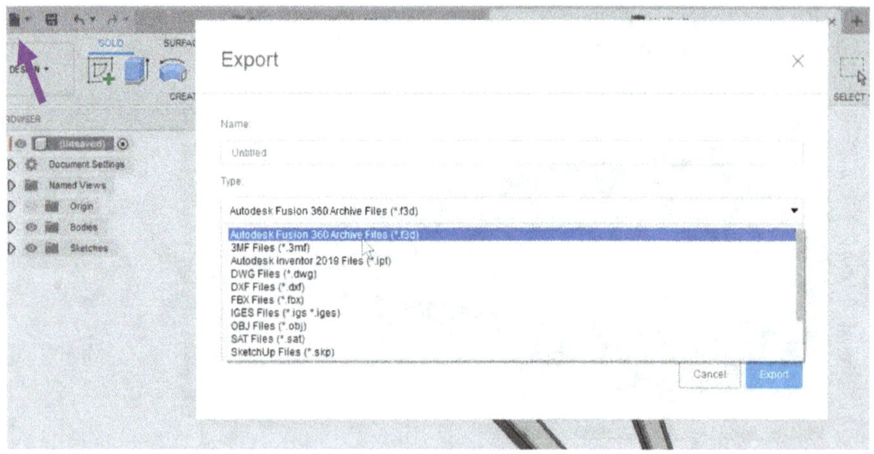

Figure 88: "Export" a file in a specified format; "File" (see arrow) -> "Export".

4.2 Design Project II: Cup with Handle

Figure 89: A cup with handle as the next design project

Before we get to the two somewhat more exciting projects, we would like to design a cup including a handle next. Pay attention to the specific combination of additive and subtractive design methods in this project. We will first design the basic shape, i.e. the cup without the handle, and then add the handle. Start with a circle geometry on a 2D sketch, for example on the x-y plane, in a new project. The diameter of the circle could be 90 mm, for example, and the center should be at the origin of the coordinate system so that the sketch will be fully defined. Then switch to the 3D environment and create a cylinder from the sketch using the Extrude function. We will use a dimension of 80 mm here.

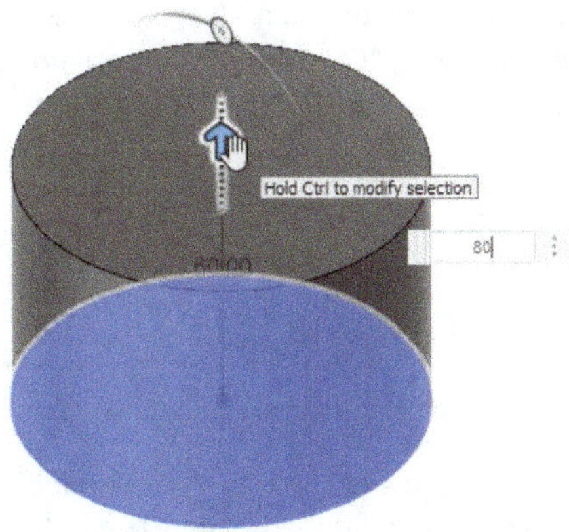

Figure 90: Extrude a 90 mm circle by 80 mm for the basic shape

To hollow out the cup, we use the "Shell" function from the "Modify" section. We select a wall thickness of 5 mm in this case. Select the upper surface, enter the wall thickness and the shell is done. By the way, at "Direction" in the options we could still specify in which direction the material for the wall should go: inwards, outwards or symmetrically in both directions. By default we use "inside" to not change the outer diameter.

Figure 91: Hollow out the cylinder to form a cup; wall thickness 5 mm

By the way, in the timeline at the bottom we can see the design progress with the individual features. As we can see at this point, we started with a sketch, continued with an extrusion, and then hollowed out. When we select a feature in the model, we also see a little shaded reference to find it along in the timeline. By right clicking on a feature, we can also edit it with "Edit Feature" if we want to change something. The sketches can also be found in the browser.

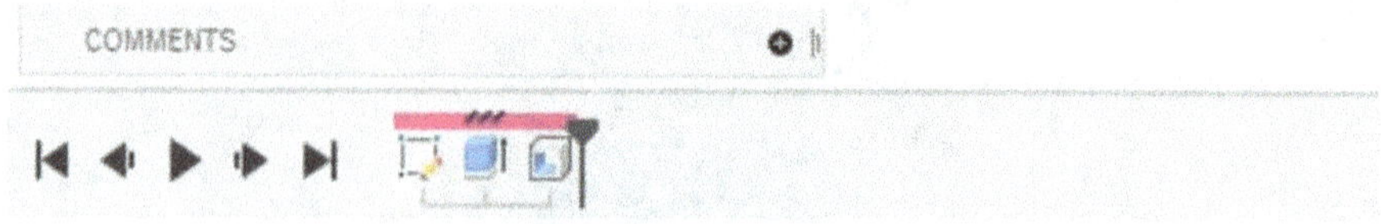

Figure 92: The timeline of our project; sketch -> extrusion -> shell

By now we have the basic shape of the cup. For the handle, we first need a parallel plane to the cup rim so that the handle sits slightly lower than the cup rim. In the menu "Construct" we select "Offset Plane" and click on the cup rim. Then we move the plane downwards by 15 mm.

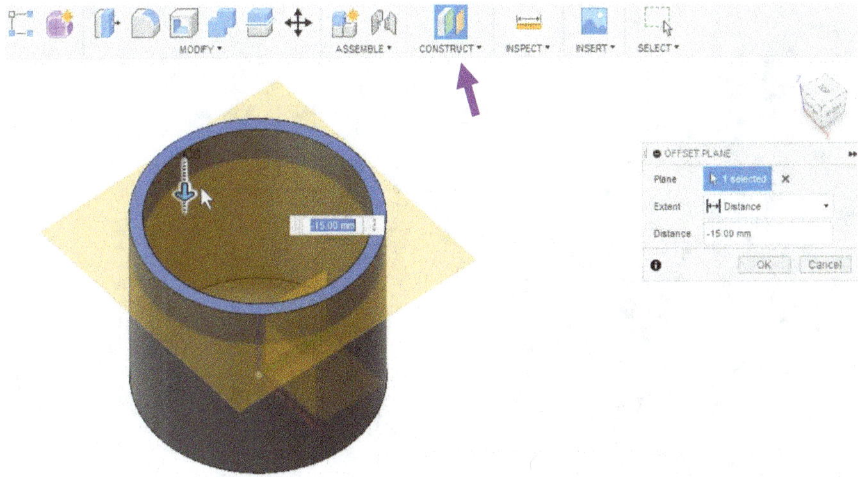

Figure 93: Create a parallel plane 15 mm lower to the cup rim

Then create a sketch on this plane (right-click -> "Create sketch") and draw a vertical line of 20 mm on this plane. The line should have a vertical constraint. If it does not already exist, simply add it and set both points coincident, i.e. congruent, on the edge of the cup.

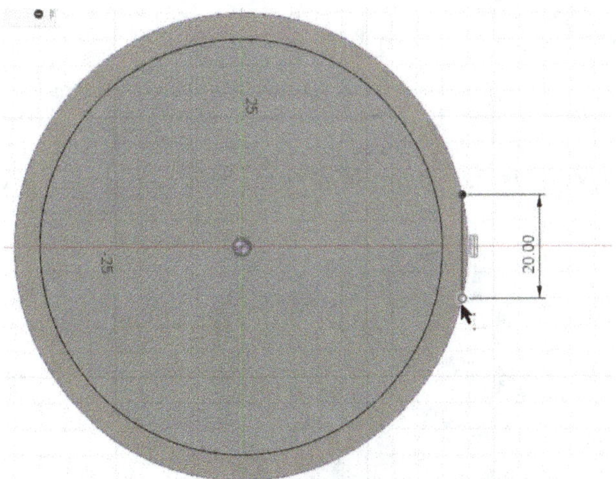

Figure 94: Draw a 20 mm vertical line on the edge of the cup

Complete the profile with two horizontal 30 mm lines and one vertical line to create a rectangle. Alternatively, draw a rectangle right away. Now you may be able to guess the shape of the handle. In this case, the element is added to the basic cylindrical element, i.e. the cup.

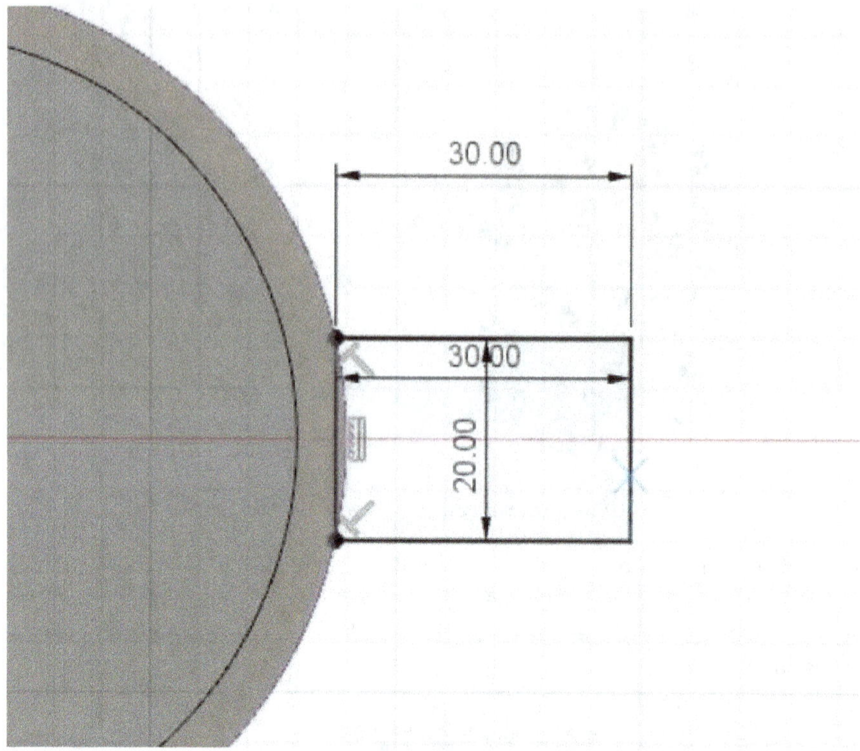

Figure 95: Complement the basic shape of the cup to the vertical line

In 3D mode, you can shape the profile of the handle three-dimensionally with "Extrude", downwards, i.e. in negative z-axis direction. Therefore we choose a dimension of -50 mm.

Figure 96: -50 mm extrusion for the handle

In the next step we start a sketch once more, but select the side face of the handle as the drawing plane this time (right click on Create Sketch plane) . Draw a rectangle 20 mm wide and 40 mm high from a center point and add the dimensions 15 mm and 25 mm to fully define the x and y position of the rectangle.

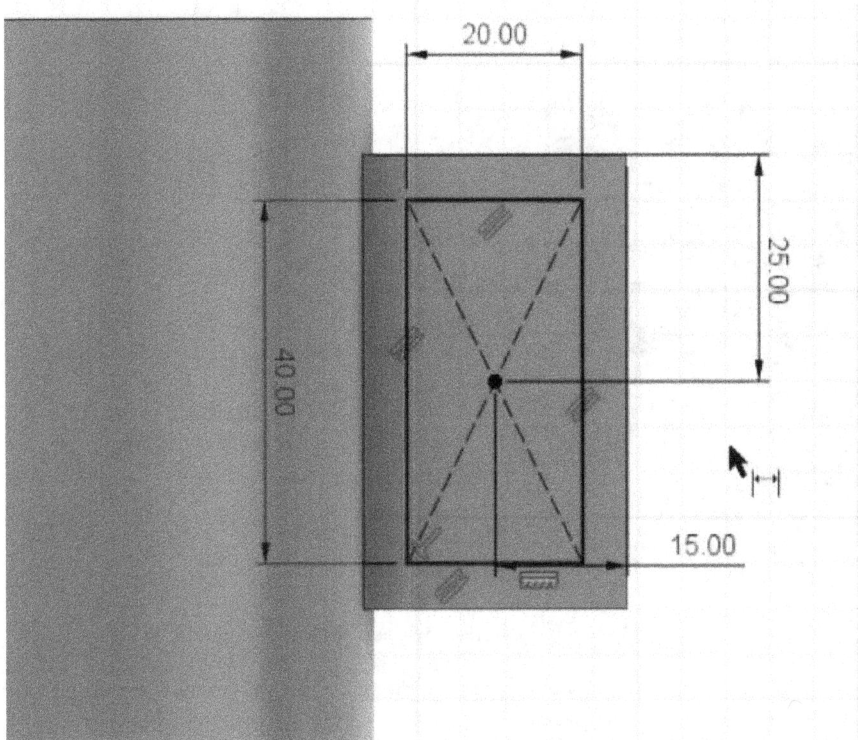

Figure 97: The sketch for the handle cutout on the previously extruded geometry

If you don't know why a sketch is not yet completely defined (black), you can simply drag the sketched geometry - choosing "Select" beforehand - to see in which direction movements are possible.

Then you can make the cutout in 3D mode to complete the handle. By the way, for the cutout, we could have sketched on the x-z plane of our cup instead of on the side surface of the handle. Then we would have simply selected "Symmetric" for the "Direction" in the "Extrusion" options and symmetrically removed material from the inside out. There are, as so often, many different ways.

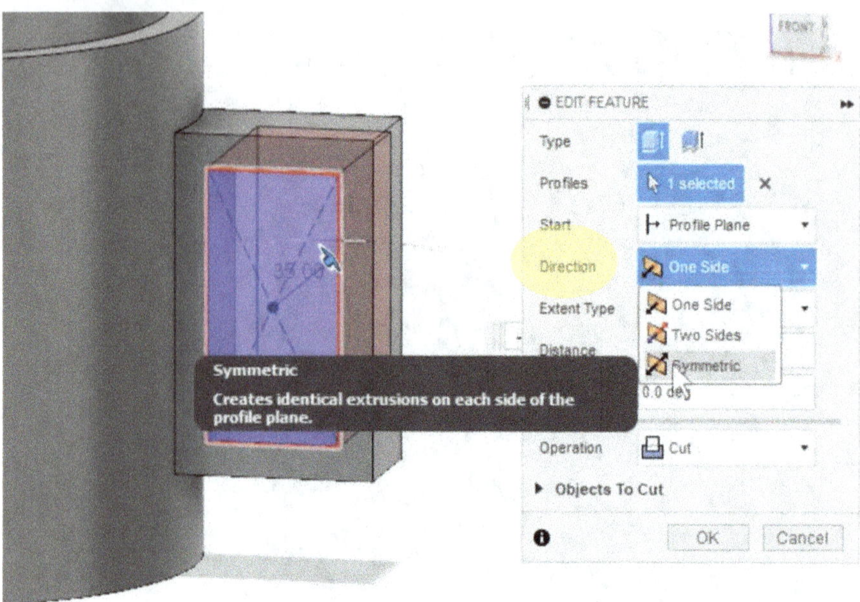

*Figure 98: Symmetrical direction; if we **had** sketched on the x-z plane*

Finally, we round off some edges of the handle and the cup. You are welcome to try this according to your own preferences. Basically, it is only a matter of design or taste in this case.

As the penultimate design project, we will make the front end of a truck with a passenger cell or driver's cab in the following chapter. This will be a bit more challenging, but for us, it will not be a problem! We will proceed step by step! Stick with it and please keep going, now it's going to get more and more exciting!

4.3 Design project III: Truck front part

Figure 99: A truck front end is to be our next design project

For the front part of the truck, we will start in a new design project. First, let's think about how to build up the model. We need a trapezoidal section for the hood, a cuboid for the actual cab and add-on parts like fenders, headlights, grille and bumper. Let us start with the section for the engine hood, for example.

To do this, we start a sketch on the x-z plane and draw a simple rectangle. The starting point should be the center point and the dimensions should be 140 mm in width and 90 mm in height.

Then we create a parallel plane to the x-z plane with an 120 mm offset.

We then sketch another rectangle, which will be a bit smaller, 75 mm wide and 80 mm high to be more specific. The distance of the center should be distanced 5 mm to the coordinate origin, so that the two lower edges of the rectangles are congruent.

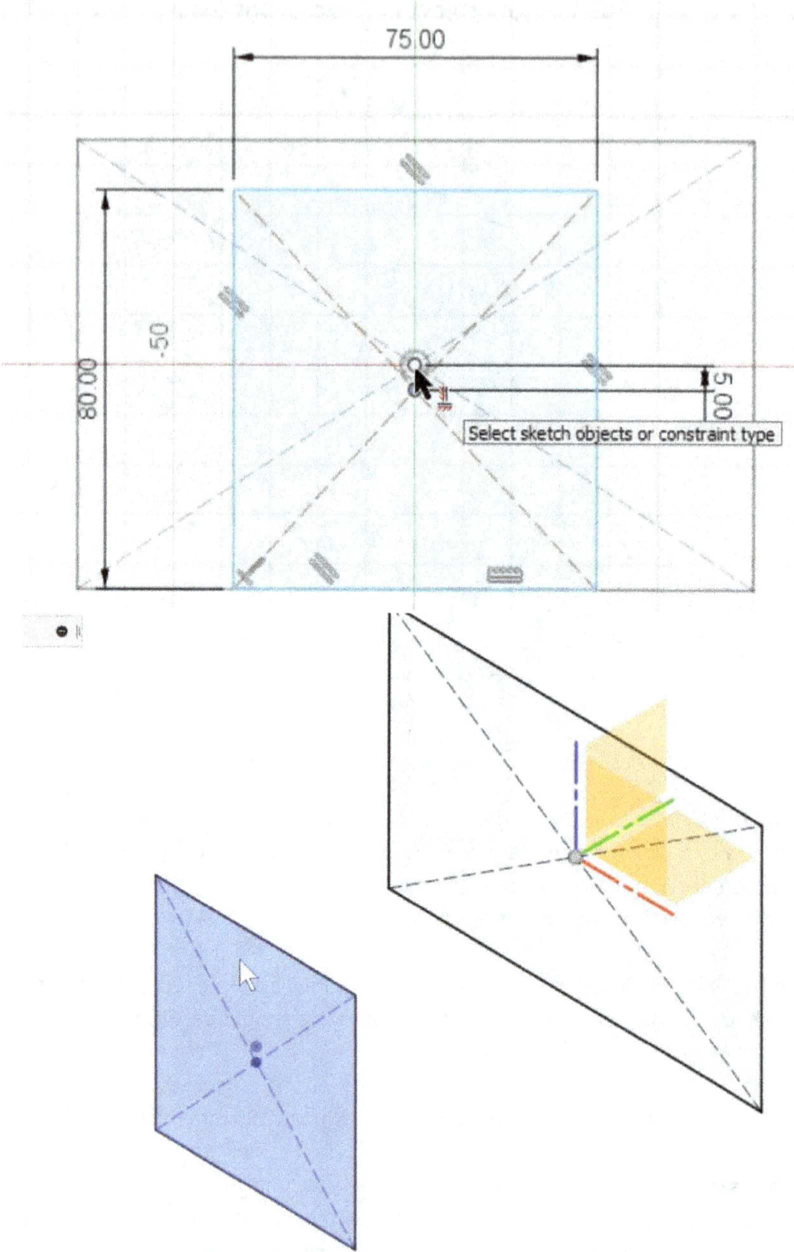

Figure 100: The second rectangle (75 x 80 mm) on the 120 mm offset plane (upper image) and the two completed rectangles in 3D mode (lower image)

With the Loft function, we then have the two rectangles connected in 3D mode to form a solid.

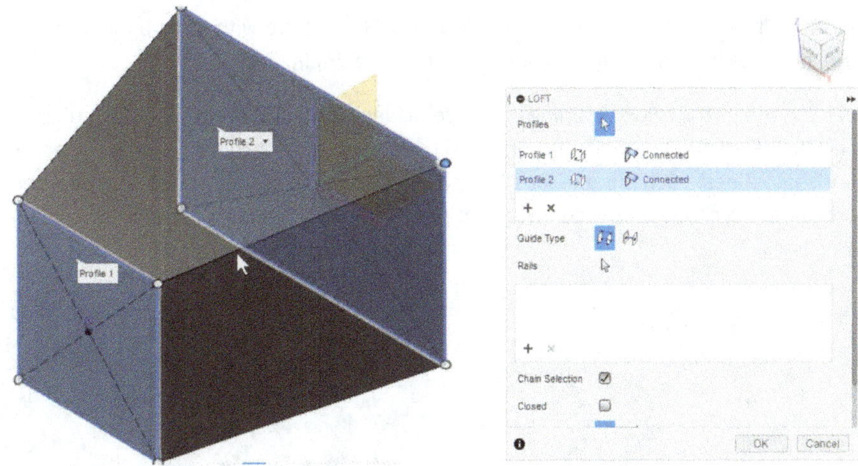

Figure 101: Use the "Loft" function to create a solid body

For the driver's cab, we draw a new sketch on the rear plane of this solid with a 140 mm wide and 170 mm high rectangle.

We then extrude this rectangle by 120 mm. At this point, we have the two basic shapes for our object.

Figure 102: The basic body of the truck's front part

For the two fenders, we draw a sketch on the y-z plane in the next step, since we want to extrude them symmetrically starting from the center.

After we have started a sketch, we first draw a 3 point arc with 50 mm radius and 72 mm distance in horizontal direction relative to the origin.

We set one of the two remaining points coincident thus congruent with the left corner and the other point with the lower line of the engine compartment. Then we need two horizontal lines, each 2.5 mm long, which start from the corner points, and another 3 point arc, which we set concentrically to the first arc and let start or end at the 2.5 mm long lines.

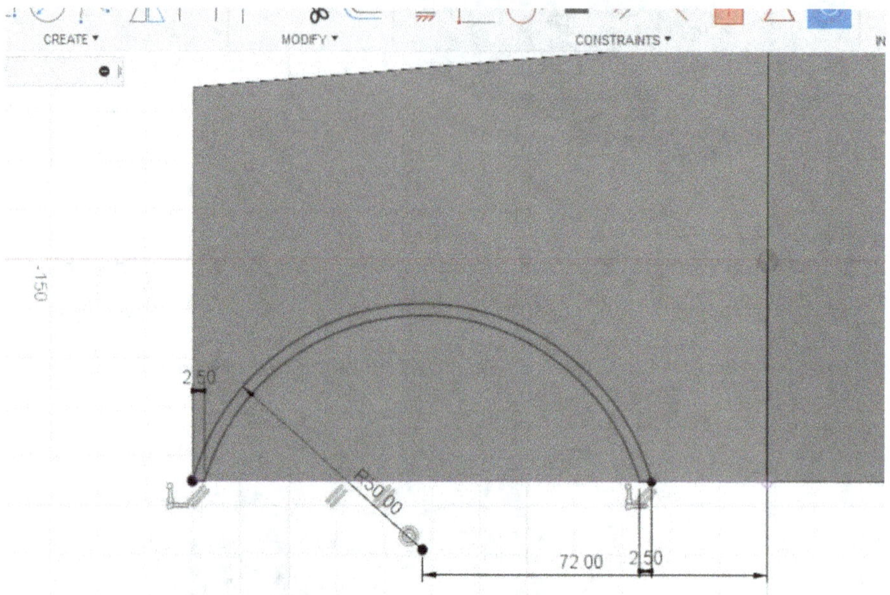

Figure 103: The profile for the two wheel housings; drawn on the y-z plane

To be able to extrude the profile in 3D mode, we must first hide the previous body, otherwise we will not be able to select the profile because it is inside.

Figure 104: Hiding a body: click on the small eye symbol in the browser

We choose a dimension of 70 mm with symmetrical direction ("Direction" -> "Symmetric"). If we want to create an independent body for the solid, we select "New

Body" at "Operation", otherwise simply "Join", which will simply merge it with the previous body. In our case, we choose "Join" because we want these fenders to be part of our basic body.

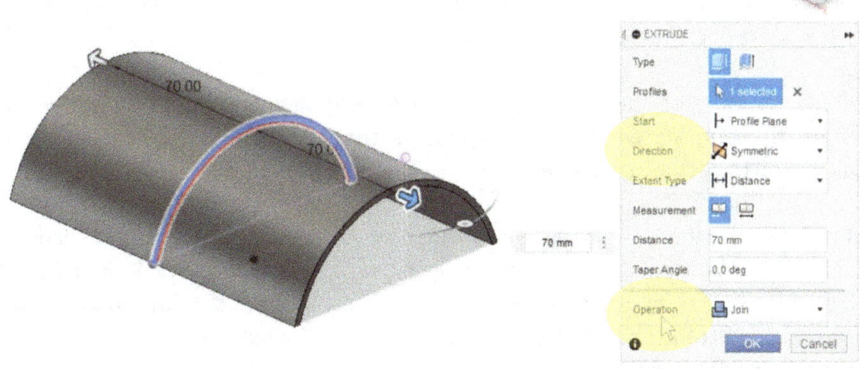

Figure 105: Symmetrical extrusion of the 2D surface for the fenders

Figure 106: Design progress so far; after the body has been faded in again

In this chapter we only want to create new bodies for each add-on part such as the radiator grille, headlights and bumper, but not components as we would do in a normal assembly. We have already briefly addressed the handling of components and their connection by using joints in an assembly in a previous chapter, and we will learn about this in more detail in the next chapter.

It should be noted that in this context, body and component represent different concepts. Confused by bodies, components and assemblies? Let's make a short digression to body vs. component:

The difference between body and component is, that each assembly is made of individual components, and each component in turn is made of bodies. So it's a kind of hierarchical detailing. For example, in a car, the parts of the chassis, the doors, the wheels, and all other individual parts, down to the smallest bolts, are components. Each of these components of a main assembly, can in turn be subdivided into multiple bodies, or solids. But you don't necessarily have to do that, you can also build a single part, a component, from just one body, especially if it is very simple in its geometry.

In this specific example, we will build our model from only one component, but since the component is somewhat more complex, we will build it from several solids. This has the advantage, that we can clearly delimit the individual bodies and, for example, hide them or slightly change the appearance of individual bodies. In the next design project we will work more closely with several components.

A brief summary: A body is a more detailed separation within a component, which in turn is a single part of an assembly. A body is primarily a part of a component, whereas a component can move freely within the parent assembly and is linked by joints within an assembly. Don't worry if you don't understand it right away, you'll understand it even better as the course progresses through practical implementation.

Back to our truck. In the next step we want to hollow out our solid, we do that with the command "Shell", a click on the lower surface and the input of 5 mm for defining the wall thickness.

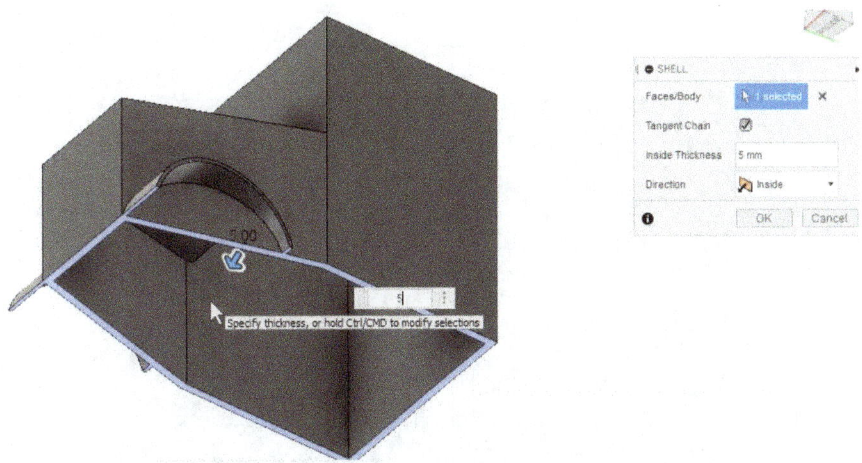

Figure 107: Apply command "Shell" to the lower surface (5 mm wall thickness)

We would also like to remove the surfaces inside the wheel housings. To do this, we could on the one hand start an extrusion as we know it. On the other hand, in this case we can also simply right-click on the surface element and remove it with "Delete".

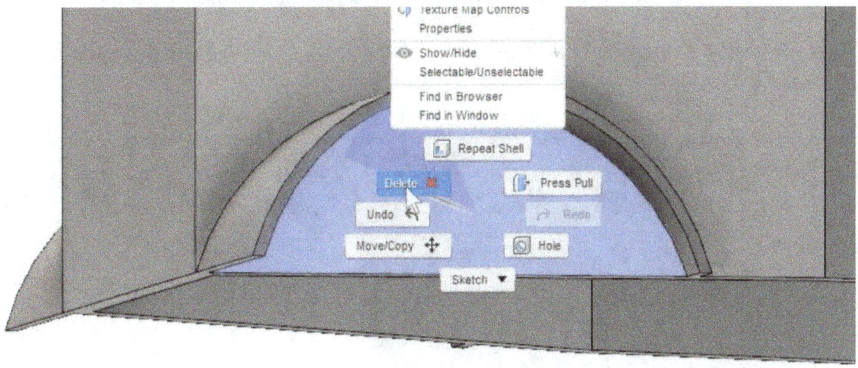

Figure 108: Delete superfluous surface sections with "Delete" (right-click on the surface)

We will then move on to the two-part windshield. We want to build it from two simple rectangles. Take the dimensions from the following profiles.

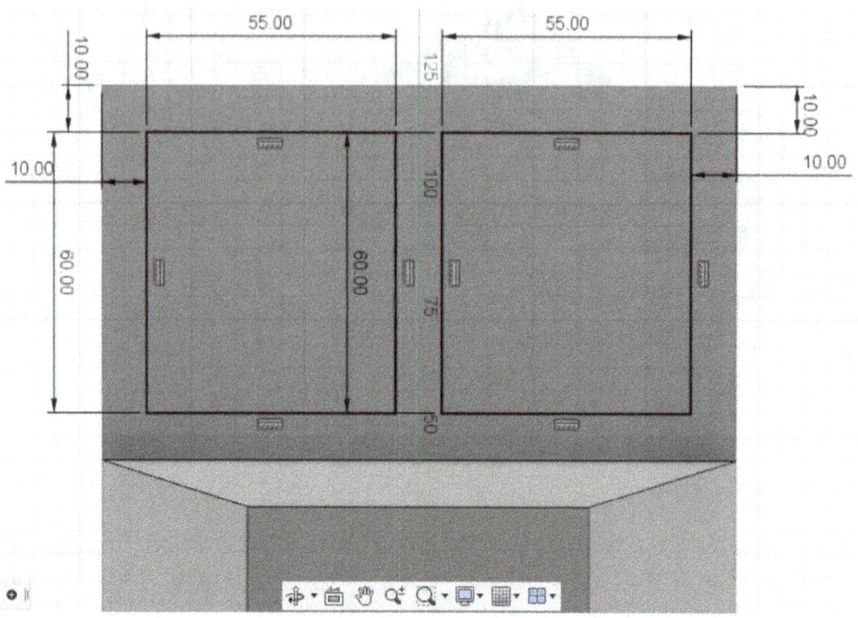

Figure 109: The two rectangular geometries for the cutout for the windshield

Then finish the sketch and cut it out with "Extrusion". The edges of the windows are rounded with 5 mm.

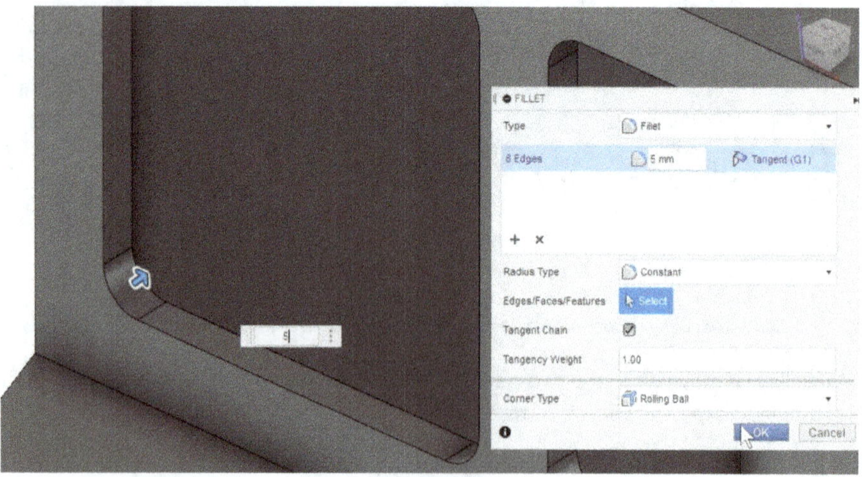

Figure 110: The inner edges of the two cutouts are rounded with 5 mm

We proceed similarly for the side windows. For this, however, we draw only a rectangle on one side and then simply cut through the entire width, since the cabin is hollow anyway. The dimensions and position of the rectangle should be as follows:

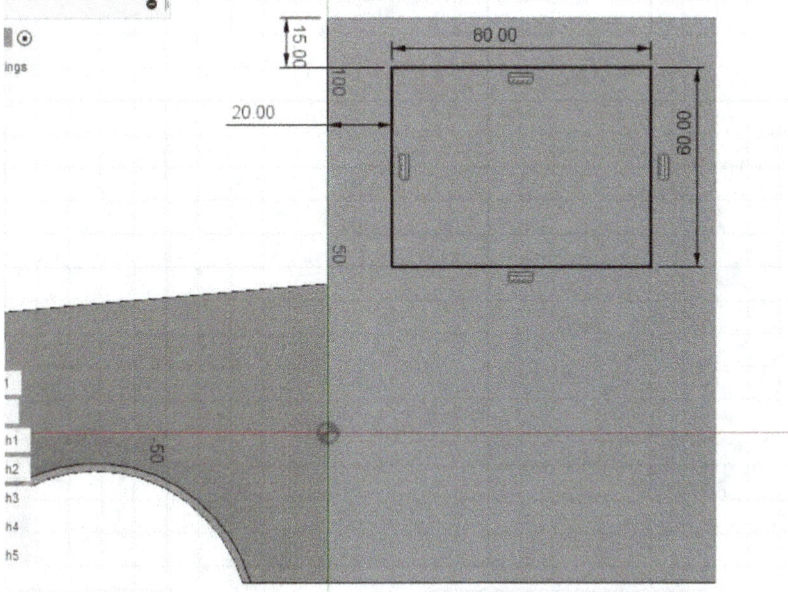

Figure 111: The dimensions for the cutout of the two windows (extrusion through complete body)

To implement at least the illusion of a door, we will learn a new function, the "Emboss" command. For this command, we first need a sketch, so we will draw a rectangle for embossing the door on the side surface of the driver's cab. The starting point should be in the lower left corner of the window and the rectangle should be 90 mm high and as wide as the window.

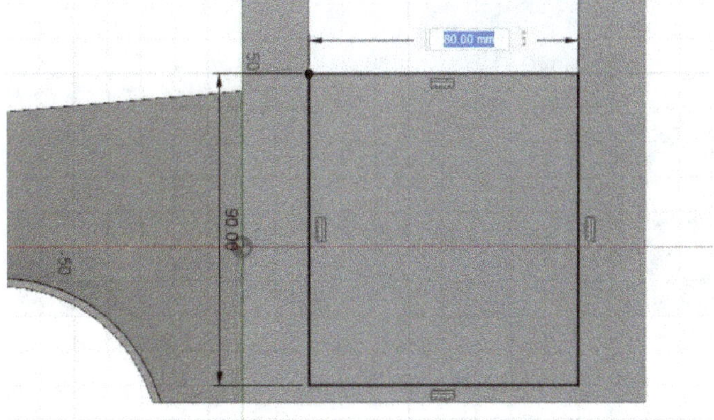

Figure 112: 80 x 90 mm rectangle on the side surface of the truck for the door

Then we select the command "Emboss" (menu: "Create") as well as the sketched profile and choose "Deboss" in the options, because we don't want an elevation but a deepening and we enter 1 mm as depth.

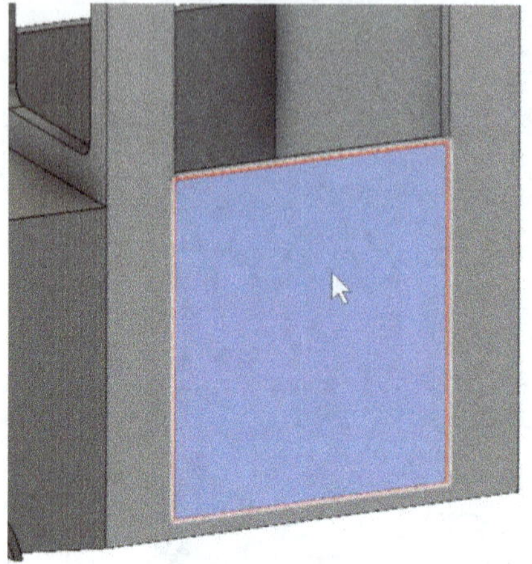
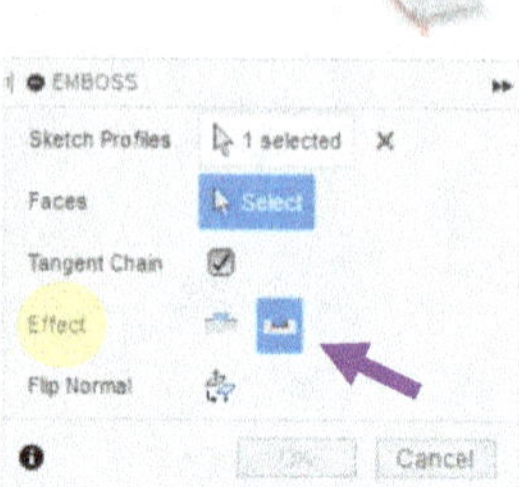

Figure 113: "Emboss" command with the "Deboss" option

As you may have recognized, this step would also have been possible with "Extrude".

For the door handle we will draw a rectangle on this surface again.
This time with the following dimensions:

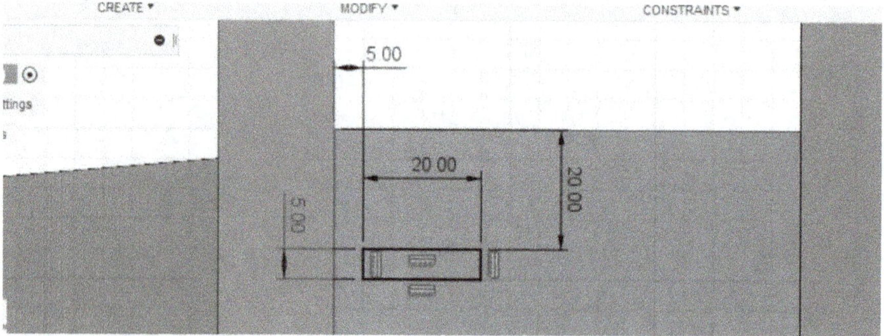

Figure 114: The rectangle for the door handle

Then we extrude the profile 5 mm and select "New Body" at Operation, because we want to create a new body for this.

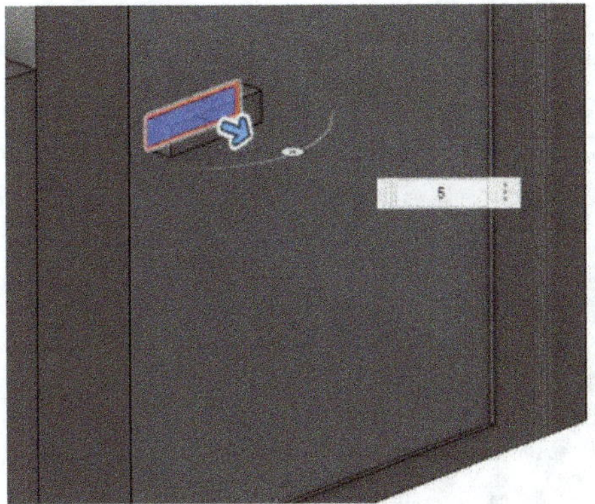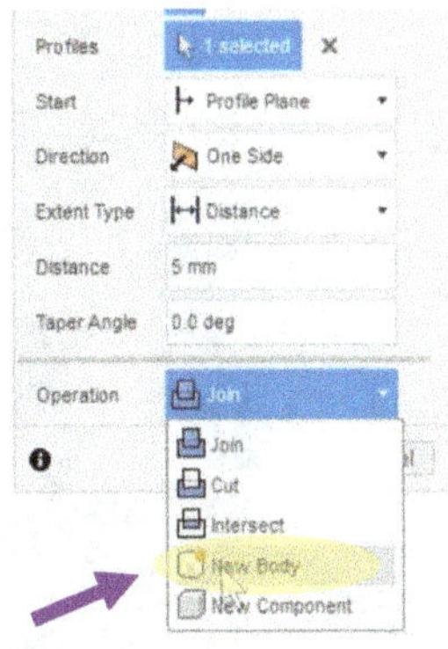

Figure 115: Extrude the door handle 5 mm and have a new body created

To make it easier for us, we simply mirror these two features to the other side. To do this, we select the "Mirror" command (menu: "Create") and in its options at "Type": "Features". We then simply select the embossing and the door handle in the timeline (below) and then switch in the mirror options to the item: "Mirror Plane" and select the y-z plane as the mirror plane.

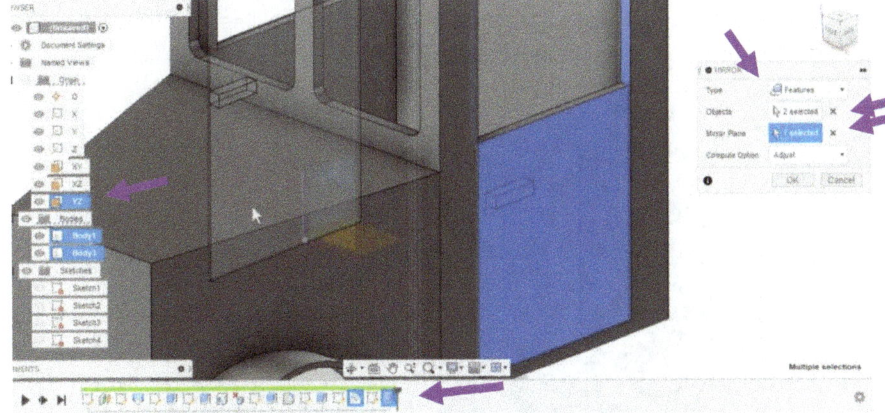

Figure 116: "Mirror" command. First select the specific Features from the Timeline, then Mirror Plane

The "Mirror" command usually saves a considerable amount of time for symmetrical parts and features, by the way, this also applies to the 2D sketching environment, so try to use it as often as possible.

We continue with two fillets, one for the two door handles with 1.5 mm each and the two upper edges of the side windows with 5 mm each.

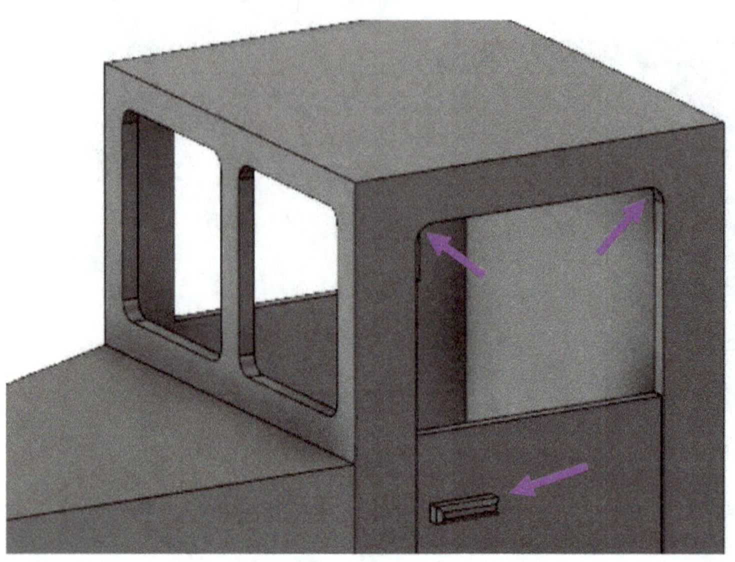

Figure 117: Add fillets (in the case of door handles, simply select the uppermost surface)

Now we draw the bumper. It should be placed at the front with the dimensions 140 mm and 15 mm. For this we will use the constraint "colinear" for the upper horizontal line, which we link to the truck front and e.g. the left vertical line, which we link to the side of the truck to fully define the sketch.

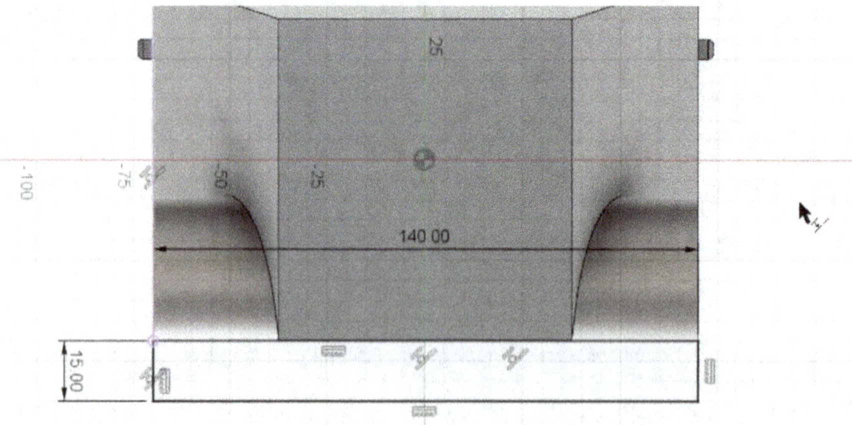

Figure 118: The 2D sketch for the bumper on the front side of the truck (just create the sketch on the front side)

Then we can extrude the profile by 8 mm, we create a new body ("Select New Body") for it, and round off with 4 mm.

Figure 119: Finished bumper (for filleting just select the top surface)

For the headlights, we first draw one of the two required on the front surface and then mirror it to the other side. The profile should have, for example, the following dimensions:

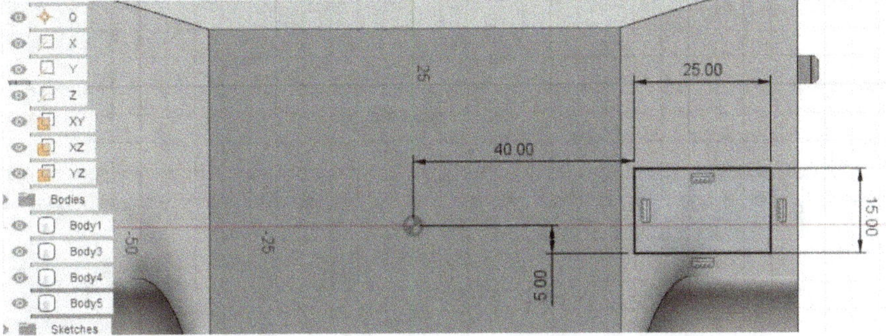

Figure 120: The sketch for one of the two headlights (sketch on the front surface of the truck)

We then extrude it by 10 mm. In addition, we draw another 2 mm cutout with a 2 mm distance to the headlight body (draw a rectangle with 2 mm distance to each edge of the headlight in a sketch) to improve the design.

Figure 121: For the cutout, draw a rectangle with 2 mm distance to the edge on the surface of the headlight and extrude 2 mm inwards ("Cut")

And a connecting strut to suggest a little more stability. For this connecting strut we need a circular geometry on the front side surface of the truck with 6 mm diameter at a distance of 83 mm and horizontally aligned to the origin.

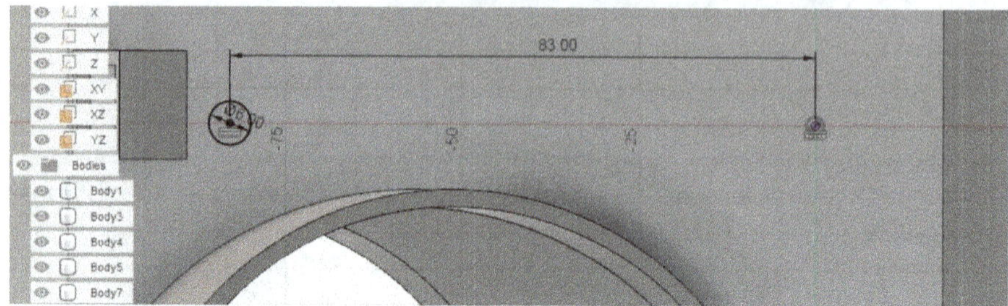

Figure 122: Create a circle geometry on the front side surface of the truck (right click on the surface -> "Create sketch")

In addition, draw another circular geometry on the back of the headlight - also 6 mm in diameter - which we simply dimension from the top and side edges with 8 mm and 12 mm.

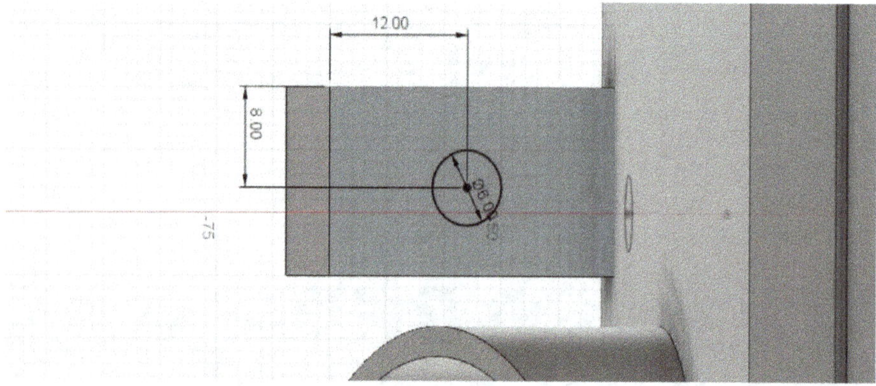

Figure 123: The second circle geometry on the back of the headlight

Then we use the "Loft" command and connect the two circular surfaces to form a three-dimensional connecting strut.

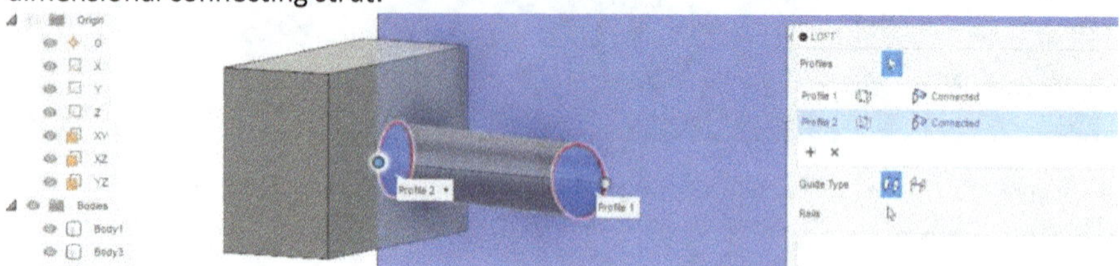

Figure 124: "Loft" command from the "Create" menu

Now we can mirror the headlight and the strut to the other side.

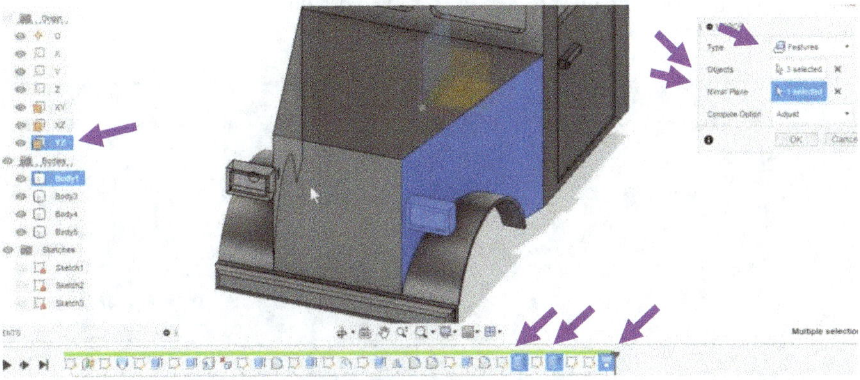

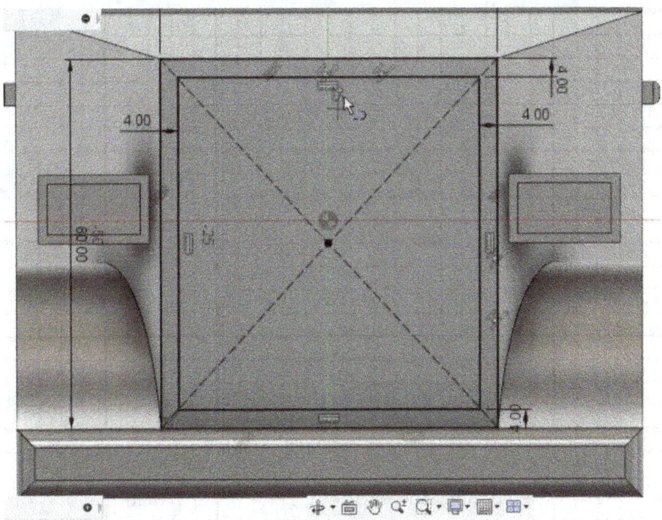

Figure 125: Mirror: Select features at "Type" in the options (top right), then switch to "Objects" and select the features in the timeline (bottom), finally switch to "Mirror Plane" in the options (top right) and select the y-z plane in the browser. Done!

As a last detail of our truck front-part we would like to draw a grille. For this we first start a new sketch on the front surface.

Then we first draw a rectangle with 75 mm width and 80 mm height, the side line and the upper line should be colinear to the lines of the front surface. In the next step another rectangle, with 4 mm distance to the edge of the first rectangle, which borders our radiator cutouts.

Figure 126: Draw two rectangles on the front surface - one of them congruent and one of them with a distance of 4 mm from the edge

Then we draw a vertical line congruent with the center line. Next, we draw a line to the left and right of the center line at a distance of 1 mm from the center line. The start and end points should be on the second rectangle drawn.

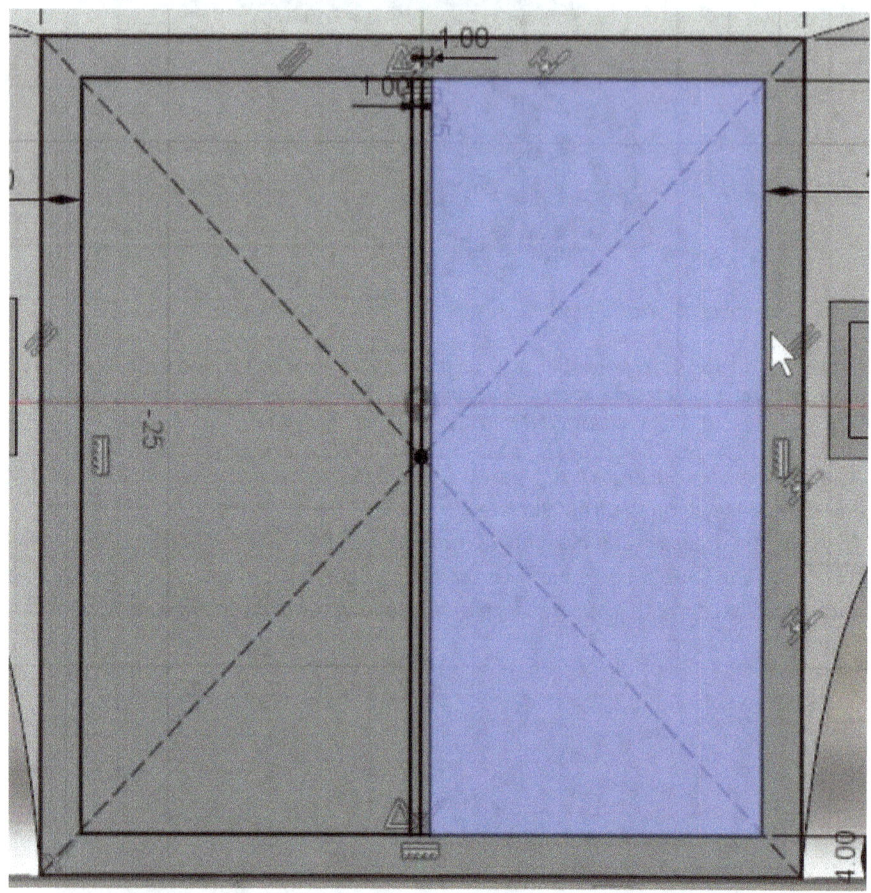

Figure 127: The center line and a line to the left and right of it, each 1 mm apart

Now we would have to draw a lot of these lines, because we want to extrude every other space between them to get the shape of the grille.

But to make it a little bit easier, we use a new command: the "Pattern" command, or "Rectangular Pattern" in this case.

To do this, we select the vertical line elements, and enter a distance of 1 mm between the elements.

Then we select for "Distance Type": "Spacing" and for "Direction Type" for the x-axis: "Symmetric", because we want to work in both x-directions, and increase the number to 65. Voila, the program does the work for us.

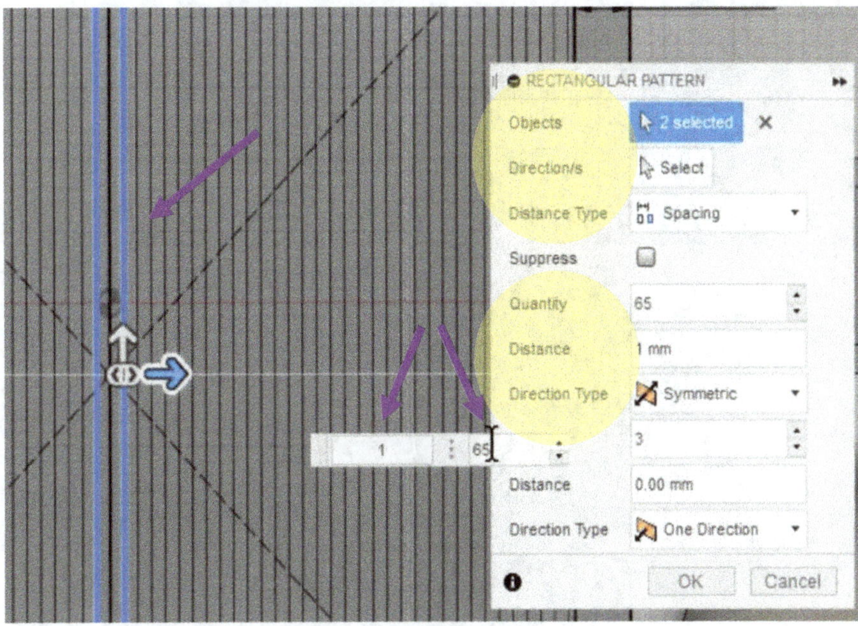

Figure 128: Command "Rectangular Pattern" (The desired lines have already been created by the program in this image)

To create the solid body of the radiator grille, we have to extrude the area between the two large rectangles as well as every second long, narrow rectangle 2 mm outwards, creating the following solid:

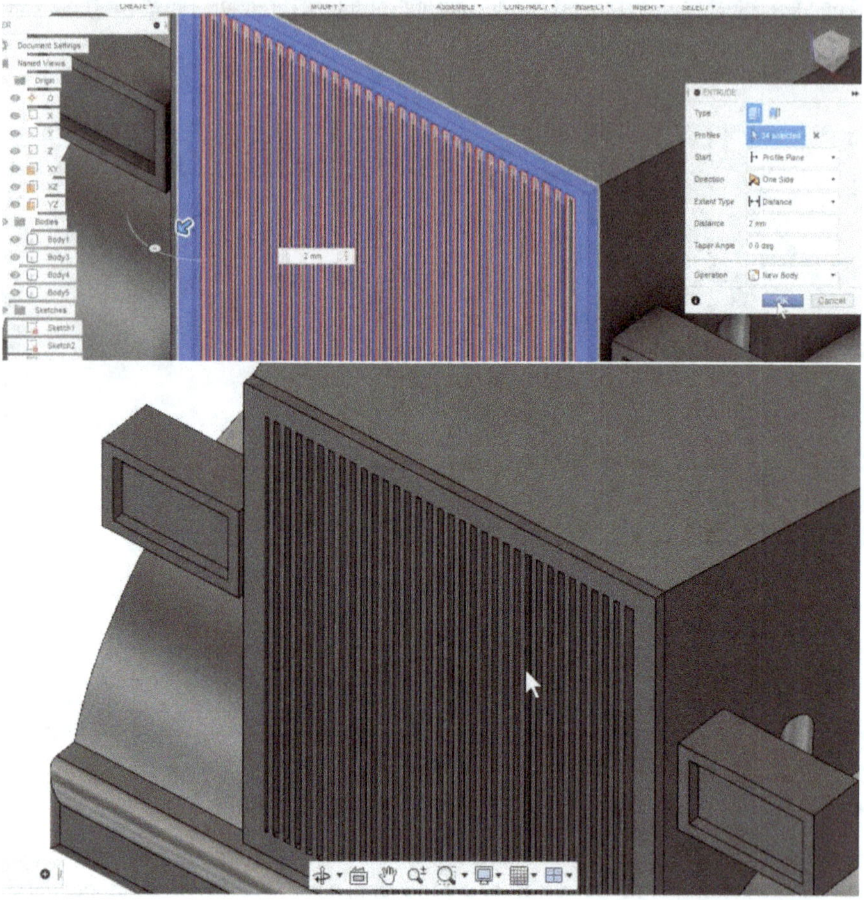

Figure 129: Extrusion of the radiator grille

Excellent! After we have rounded the surfaces of the driver's cab with 2 mm each, we take a quick look at the individual bodies and then will have finished this lesson! Great if you stayed with it!

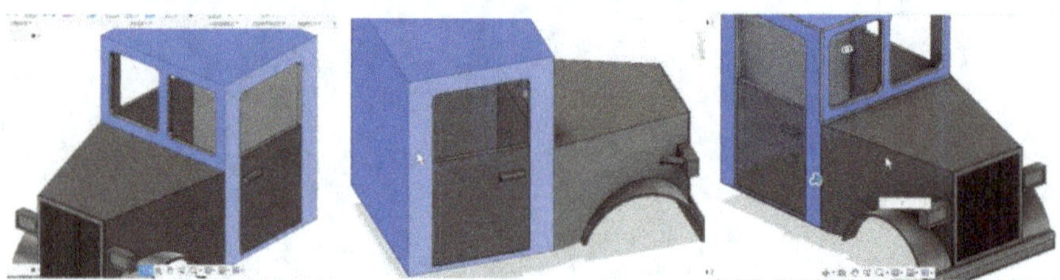

Figure 130: Round off the surfaces for the driver's cab (light blue surfaces and 2 mm radius)

As we can see, we have now created several bodies, which are located in the "Bodies" folder in the browser. More precisely, one each for the door handles, the cabin, the headlights, the struts, the bumper and the grille. We can hide/show these bodies as we wish, or right-click to change the material or appearance per body.

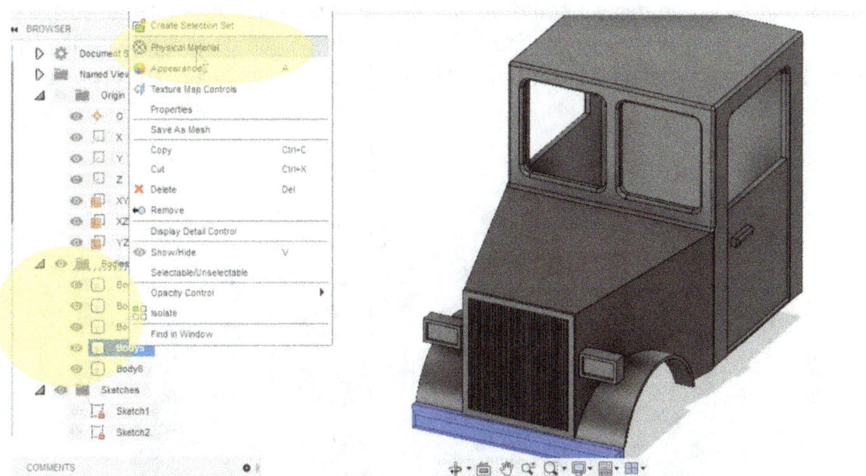

Figure 131: Change the material of a body (right click on the body and "Select Physical Material". In the menu then simply "drag" a material onto the body with the mouse button pressed)

If we want we can print the model as it is with a 3D printer. If you are interested in 3D printing, feel free to take a look at the book "3D Printing | 101".

However, if you prefer to design the bumper, grille and headlights as separate components and then assemble them later, take a look at the next lesson first. In the upcoming lesson, we'll take a step-by-step look at how to work with components in an assembly. We'll design a simplified model of a 4-cylinder internal combustion engine.

This is going to be pretty awesome! Let's get right to it!

4.4 Design Project IV: 4 Cylinder Internal Combustion Engine Model

In this chapter, as announced, we want to design a simplified model of a 4-cylinder combustion engine. We want to build this model from several main components, as in reality, but will then neglect some details so that the design does not become too complex. We need a crankcase, four pistons, four connecting rods, four piston pins and a crankshaft. We will dispense with the oil pan and the cylinder head in this course.

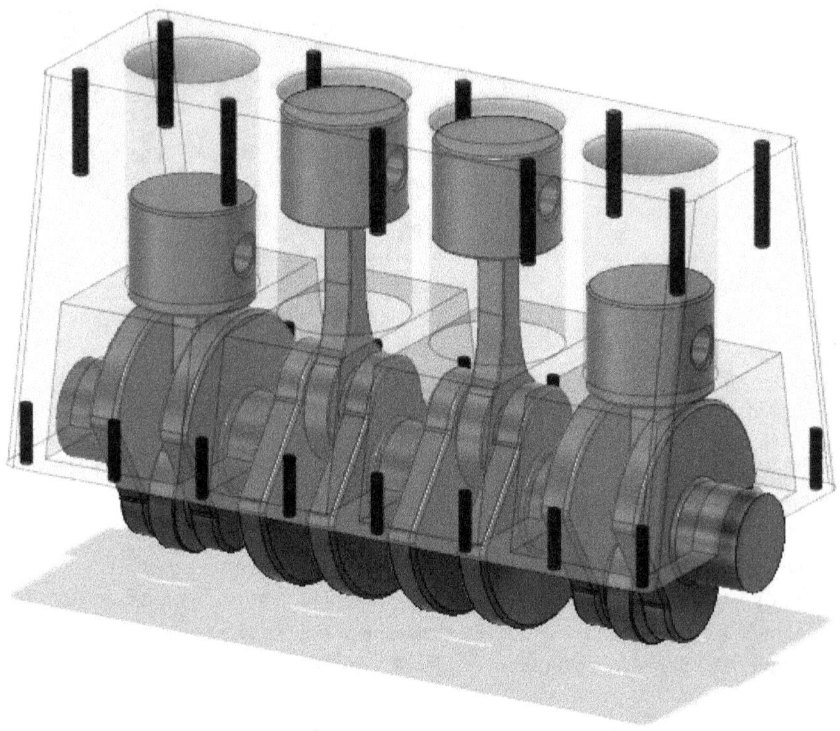

Figure 132: The model of the 4-cylinder engine we will design in this chapter

4.4.1 Part 1: Crankcase

Figure 133: The crankcase of the engine model

The first component we design is the crankcase, as it creates a central starting point. To do this, we start on the x-y plane with a sketch.

To create the shape for the crankcase as the basic body, we first span a rectangle from the center point (coordinate origin) and can immediately enter 500 mm as the width and 150 mm as the height as dimensions. As we can see, after entering the dimensions, the sketched profile becomes black, i.e. completely defined.

Then we finish the sketch and in 3D mode we create a plane parallel to the x-y plane with a distance of -250 mm, as we have already learned in one of the previous lessons.

On this plane we then draw another rectangle with identical width, i.e. 500 mm, but a height of 250 mm (coordinate center as starting point).

After closing the sketch, we use the "Loft" command to create a trapezoidal solid.

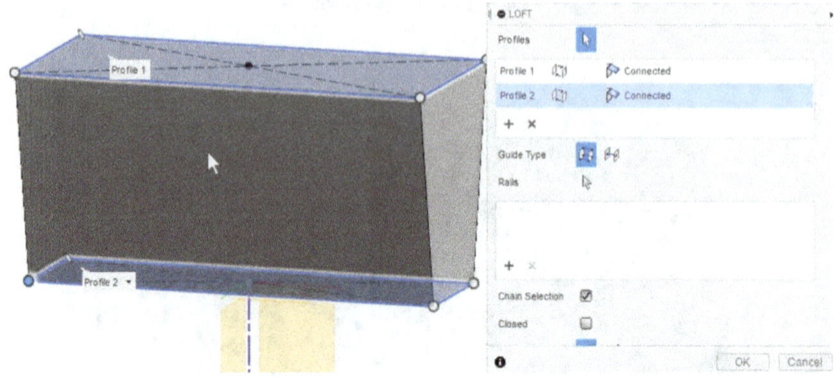

Figure 134: Connect the two sketches on the different planes with the "Loft" command

Now we take care of the holes for the pistons, i.e. the cylinders. We can make them in two ways, either with the "Hole" command or as a circular cutouts with "Extrude".

Since the holes have to go completely through the cuboid, we simply use cutouts in this case. For this we start a sketch on the upper surface.

We want to create cylinders with 90 mm diameter and design a 4-cylinder engine. Therefore we need the following dimensions and geometries:

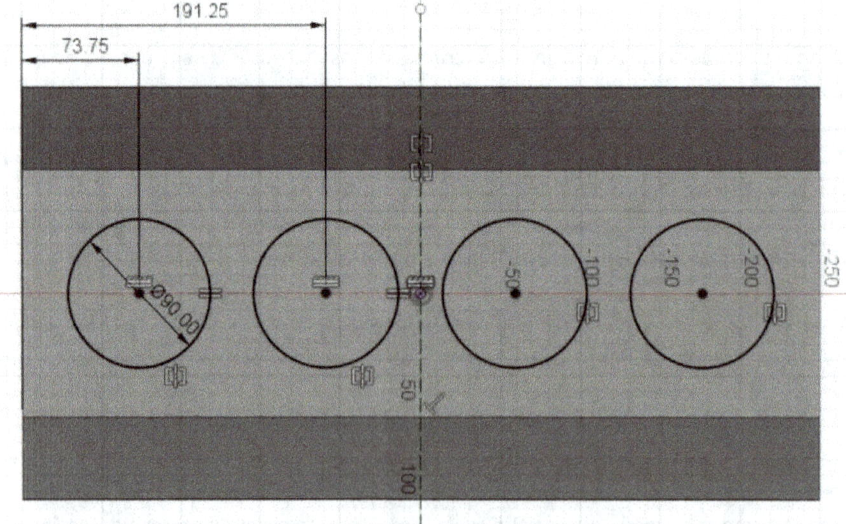

Figure 135: The circles for the cutouts of the cylinders; sketched on the upper surface

What is the easiest way to draw these circles? First we draw a circle with a diameter of 90 mm and define its position in x-axis direction with a dimension of 73.75 mm from the center to the edge. To fully define the position of the circle, we need not only the diameter and a dimension to a fixed point in the x-direction, but also a position in the y-direction. Since the center of the circle should be on the x-axis, we use a constraint instead of a dimension. Select the center of the circle as well as the origin, and select the constraint "horizontal". Then the profile gets black and thus completely defined.

For the second circle we use conditions again. First simply draw a circle and then set the condition "Equal", so the circle gets the same dimension, without further dimensioning (select condition and both circles). Then again the condition "Horizontal" for the y-position of the circle. And a dimension in x, for the x-position in the coordinate system. In this case 191.25 mm, to create an even distance of 117.5 mm between the cylinders.

Since our geometry of the four circles is axisymmetric about the y-axis, we can now create the other two circles very quickly and easily using the "Mirror" command. For the command we first have to create an axis around which we want to mirror, because the y-axis is not selectable in this case. We do this by drawing a line congruent to the y-axis and linking it with "coincident" to the origin.
We then convert this line into a construction line by right-clicking and selecting "Normal/Construction". You can recognize this by the dashed line type.

We will not fully define construction lines, since they are not necessarily relevant. We only need a defined position in x-direction, which we already have.

Then select the "Mirror" command in the "Create" menu and select the two circles, switch the selection to "Mirror Line" in the options and then select the just created construction line. Voila, the other two circles are created and already fully defined.

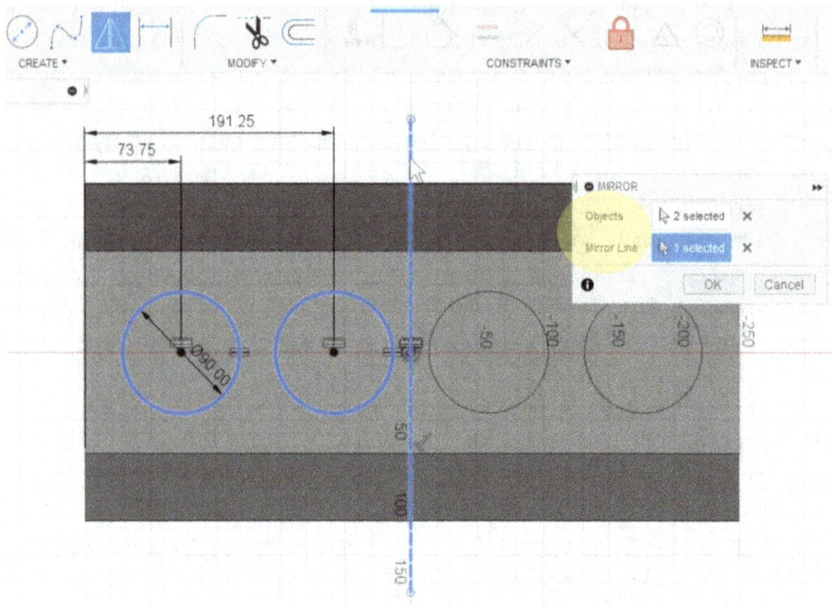

Figure 136: Select "Mirror"; select objects; switch to "Mirror Line" (in the options on the right) and then select the construction line; mirrored circles are created

We close the 2D sketch and create the cutouts with "Extrude" by selecting the four circular areas. In the options we can select "To Object" for "Extent Type" and then select the surface to which the cutouts should be made. In our case we select the bottom surface. By the way, "Operation" must then be set to "Cut".

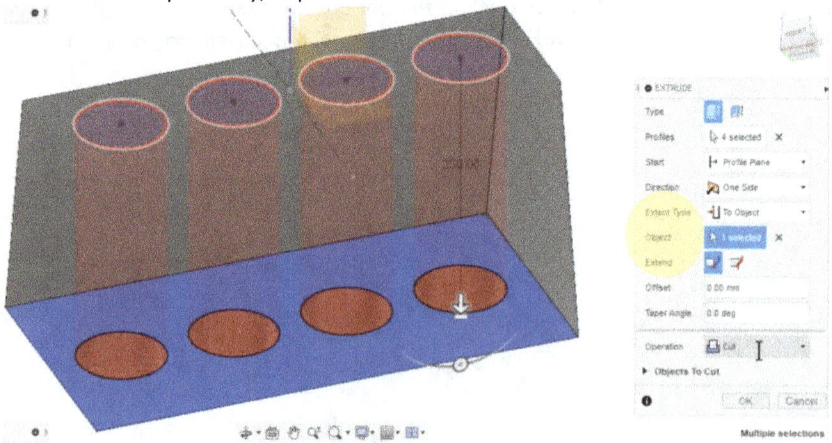

Figure 137: Make the cut to the bottom surface ("To Object")

By the way, we could have integrated these circular surfaces into the first sketch right away and thus could have saved a step.

Then we work on the lower part of the crankcase, in which the crankshaft will later find its place. To do this, we create a trapezoidal cutout that spans symmetrically from the center of the housing (sketch on y-z plane).

First, we draw a base line and set it colinear with the crankcase bottom. The length is unimportant for now.

Then we draw the trapezoid as shown and dimension the height with 100 mm.

Then dimension the lower corner points with 25 mm to the wall.

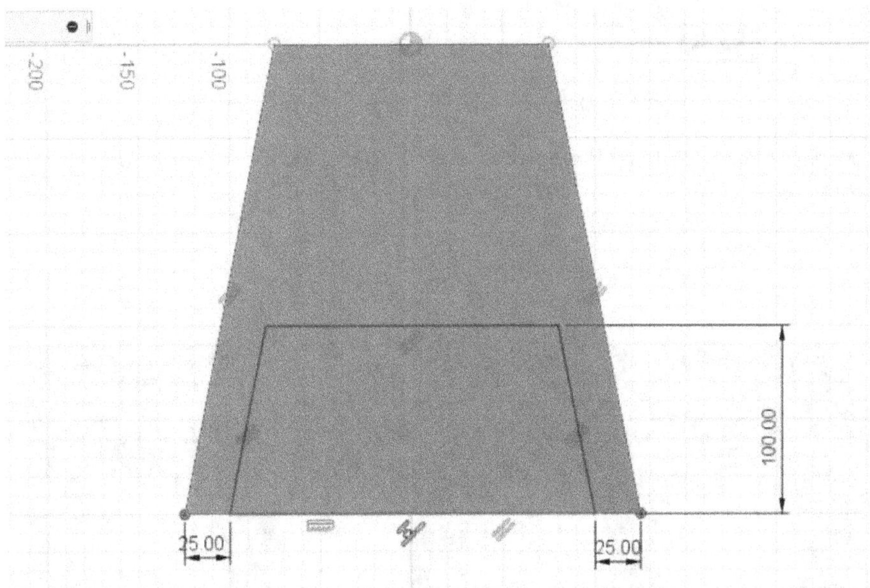

Figure 138: The trapezoid on the y-z plane

To be able to select the surface in 3D mode, we hide the body for a moment. In 3D mode, use the "Extrude" command once again and select the surface. Then show the body. Afterwards we select the option "Symmetric" for "Direction" and "Cut" for "Operation".

We also enter a dimension of 230 mm, since we have a length of 500 mm and want to leave 25 mm of wall thickness for each. So the calculation is: 225 mm x 2 = 450 + 2x 25 makes 500 mm. Confirm and you are done.

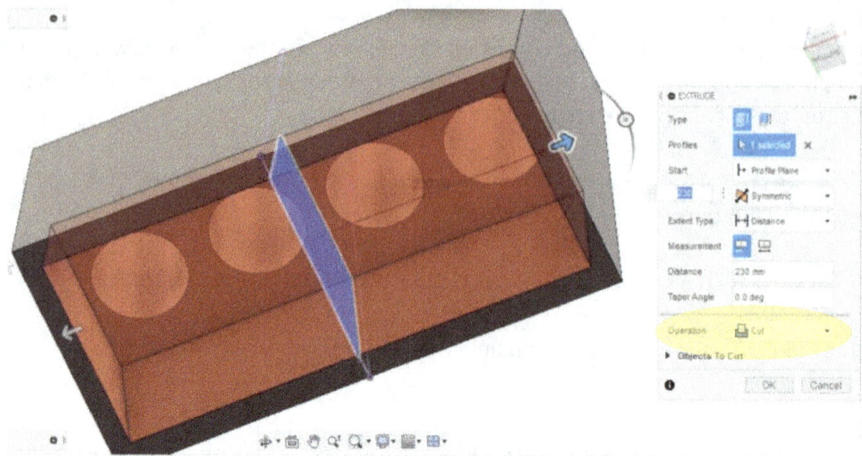

Figure 139: Make the cutout in the lower area of the crankcase

We now need to add material again for the crankshaft mounts. We draw the following three rectangular profiles on the lower surface of the housing:

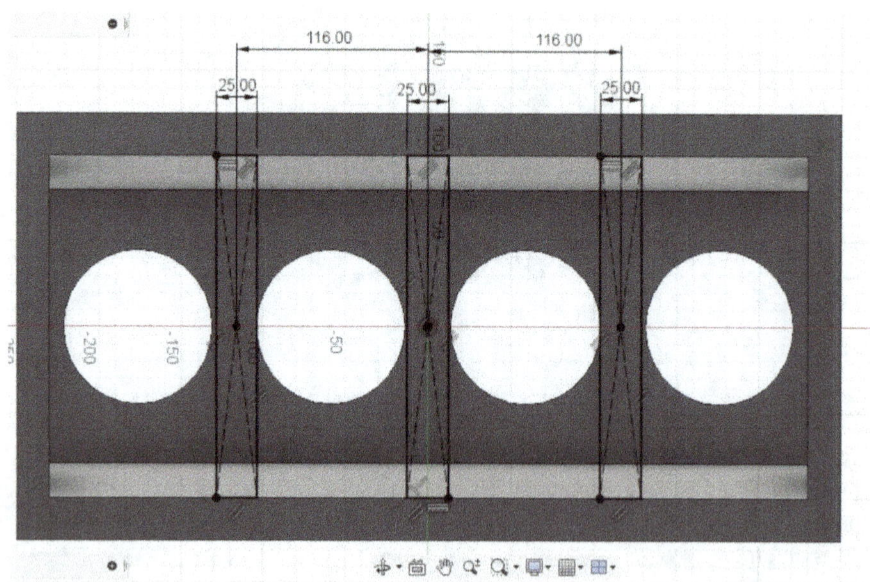

Figure 140: The three rectangular profiles; sketch on the bottom of the case

We then extrude this in 3D mode by selecting "To Object" for "Extent Type", as well as "Join" for "Operation", in the extrusion options. This allows us to select the bottom face of the cylinder and extrude the three ribs to it.

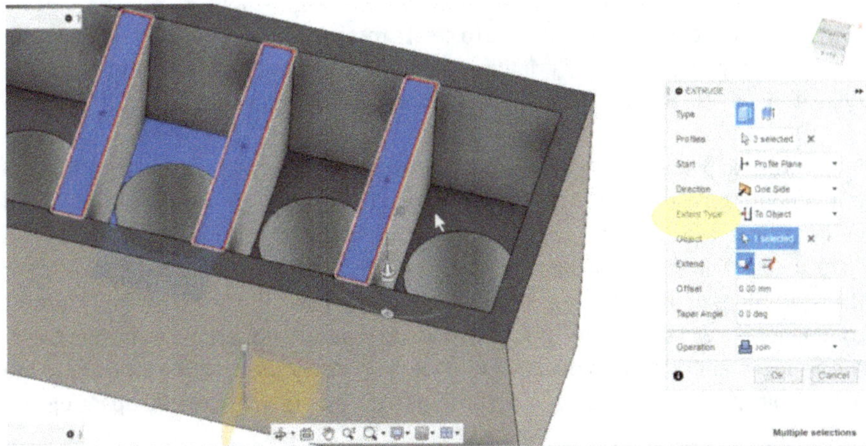

Figure 141: Extrude the three ribs to the inner surface

In the next step, we create a circular cutout for the bearing surfaces of the crankshaft. To do this, we draw a circle with a diameter of 70 mm and a distance of 125 mm from the corner point on the side wall of the housing. The center of the circle should be congruent with the bottom line.

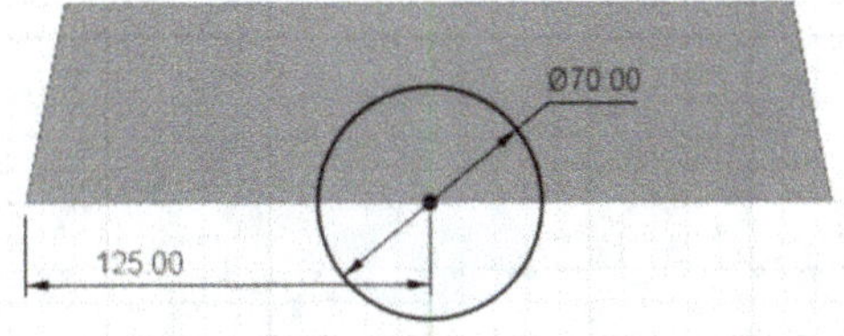

Figure 142: Circular geometry for crankshaft support; sketch on side face

We then extrude this completely through the entire housing using the "Cut" option.

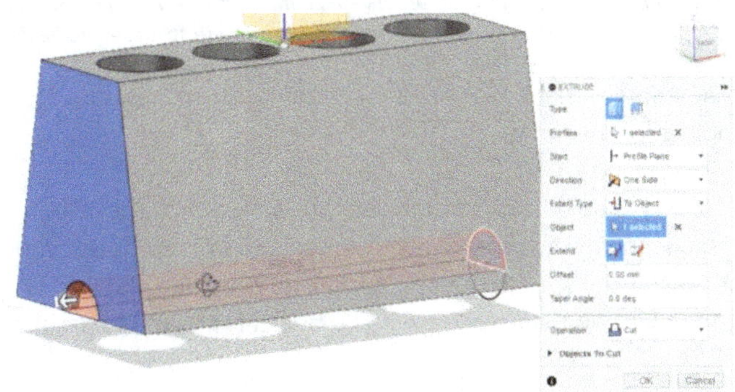

Figure 143: Create the cutout for the crankshaft

In the penultimate step, we would like to create threaded holes for mounting a cylinder head and oil pan to our very primitive crankcase. First, we create the holes for the cylinder head. We use the "Hole" function in 3D mode.

But in order to place the holes correctly, we first start a 2D sketch on the upper surface of the housing. We need ten holes for the cylinder head. To create them quickly and easily we use the "Pattern" command from the "Create" section. For this we need "Rectangular Pattern". First we create a point with a distance of 20 mm from each of the lateral lines of the cylinder head surface. Then we select the point and the "Pattern" command. We will see two arrows, as well as input options for distance and number of the arrangement or pattern popping up. If we simply drag the arrows a little and in the desired direction, we will see that a matrix with the points to be created opens up.

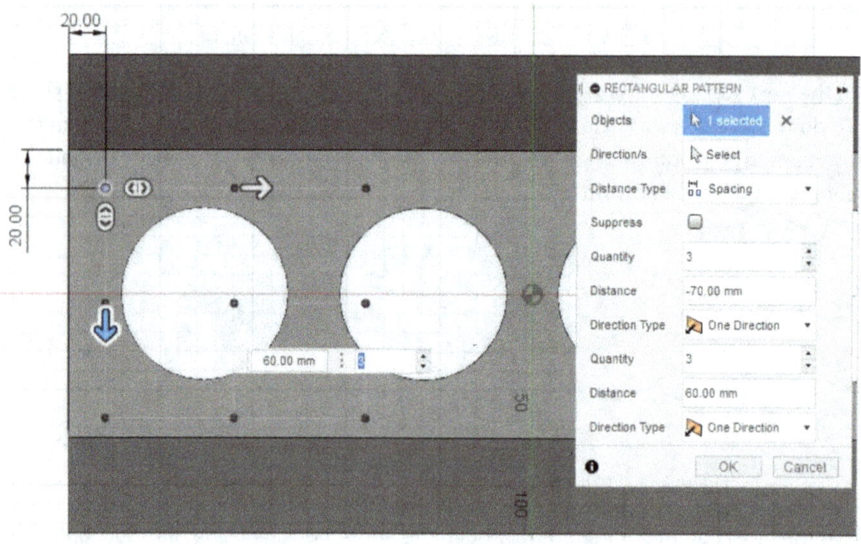

Figure 144: A point ("Create" in the 2D area) with 20 mm distance was created, as well as the command "Rectangular Pattern" was selected and the arrows were stretched in the desired direction

Think of it like a spreadsheet. In y-direction we need 2 rows. In x-direction 5 lines. 2 x 5 equals 10 points for the holes.

The corner points should have a distance of 20 mm each to the edge, i.e. we need a distance of -460 mm for the pattern in x-direction and 110 mm in y-direction. We could also set the "Distance Type" in the options bar to "Spacing", then we would measure from point to point. We then confirm with Ok and get the desired pattern.

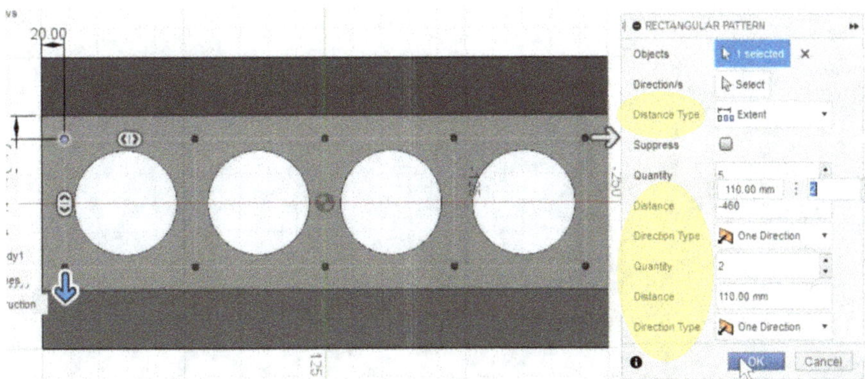

Figure 145: Select "Extent" for "Distance Type" and enter distance & quantity for x- and y-direction in the respective "Distance" fields (-460 mm in x; 110mm in y-direction)

Then we select the "Hole" command in 3D mode and create the holes by entering the specifications and selecting the points. At "Placement" we must select "From Sketch". First we select the hole type, namely "simple" and then "tapped", since we want to create a threaded hole. We want a full thread and a so-called blind hole as a drill hole ("angle" for "drill point").

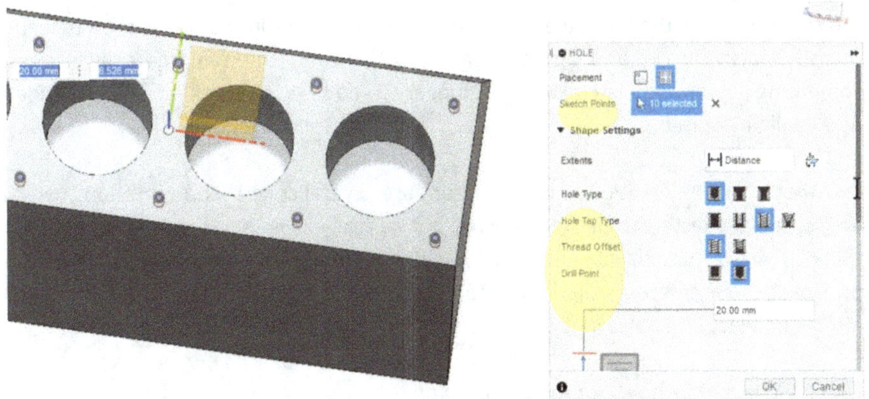

Figure 146: Select specifications for the holes

In the lower selection fields we can then choose which dimension the threaded hole should have. For example, our holes should be 70 mm long and have a diameter of 10 mm for a metric M10 thread. Also a thread pitch of 1.5.

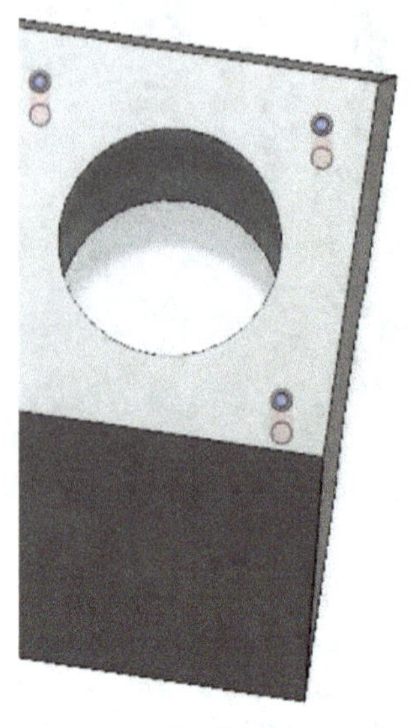
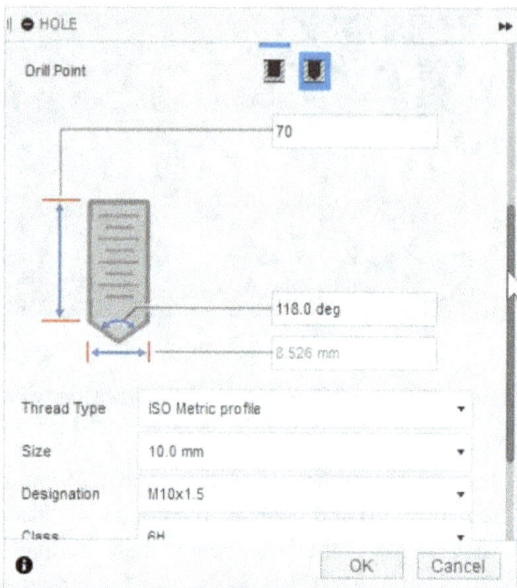

Figure 147: Choose further specifications for the holes

We can also check the "Modeled" box (scroll down further in the options) so that the thread is actually cut and displayed as real. However, this requires a little more computing power and may take a little longer. Confirm with "Enter" and the threaded holes will be created.

One more hint: As mentioned before, there are several construction methods, which are sometimes faster, sometimes slower, but basically all lead to the goal. It is best to think along, so that you can see other ways, too. For the holes, for example, it is also possible to first create a hole in 3D mode and then use the "Pattern" function of 3D mode and place the holes in the same way as the previously sketched points.

Let's try this for the holes for mounting an oil pan.
We select "Hole" and then first the drilling surface, i.e. the bottom side of the housing. Then the hole type, as well as the specifications as before. However, here we want, for example, only M8 threaded holes and a dimension of 40 mm. Then we simply select two edges for the positioning of the hole and enter the desired dimension in x- and y-direction for the positioning of the first hole. In each case 12.5 mm. Confirm with Enter and the hole is created.

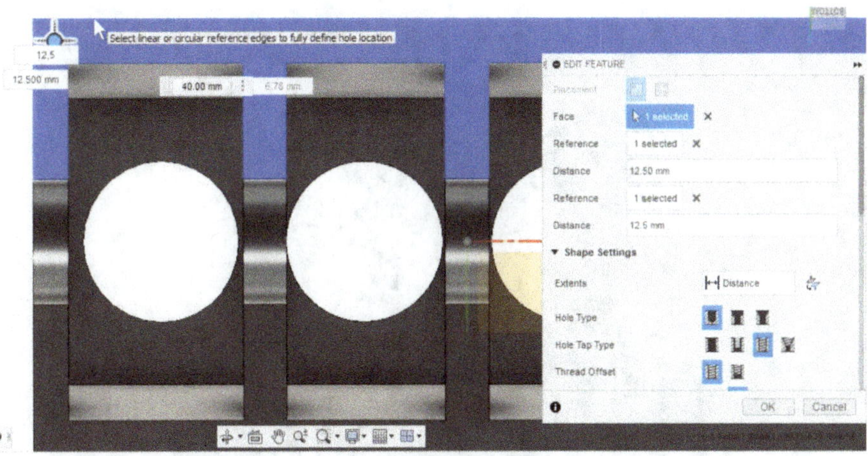

Figure 148: Dimension holes in 3D mode without a 2D sketch; simply select an edge for reference for the x position and enter a dimension value; then repeat analogously for the y position

Then we select the hole and use the "Pattern" command. In the next step, we switch to "Directions" in the options and then click on the x-axis to specify the first direction. The arrows appear and we can proceed in the same way as in the 2D sketch before. In the x-direction we want 8 holes with a total distance of 475 mm and in the y-direction we want 2 holes with a distance of -225 mm; in total 16 holes.

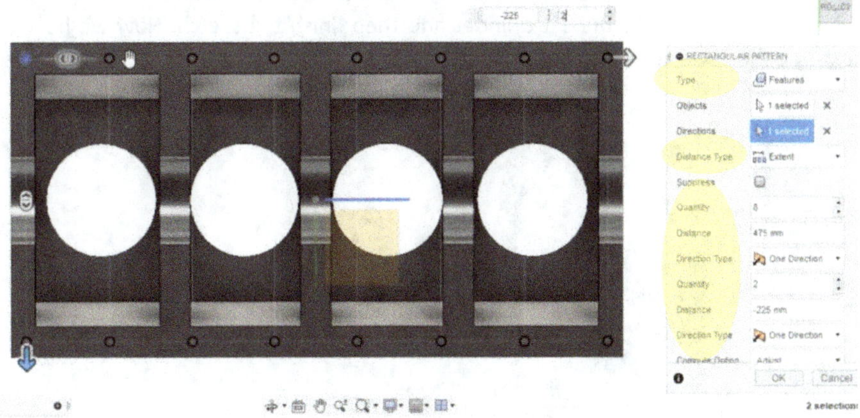

Figure 149:16 holes were created by using "Pattern" directly in 3D mode

In the last step for the crankcase and this lesson, we will use the Fillet command to round corners. Select the command, select some desired edges (e.g. the lateral ones) and enter a rounding radius of e.g. 10 mm. The crankcase is done! Let us continue in the next lesson with pistons, connecting rods and piston pins. Keep it up!

4.4.2 Part 2: Connecting rod, Piston and Piston pin

Figure 150: Connecting rod, piston and piston pin (not visible)

In this section we are interested in building the connecting rods, pistons and piston pins. For this we start with the creation of the pistons. To do this, we select the bottom of the crankcase and start a new component by right-clicking on the case in the browser ("New Component"). Then we start a sketch on the inner bottom surface of the crankcase (start sketch on a plane of the new component) and draw a circle of 85 mm diameter concentric to the 1st cylinder and then finish the sketch. Now we have to extrude the circle area, we choose e.g. 70 mm.

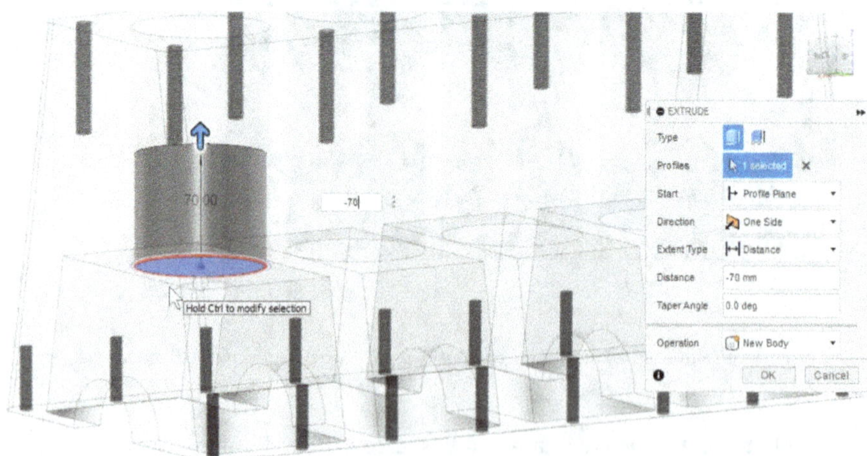

Figure 151: Already extruded piston (70 mm extrusion)

In the next step, we hollow out the piston and give it a wall thickness of 5 mm (use "Shell").

Then we start a sketch on the y-z plane of the piston to make a cutout for the piston pin, which later connects piston and connecting rod. For example, we choose a diameter of 30 mm and dimension the circle with 35 mm to the lower edge so that it is centered. We also link the center point with a horizontal constraint to the center point of the piston edge.

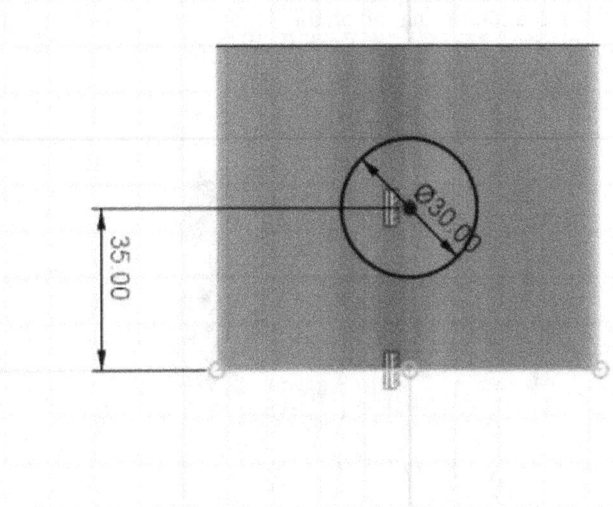

Figure 152: The sketch for the cutout for the piston pin on the y-z plane of the piston.
The piston was simply moved a little in 3D space beforehand to make it easier to draw

Then we extrude the cutout in 3D mode, creating an opening. Finally, we round off the upper and lower edges of the piston with 2 mm.

Figure 153: The finished, hollowed-out piston with cutout and fillets

We will dispense with piston rings and further detailing for reasons of complexity and time.

Instead we'll continue with the connecting rod and the piston pin, and wil then simply copy the other required components for the other cylinders, since they're identical.

For the connecting rod, we once again create a new component. Sketch the following cross-sectional profile of the connecting rod on the y-z plane of this new component.

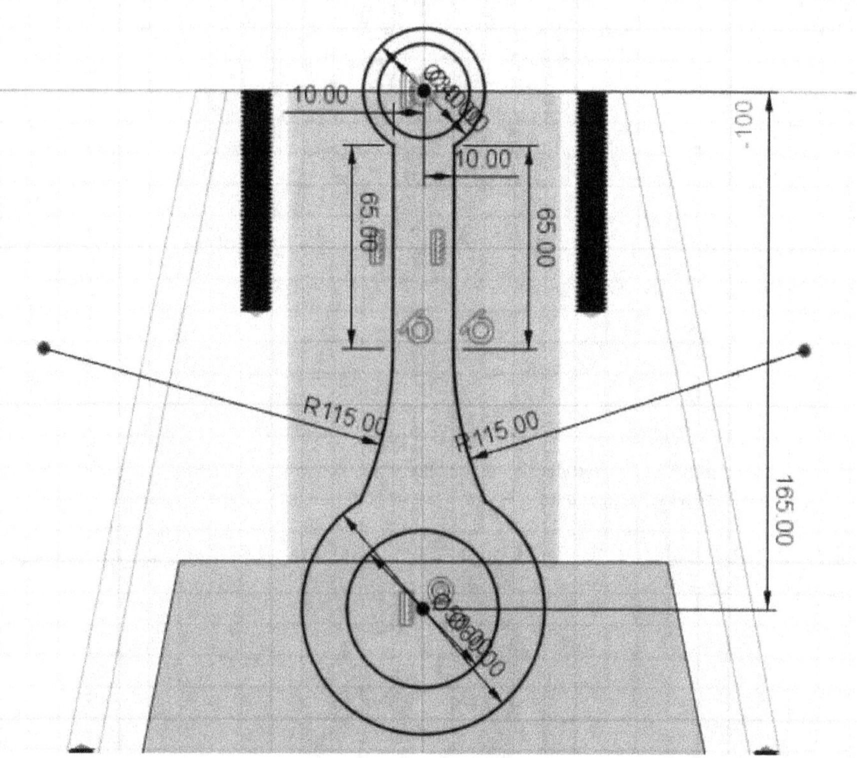

Figure 154: The geometry of the connecting rod; detailed steps and further dimensions follow

We will first start with the two "eyes". The upper connecting rod eye should have a diameter of 30 mm inside and 40 mm outside.

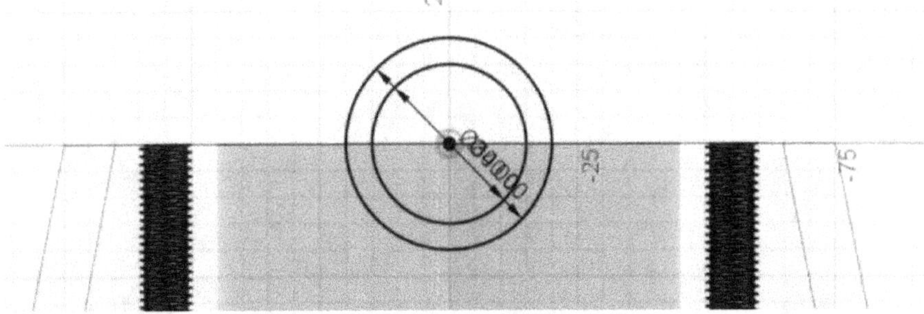

Figure 155: The upper connecting rod eye consists of two congruent circles (30 mm & 40 mm). The starting point should be the coordinate origin

For the lower connecting rod eye sketch circles with 50 mm inside and 80 mm outside. Then we set the two centers vertically to each other and dimension the distance as 165 mm.

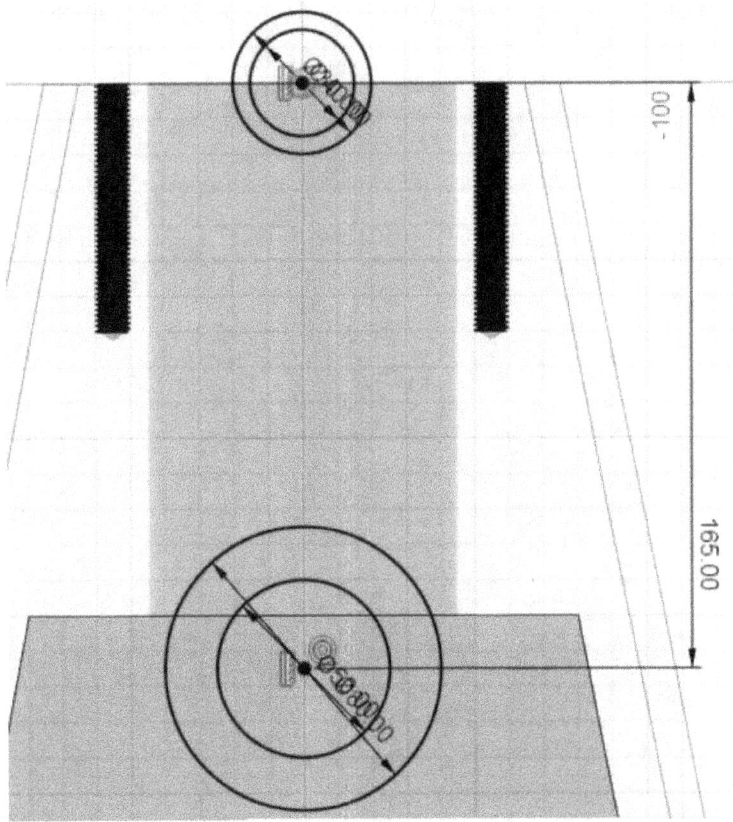

Figure 156: The lower connecting rod eye also consists of two congruent circles (50 mm & 80 mm). The distance to the coordinate origin should be 165 mm

Then we draw two vertical lines 65 mm long, each of which should have a horizontal distance of 10 mm from the center of the upper connecting rod eye.

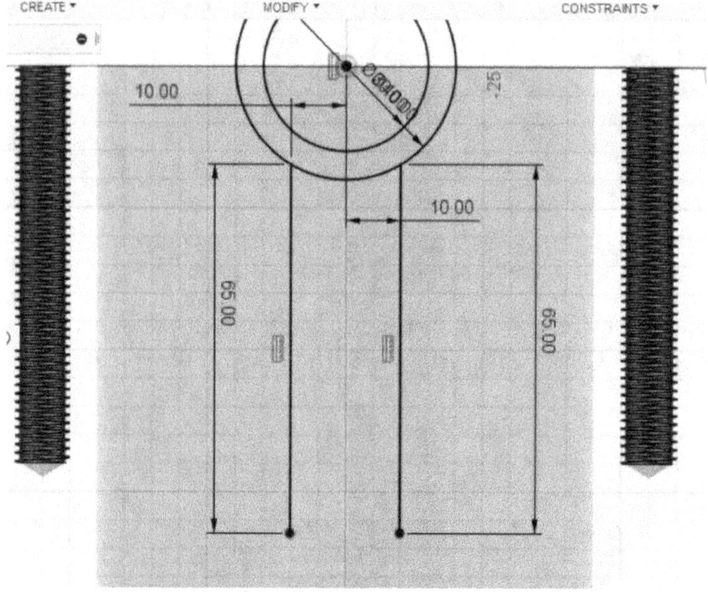

Figure 157: two vertical lines, each 65 mm long, for the connecting rod shaft

We complete the profile with two tangential arcs, each of which should have a radius of R=115 mm.

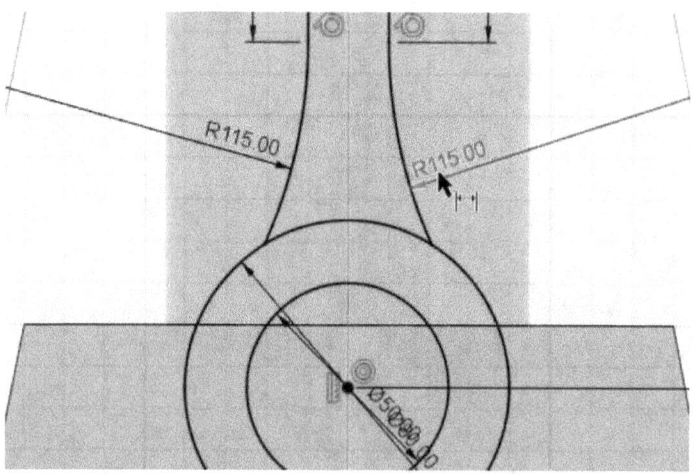

Figure 158: Draw two tangential arcs (start and end points on the vertical lines and the 80 mm circle, respectively) and dimension each with 115 mm

Finally, we use the "Trim" function and remove excess lines.

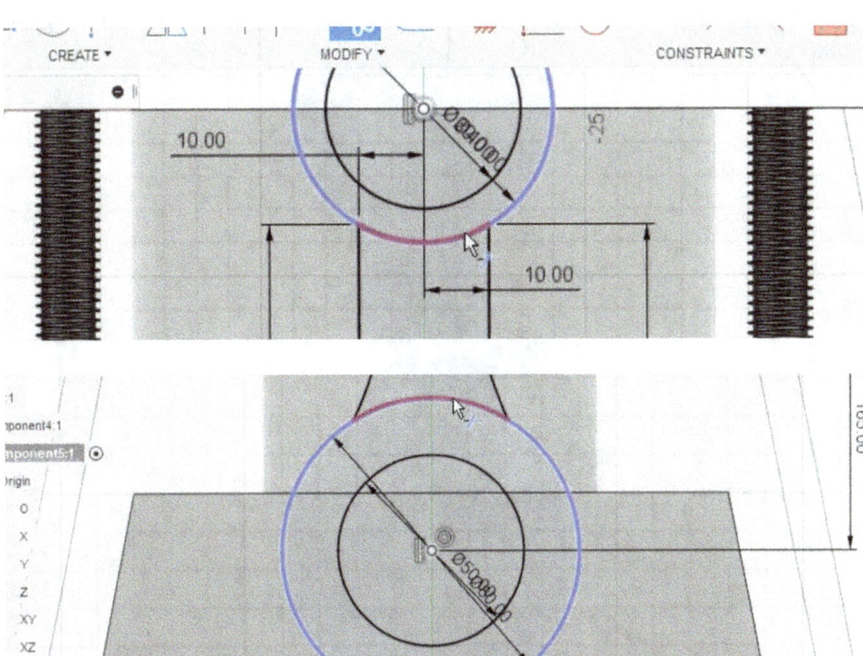

Figure 159: Remove the two excess lines (red) using the "Trim" tool

When this is done, we can finish the sketch and extrude the connecting rod by 20 mm. To ensure that the transitions are not too extreme, we can round off the transitions in the area of the connecting rod at the bottom and top with 20 mm.

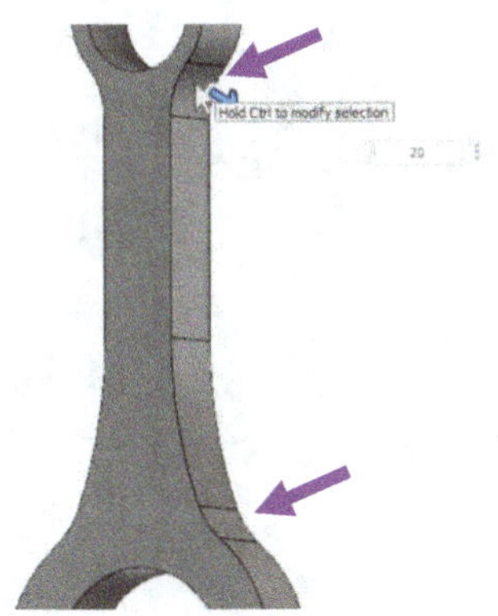

Figure 160: Round off the edges of the transitions at the top and bottom with 20 mm (already done)

Also, round the edges of the two surfaces with 1 mm each. This connecting rod is also a significantly simplified model. Normally, a connecting rod looks like the following one in this picture:

Figure 161: Connecting rod (without main bearing shells) of a real engine

In the lower area it is divided into two parts, the geometry is more functional and there would also be some bearing shells, which would sit in the lower eye.

Let's then draw the piston pin first before linking the connecting rod to the piston. To do this, we create a new component and draw a circle with 30 mm diameter on its y-z plane, which we then extrude 77.5 mm symmetrically and hollow out to a wall thickness of 3 mm.

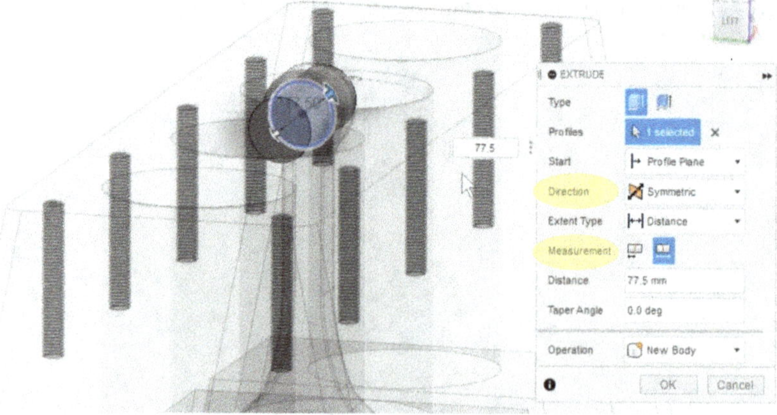

Figure 162: Extrude the piston pin 77.5 mm symmetrically (Measurement: "Whole Length")

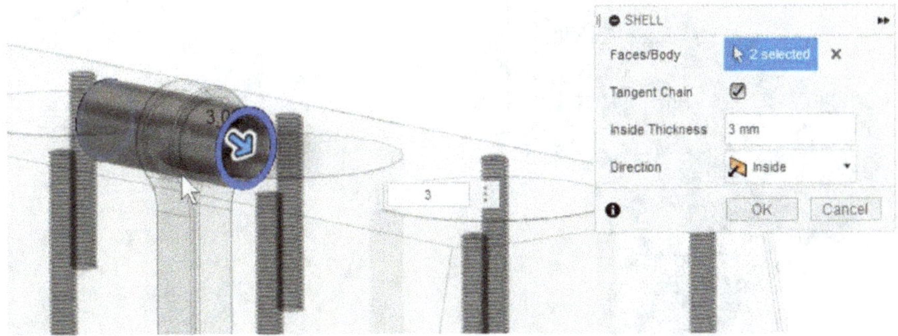

Figure 163: Hollow out the piston pin (select both sides and enter 3 mm)

Then we first mount the connecting rod to the piston pin by selecting the following points as joint origins and selecting the joint type "Revolute" (first activate the command "Joint").

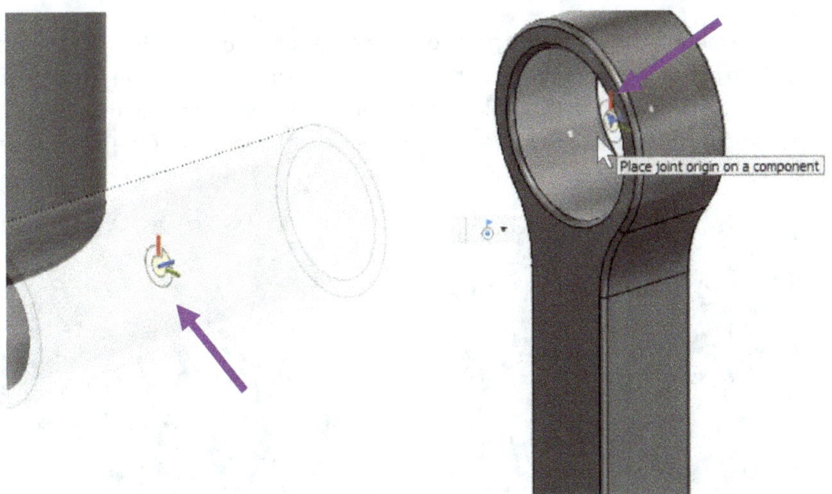

Figure 164: When selecting the joint origins, make sure that you select the middle surface and that the orientation matches the Figure

Figure 165: Joint has been created; use "Revolute" as joint type

And then we mount the package of pin and connecting rod in to the piston. We do this with the help of a lateral joint origin on the pin and in the middle of the pin opening on the piston. A little patience is required here until the two correct joint origins are selected or found. Especially pay attention to the correct alignment of the axes at the joint origins.

Figure 166: Placing the two joint origins; at the top in the center of the side face of the piston pin and at the bottom in the center of the bore of the piston

In the penultimate step of this lesson, we copy the already connected group of piston, connecting rod and piston pin three more times. To do this, we select the three components in the browser after naming them, and copy them with CTRL-C. With CTRL-V we paste them into the design environment. We do not need the window that opens, therefore just close it. The components have been inserted congruently, i.e. we must first bring them to view by simply moving each component with the mouse.

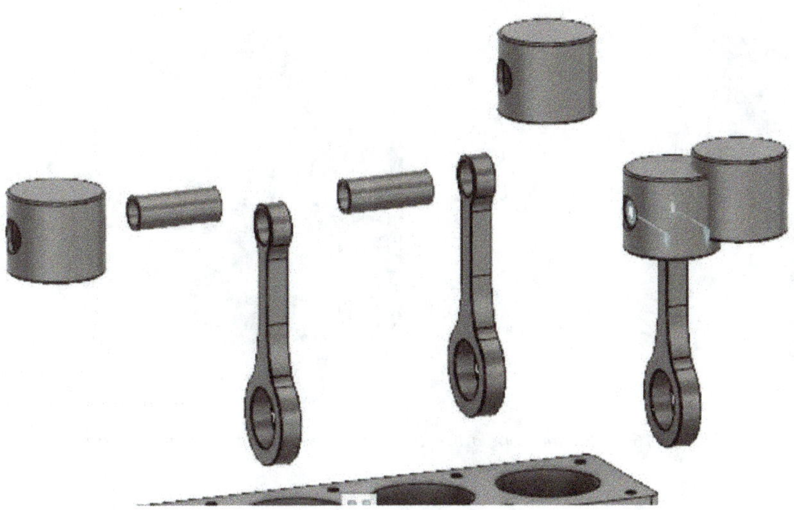

Figure 167: The new components for the other three cylinders that have not yet been sorted and linked

After sorting the components, create the same joints for the copied components as in the first set of pistons, connecting rods and piston pins.

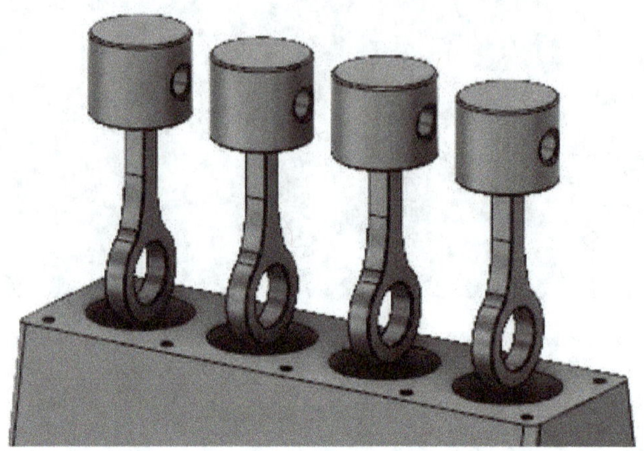

Figure 168: Pistons, connecting rods and piston pins connected and sorted

In the last step of this chapter, we link the pistons in the cylinder so that they can only perform a linear movement in the cylinder. To do this, we - for example - select the center of the upper piston surface and the center of the cylinder as joint origins and the joint type "Slider".

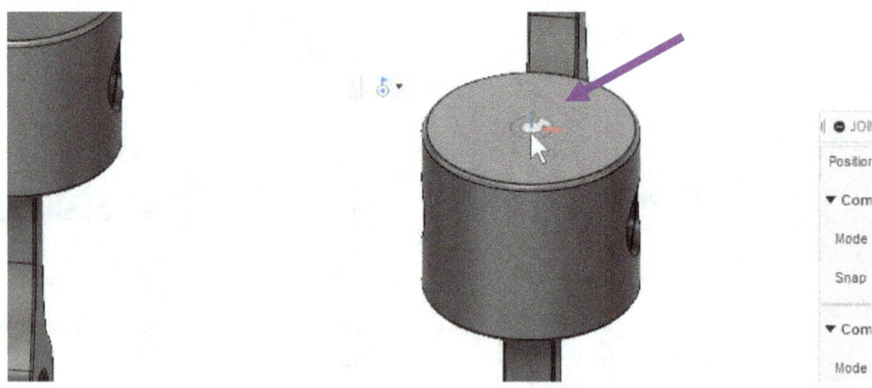

Figure 169: Place joint origin 1 on the piston (centered on the upper surface)

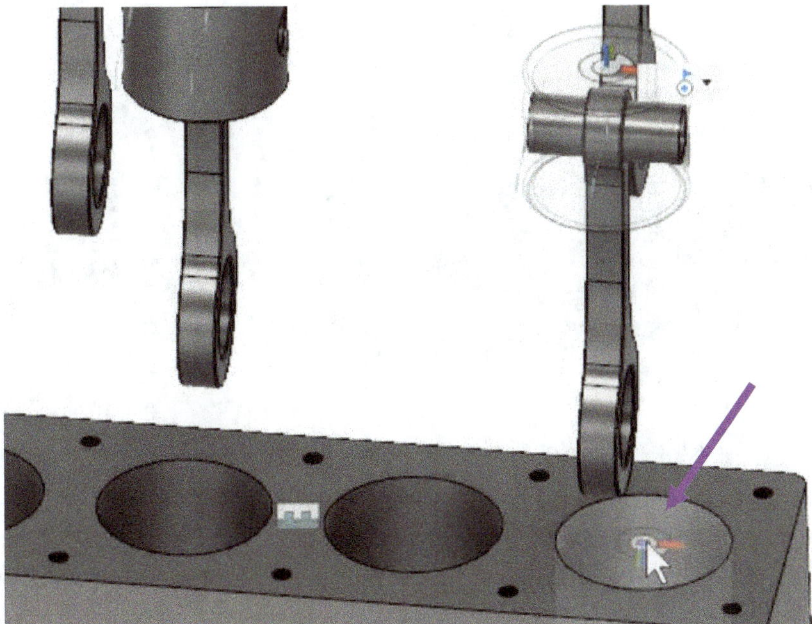

Figure 170: Place joint origin 2 on the crankcase centered on the upper cylinder surface

We proceed in the same way with the other three pistons. By the way, by right-clicking on a joint (browser) and selecting "Edit Joint Limits", we could also define a maximum and minimum for the movement range, i.e. limits in which the piston may move. But since this is set by the connection to the crankshaft and connecting rod anyway, we don't need it here.

Gradually it's getting quite full of joints, and their display can be a bit of a distraction, so I'm just hiding them at the moment and only putting them back in when I need them.

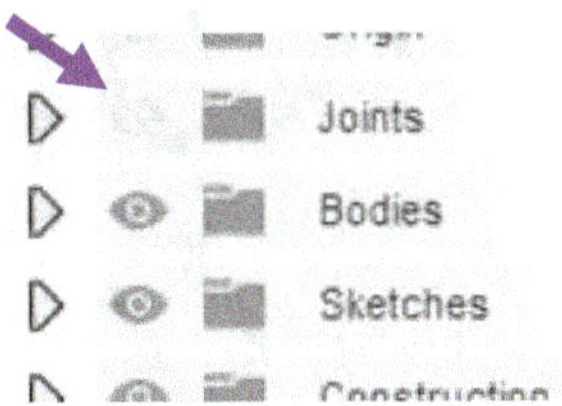

Figure 171: Hide/show joints in the browser with a click on the eye symbol

Now we are almost done with our very simple 4-cylinder internal combustion engine. In the next lesson we will draw the crankshaft. Let's go!

4.4.3 Part 3: Crankshaft

Figure 172: The model of our crankshaft should look like this when it is finished

Before we start with the crankshaft in this lesson, first hide all components that are not needed, only the crankshaft housing should remain. Then we will start a new component for the crankshaft. In the end, the crankshaft should look something like this picture:

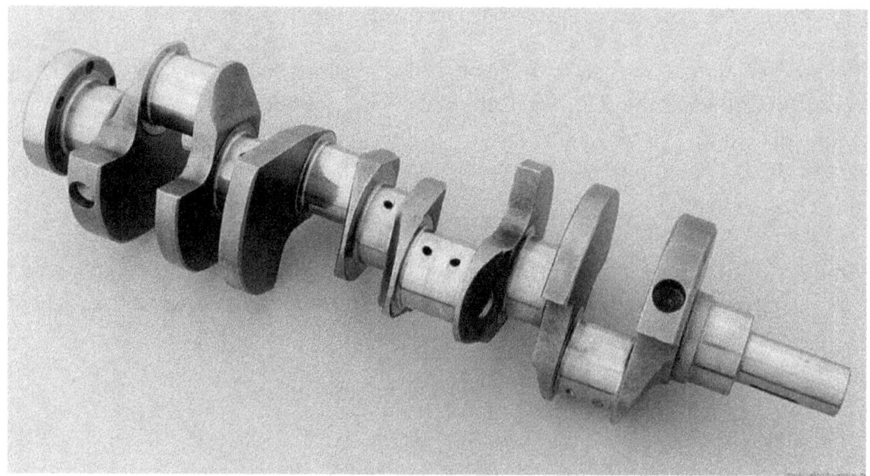

Figure 173: A real crankshaft for a 4-cylinder-engine

Of course, we will do the crankshaft in a somewhat simplified way. We start a new sketch in the side view on the y-z plane of the new component. Then we draw the first crankshaft journal with a simple circle of 65 mm diameter and set a concentric constraint.

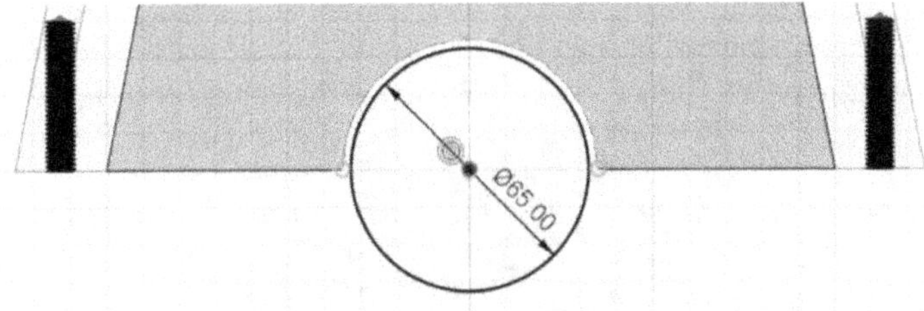

Figure 174: The beginning of our new component

In 3D mode we extrude this circular surface and select a distance of 20 mm in one direction and confirm with "Ok".

Since our crankshaft is to be symmetrical, we will draw only one half of it for the time being and will simply mirror it later on the y-z plane. We will build up the crankshaft section by section using extrusions. You can also think about how you could construct the crankshaft using the "Revolve" command, i.e. as a rotational part, and whether this is possible at all?

We start a sketch on the previously created shaft journal, for the next section, the first crankshaft part. For this we create two circles, one with 70 mm and one with 160 mm diameter at a distance of 45 mm from each other including a vertical constraint between their two centers. The center of the upper circle should also be 40 mm vertical from the center of the shaft journal and sit in line with it, i.e. be vertically constrained.

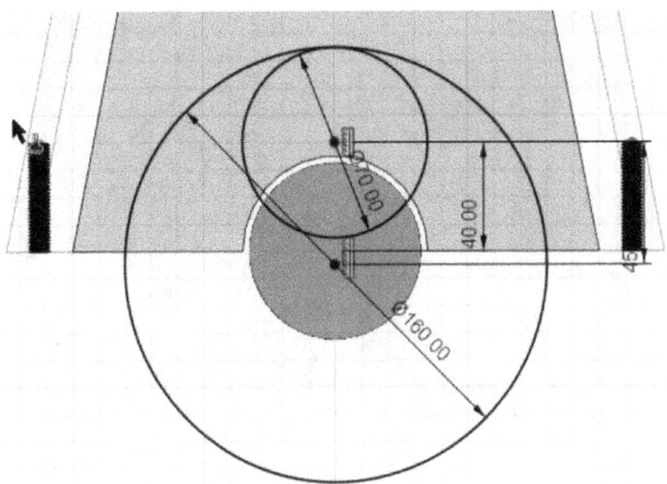

Figure 175: Two circles (70 & 160 mm) at a distance of 40 mm from each other. The upper circle has a distance of 45 mm to the coordinate origin. Vertical constraints are present.

Then we draw two connecting lines and dimension them vertically with 60 mm length and by means of parallel dimension with 30 mm to the upper circle center.

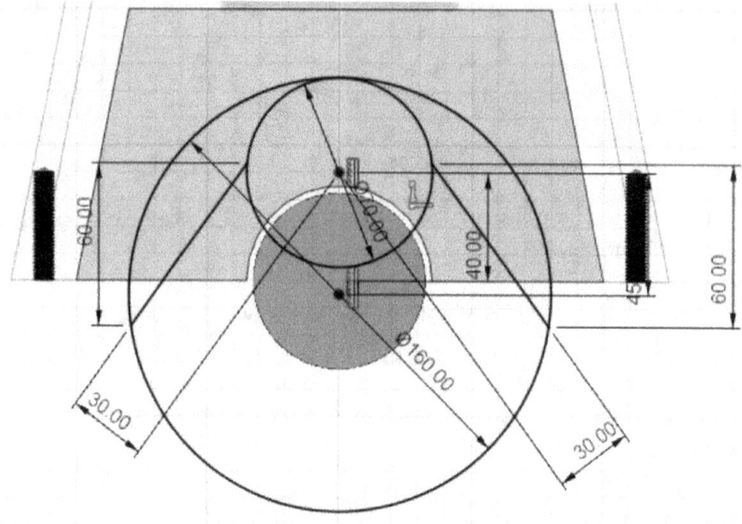

Figure 176: Two connecting lines (60 mm vertical dimension, 30 mm parallel dimension)

In the last step we use the "Trim" function to cut away all superfluous lines and sections.

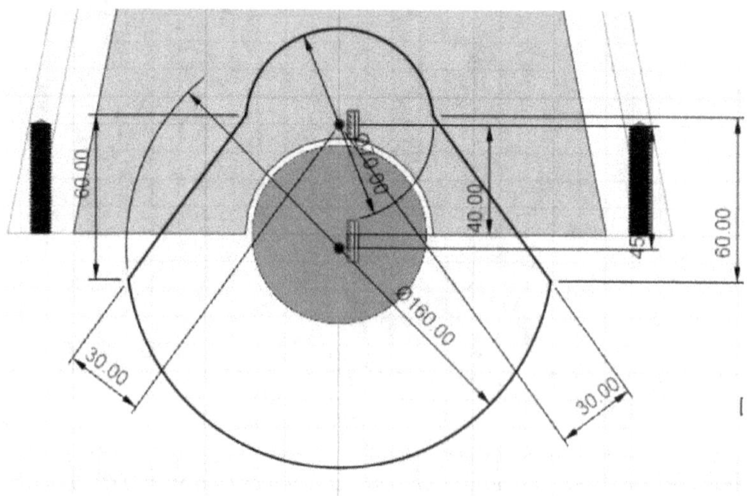

Figure 177: the superfluous arcs have already been removed with the "Trim" tool

Then we extrude this crankshaft part by 22 mm. In the next step, we draw the shaft journal for the connecting rod on this part. For this we draw a 50 mm circle, which should sit concentric to the upper curve of the crankshaft. We need a dimension of 16 mm for the extrusion.

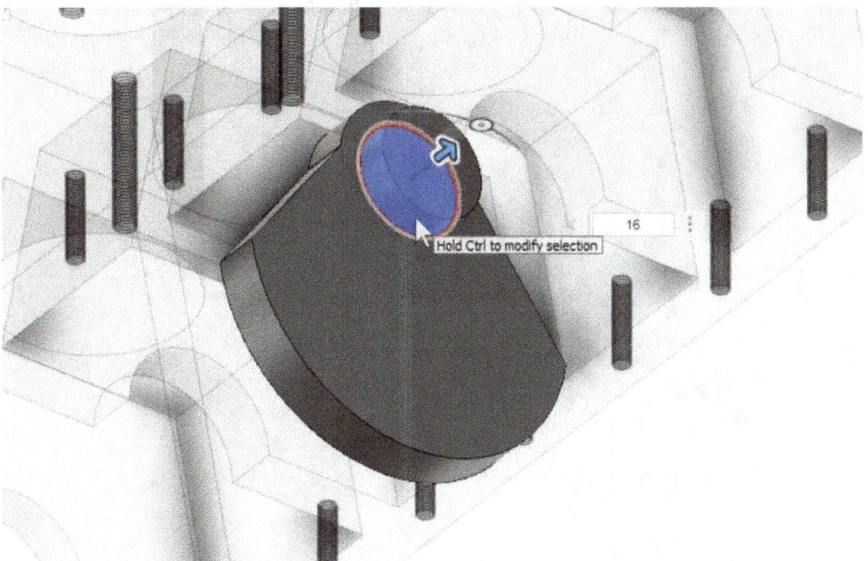

Figure 178: The crankshaft journal for the connecting rod on the crankshaft part; 16 mm extruded

Now we could draw part by part and shaft journal by shaft journal on top of each other as a 2D sketch and extrude them, just as we have done up to this point. However, it is much easier now to use the existing half again for the shaft journal of the first connecting rod. This body represents more or less 1/8 of the entire crankshaft.

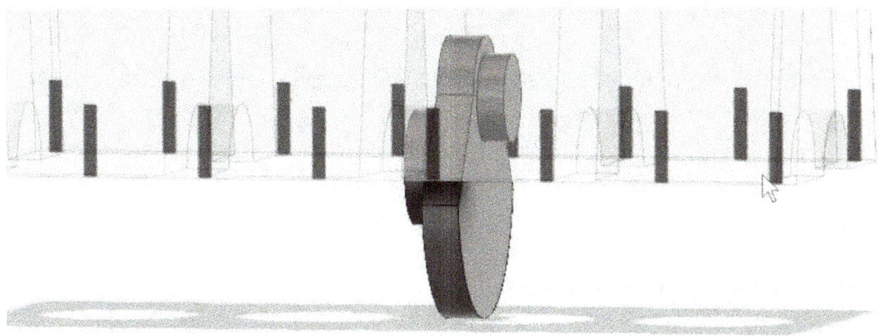

Figure 179: The first 1/8 of the entire crankshaft is finished and will now be mirrored

In the following we will skillfully use the "mirror" function to save us some work. So for the second crankshaft part and adjacent shaft journal sections we simply mirror the first body by selecting it.

In the options window, you may need to select "Bodies" as the "Type" selection and choose the side surface of the half crankshaft journal as the "Mirror Plane".

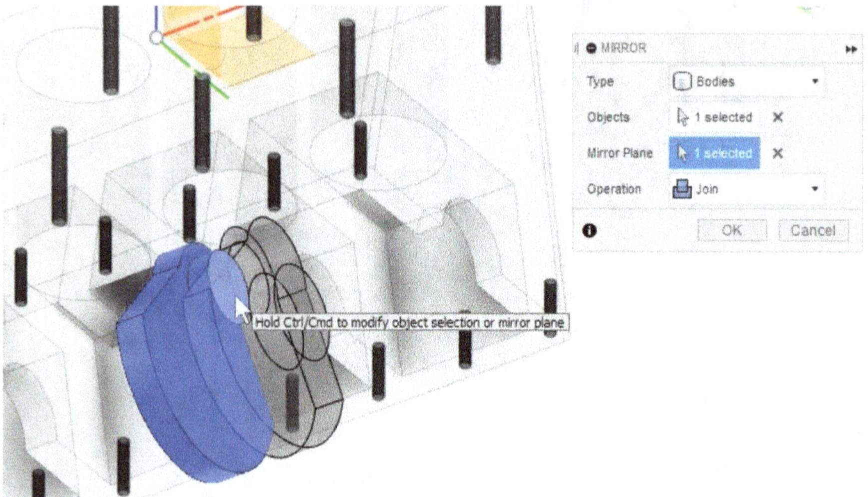

Figure 180: Mirror the first 1/8 of the crankshaft, at "Type": select "Bodies", mirror plane must be the shaft journal (see mouse pointer)

At "Operation" in the "Options" we can leave "Join" forthis step, because we want to get only one body and the new part is already aligned correctly. That means the second eighth of the crankshaft is done. For the next 2/8, we mirror the previously created crankshaft part in this step once again. Select the body, select "Mirror Plane", in this case the side of the shaft journal that rests in the crankcase.

Now, however, we have to make a small change in "Operation", since we want to create a new body for the time being, so select "New Body".

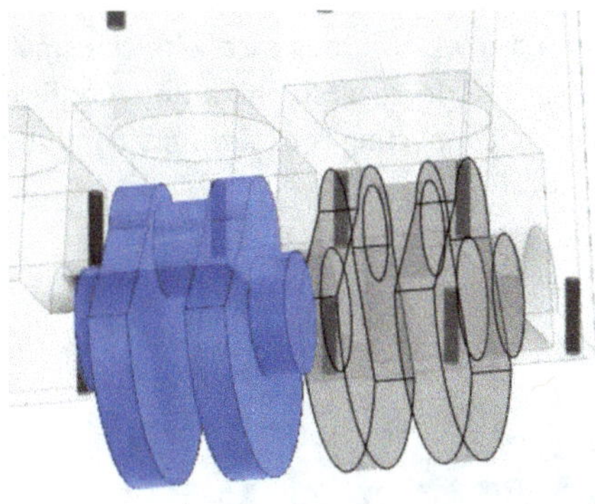

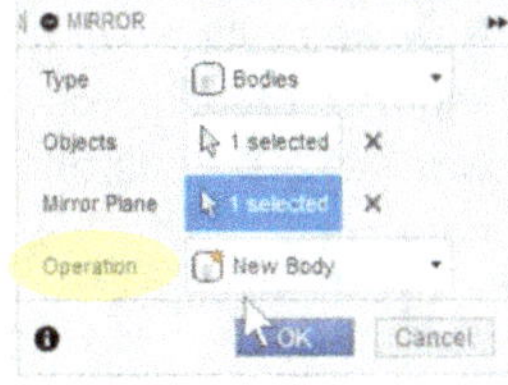

Figure 181: Create the second quarter of the crankshaft; in "Operation": select "New Body"

Why a new body? Because, as we can now see, this quarter of the crankshaft has to be rotated 180 degrees around - in this case - the x-axis so that it is in opposition to the other quarter. Otherwise, all pistons would run in the same way, but only two of the four pistons may always be in the same position. For this reason we have created the new body, because otherwise we would not be able to rotate this quarter of the shaft independently of the other. For rotation we simply use the command "Move/Copy" from the menu "Modify". Then we simply have to select an origin for the move or in our case the rotation. To do this, we hide the first body of the crankshaft to better select the center of the crankshaft journal of the second body as the origin. We need the center of the shaft journal of the main bearing.

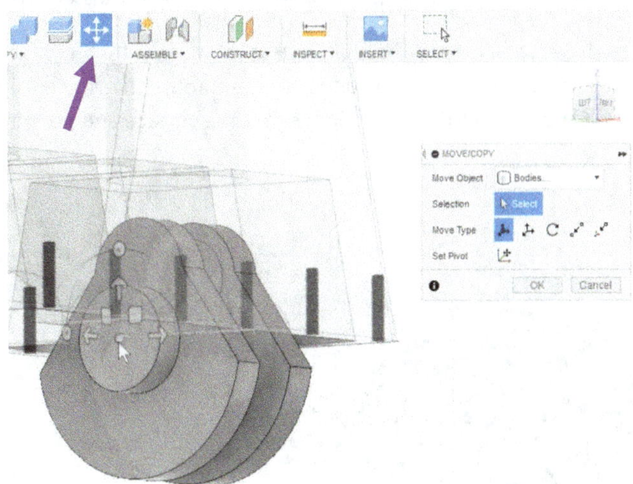

*Figure 182: Select the center of the main bearing of the second quarter of the crankshaft
(see mouse pointer; first quarter of the crankshaft is hidden)*

Now we could move the body by means of the arrows or in our case with the small knob, to rotate it around the right axis. We need 180 degrees, so half a turn. Confirm with "OK". We see that the shaft journals for the connecting rods are now correctly positioned.

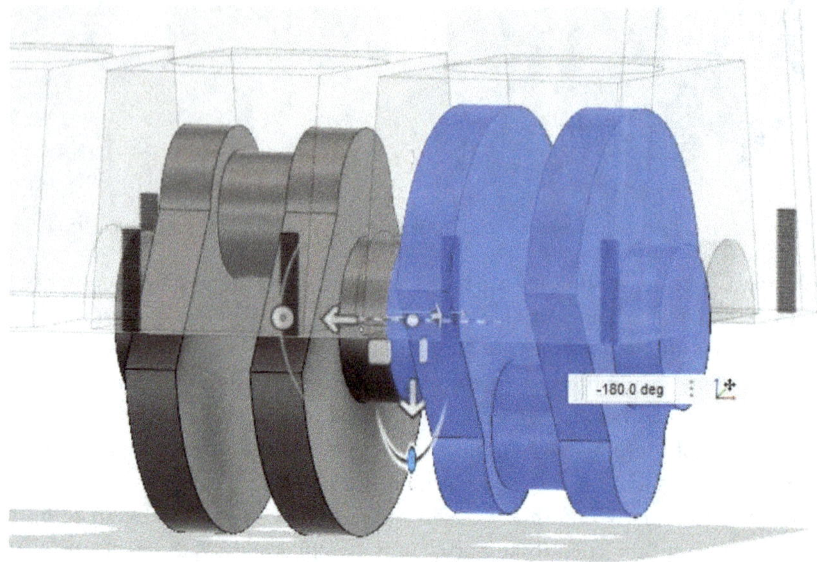

Figure 183: Rotation of the second quarter of the crankshaft around the x-axis by -180 °.

Before we continue, we'll extend the shaft journal of the crankshaft, which is a bit too short due to the mirroring. This can be done easily without a 2D sketch using "Extrude" or "Press Pull". Simply select the command, select the surface and pull the arrow, e.g. 30 mm long.

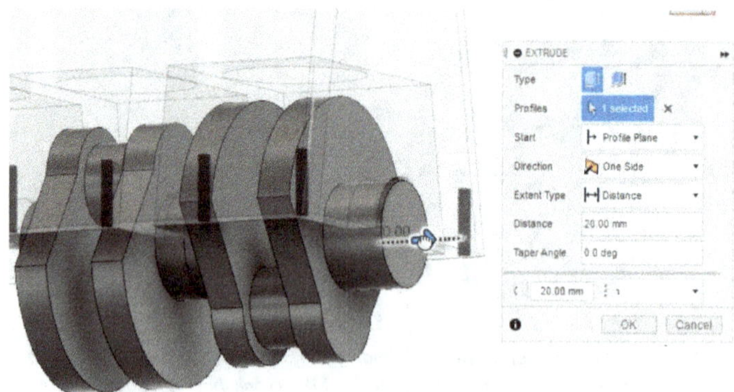

Figure 184: Extend the outer main bearing of the half crankshaft by 30 mm

Now we want to join the two existing parts of the half crankshaft again to reunite the two bodies. For this we use the function "Combine" from the menu "Modify". Select body and command, in the options at "Operation" select "Join", and press "OK".

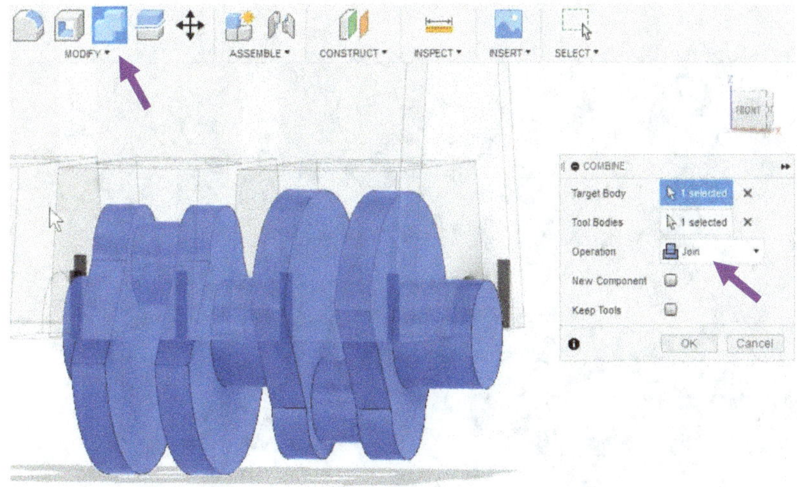

Figure 185: Reunite the two crankshaft segments with "Combine"

This approach has saved us quite a bit of work. To continue at exponential speed, we double our half-finished crankshaft one last time. This time we can again leave "Join" instead of "New Body" as the connection type, since the alignment is correct. With one click, the crankshaft is finally almost finished.

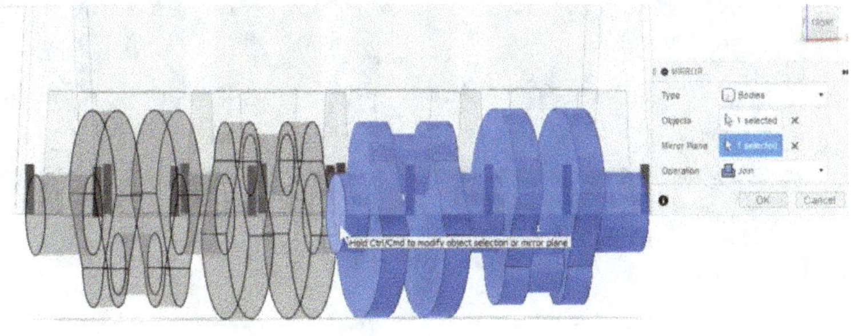

Figure 186: Create the second half of the crankshaft by "mirroring" on the middle main bearing

What is still missing? First, a few fillets, which we would like to make as follows: 10 mm at the edges of the transitions in the lower areas of the parts and 5 mm at the edges of the transitions in the upper areas. We could have also integrated these fillets into the 2D sketches.

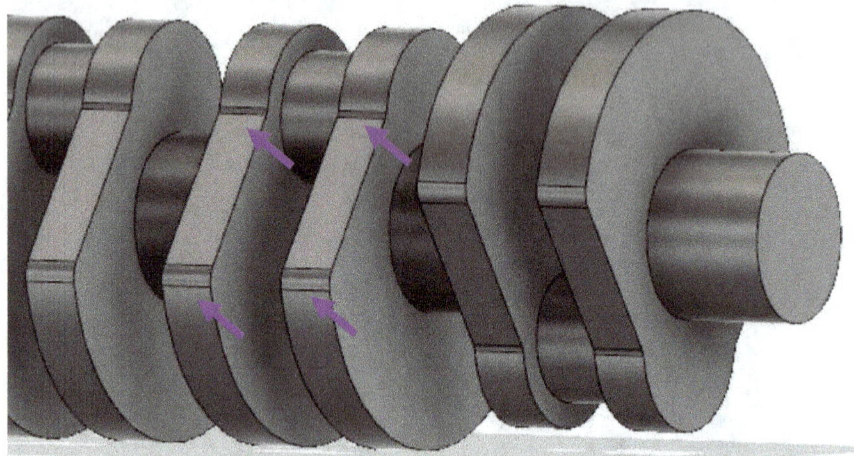

Figure 187: Round off edges with 10 mm and 5 mm, or at your own discretion

And then 3 mm fillets for the edges on the side faces and shaft journals. To do this, simply select all side faces.

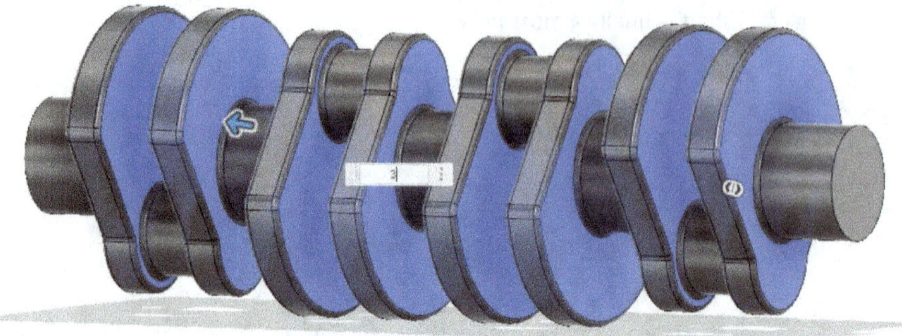

Figure 188: 3 mm fillets for the edges of the side faces (already created here)

In addition, the joint to the crankshaft housing is still missing. To do this, we simply select the first joint origin centered on the shaft journal with which we started, and select the second origin centered on middle crankshaft journal. As joint type we select "Revolute". Perfect, finally all components for our simplified engine model are done.

118

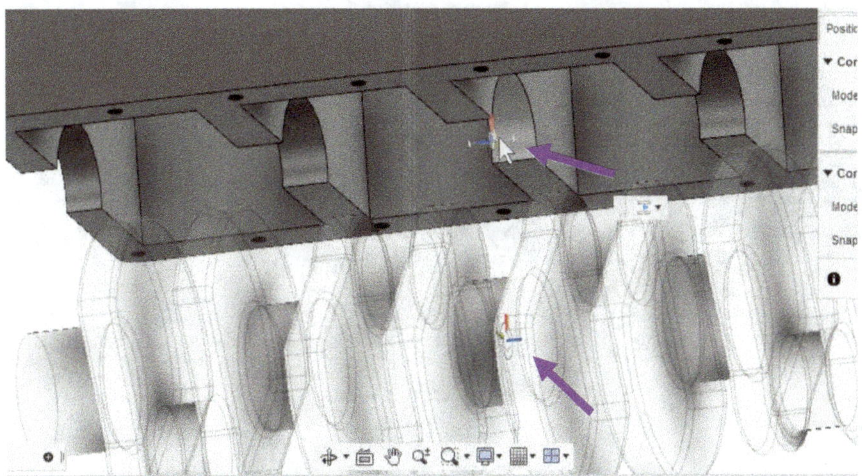

Figure 189: The joint origins for the joint between crankshaft and housing

At the end of the chapter, we would of course like to link all the connecting rods to the crankshaft and let our engine run in virtual mode. Final sprint!

For a better overview, we will only show the connecting rods of the individual cylinders one after the other and link them to the crankshaft. Before we do this, we will hide the crankcase.

The joint creation is rather unspectacular. Center the first joint origin in the lower eye of the connecting rod and center the second origin on the shaft journal of the crankshaft.

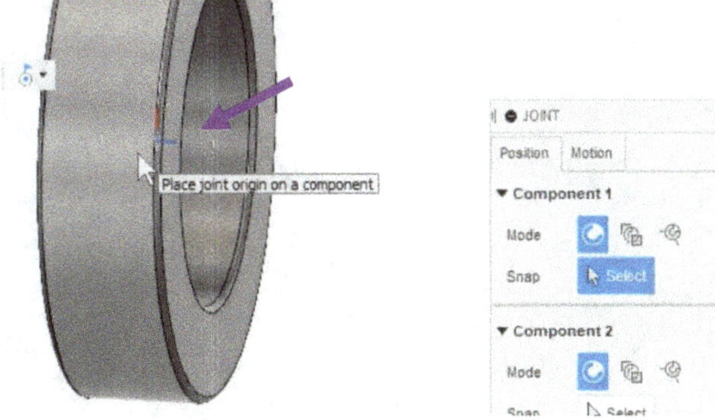

Figure 190: The first joint origin must be in the lower eye of a connecting rod (centered)

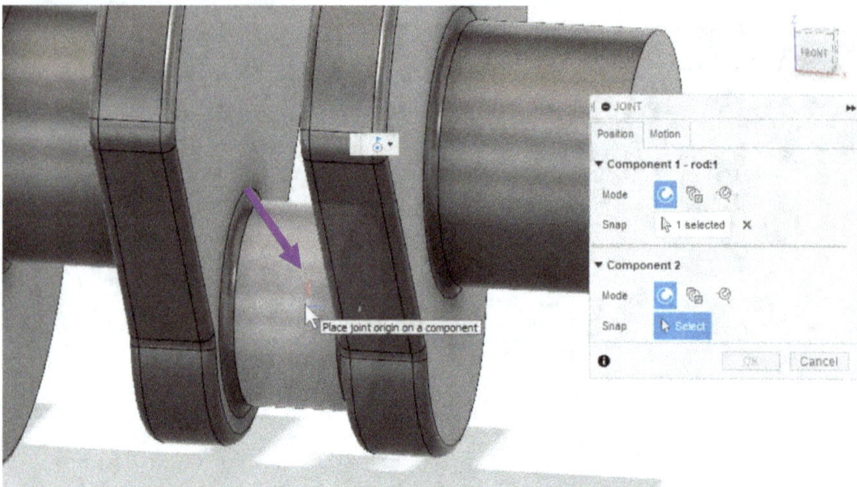

Figure 191: The second joint origin must be centered on the respective main bearing of the crankshaft

The joint type in this case is "Cylindrical". Then a warning appears because we have selected the joint type "Revolute" for the piston and a lateral movement will therefore not be possible. However, we do not need this in this here and the warning can therefore be ignored. In reality, however, a slight sideways play is necessary. But by far not as much lateral play as we would have in our model. We proceed analogously for the other connecting rods. When everything is connected, we can first show all parts and make the crankcase transparent with a right click on its body and the selection of "Opacity Control", according to taste, e.g. 30 %.

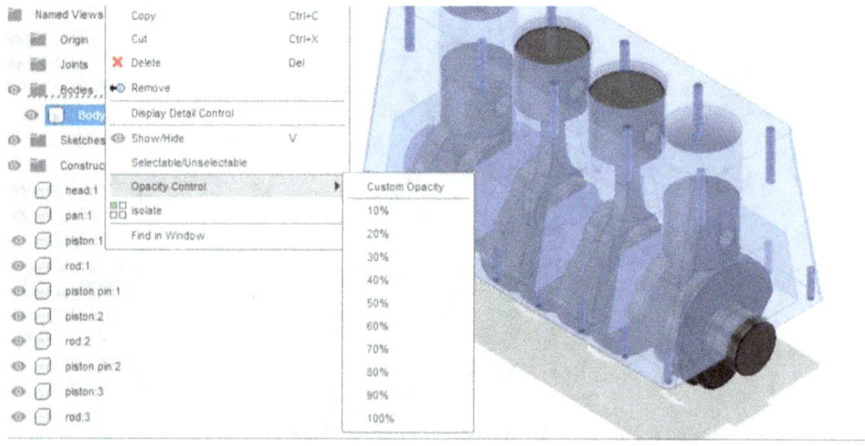

Figure 192: Making the crankcase transparent

At the end of the chapter, we want to run our motor virtually. If we have placed all the joints correctly, this should be no problem. To do this, we search for the joint between the crankshaft and the crankshaft housing and right-click on it.

We then select "Animate Model" and, buckle up please, the engine runs! Respect, if you got this far, you can really be proud of yourself! By the way, you can end the animation of the joint simply by pressing the "ESC" key.

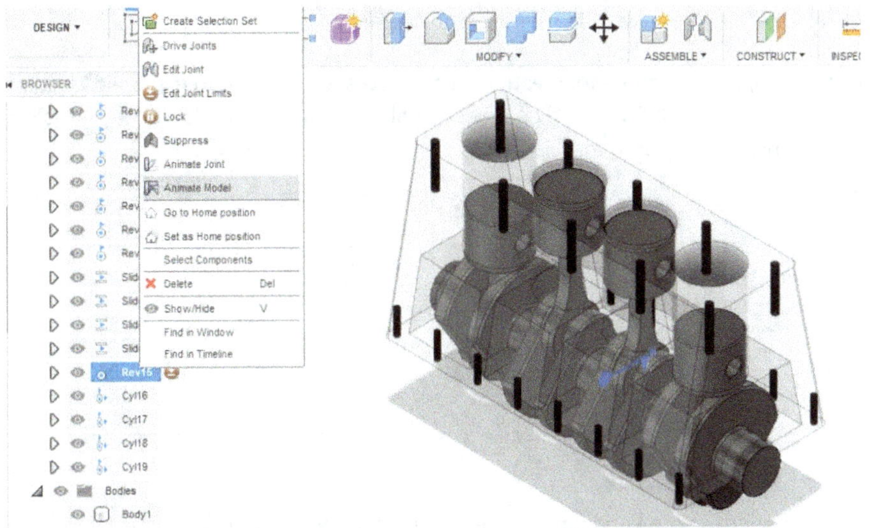

Figure 193: Animate the joint of the crankshaft: Right-click on joint -> "Animate Model"

Before we move on to the next sections of Fusion 360 , we will first have a look at the "Surface" & "Sheet Metals" menu tabs from the "Design" section in the following chapters.

5 "Surface" & "Sheet Metal"

5.1 Surface

In the design projects, we have exclusively worked in the "Solid" tab. This is probably the tab you will use most often. In the "Surface" tab, you can only work with surfaces. The difference to "Solid" is basically only the thickness of the construction elements. In fact, however, we are dealing with actual surfaces.

In principle, the procedure for creating such surfaces is analogous to the "Solid" section, i.e. when you start a 2D sketch on a desired plane, you will find the identical tools in the 2D environment as in the "Solid" tab.

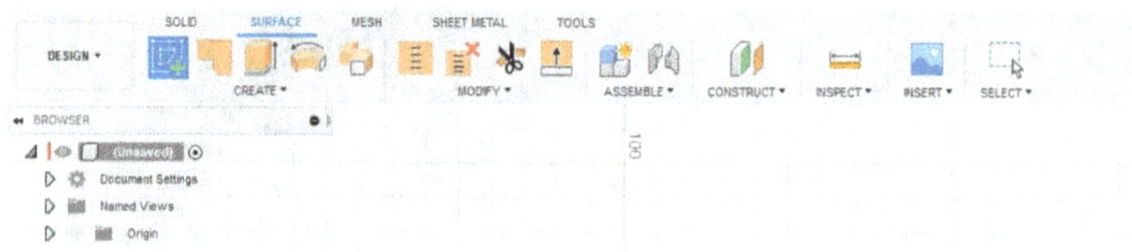

Figure 194: The "Surface" tab of the "Design" section with commands and functions

If you now draw a line and a rectangle, for example, you can then create a surface in 3D mode using the "Extrude" function, which is familiar to us.

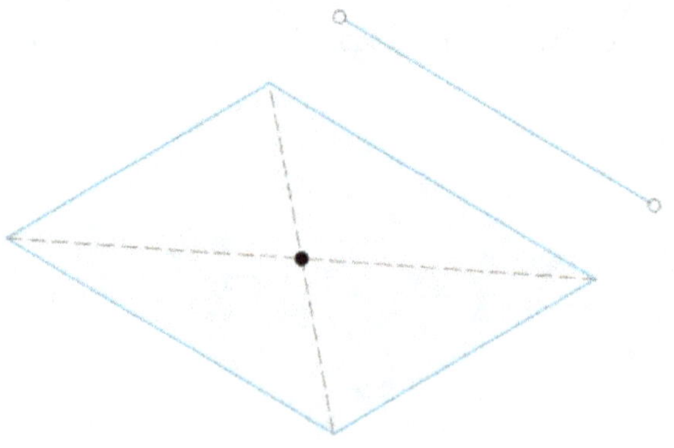

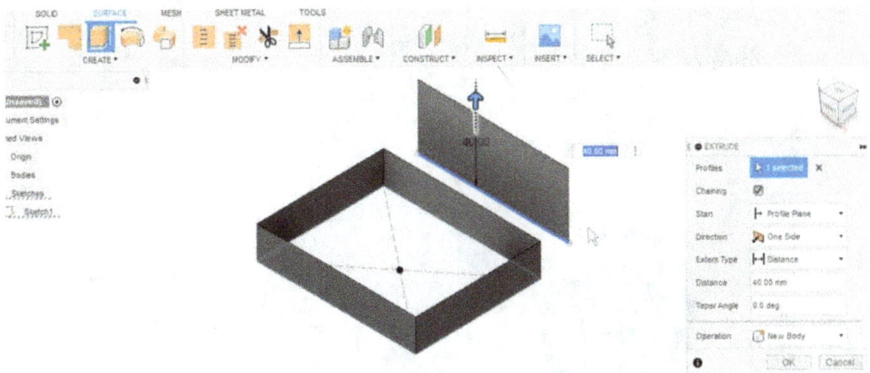

Figure 195: Draw rectangle and line (top); Create 3D surface elements with Extrude

As you will notice, the element has no depth/thickness because, as mentioned, it is only a surface element.

You will find many familiar functions in the "Create" section, as well as in the "Modify" section. There are also a few new commands here and there, such as "Stitch" and "Unstitch".

With "Stitch" you can very quickly turn a closed surface shape into a solid body. I.e. you could model a complex surface in the "Surface" area and then transform it into a solid body using the "Stitch" or "Unstitch" command.

Let's try this on a spherical surface. To do this, draw a half of a circle on any plane and rotate it 360 degrees in the "Surface" "Create" area. As we can see in the section view, we have only created a spherical surface.

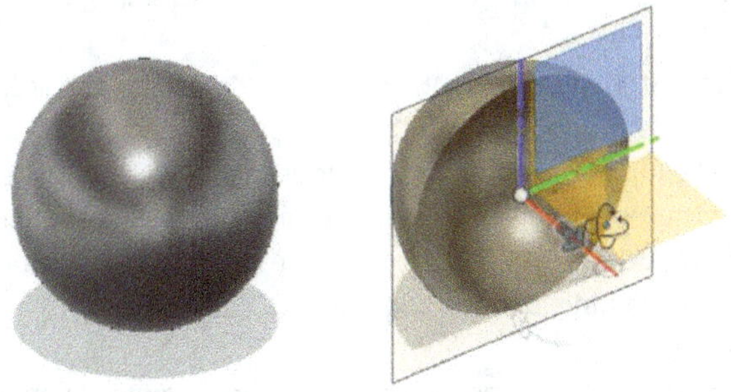

Figure 196: Create a sphere and display the section view

However, we can turn these into a solid body by using the "Stitch" command and selecting the surface or all surfaces for a more complex part.

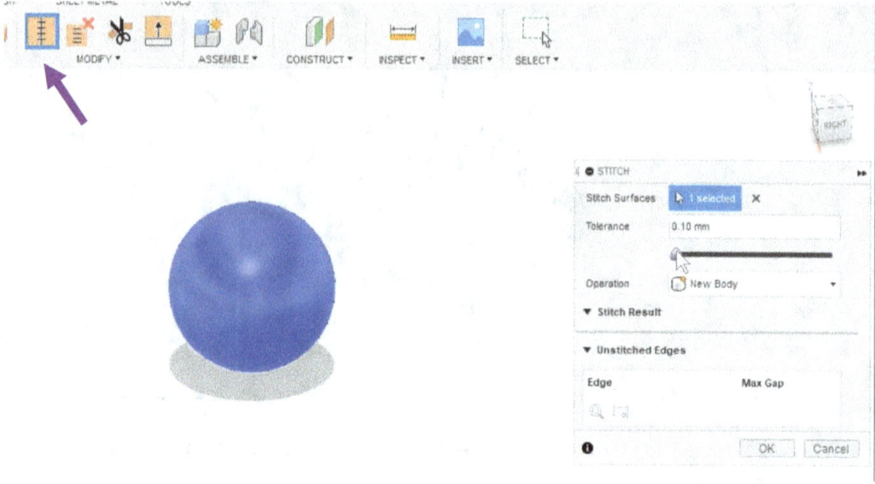

Figure 197: Run the "Stitch" command to create a solid body

If we activate the section view again, we see this through the hatching, which indicates a solid body.

Figure 198: The hatching in the section view tells us that we have a solid body

The command "Unstitch" would work analogously in reverse application.

With "Extend" or "Stretch", on the other hand, you could extend individual surfaces.

Since I personally do not need the surface modeling very often, this short introduction should suffice. The only thing you have to remember is that for surfaces you should always use the tab "Surface" and that it can be used relatively analogous to the tab "Solid" with regard to functions and commands.

You can use the surface modeling methodology, for example, if you want to recreate a complex shape from surfaces, i.e. if you want to create only the shell of a part, because the part would be difficult to build up as a solid body, and afterwards turn it into a solid part.

In other words, "Surface" takes on meaning only for solids with complex structures, because you can then use many small individual surface elements to better model very complex shapes.

5.2 Sheet Metal

Let's turn to designing Sheet Metal. This is of great importance if you want to design sheet metal. The commands and functions in this tab are designed for this purpose.

Of course, you could also use "Solid" to design sheet metal, but you will see in a moment why you should rather work with "Sheet Metal" for this purpose. A first hint: It makes it much easier to deal with bends, flanges, flat patterns and other sheet metal specific elements and features.

If you want to design a bent sheet metal element, such as this element,

Figure 199: Example for designing in the "Sheet Metal" tab

you will need a cut piece of sheet metal in basic form, which you would then bend or machine into shape in real life. This basic shape, also called flat pattern, can easily be created in Fusion 360 in this section after simply designing the already bent sheet metal.

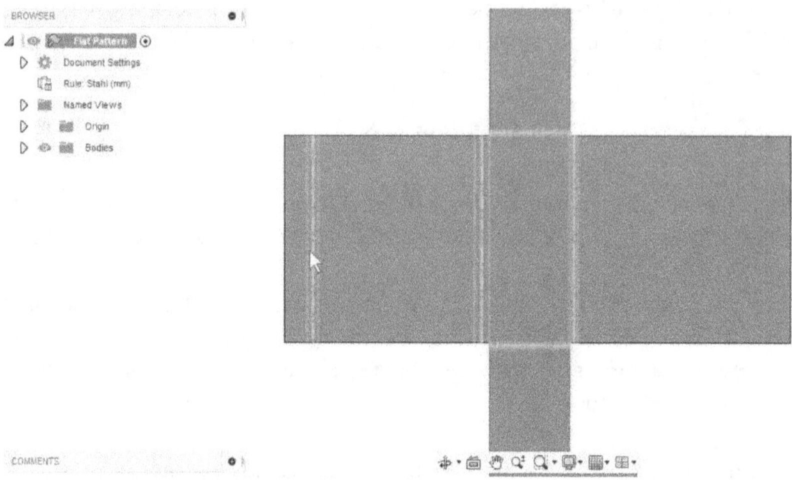

Figure 200: Die The unfolding of the previously illustrated example; generated by the software

This means that you design the desired, finished sheet metal body and then simply have the software generate the unfolding, i.e. the geometry for the production.

Let's look at this using the previous example. The procedure for the design is very similar, but a bit different compared to working in the "Solid" section of the program. Let's go!

For the base element, we create a sheet by starting a new sketch on a plane. We then draw, for example, a rectangular profile for this base element.

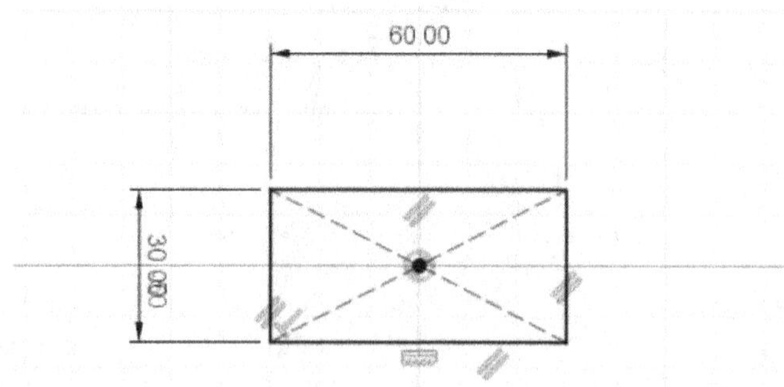

Figure 201: Sketch a rectangular profile on a plane as usual (60 mm x 30 mm)

At this point, we would normally use the Extrude command, but we won't do that here in Sheet metal. This is one of the biggest differences in sheet metal design. Instead, we are building our sheet metal body using the "Flange" command. To do this, select the command and the sketched profile. You just have to click on it, the thickness is already preselected. We will see why it is, and how you can change the thickness, in a moment.

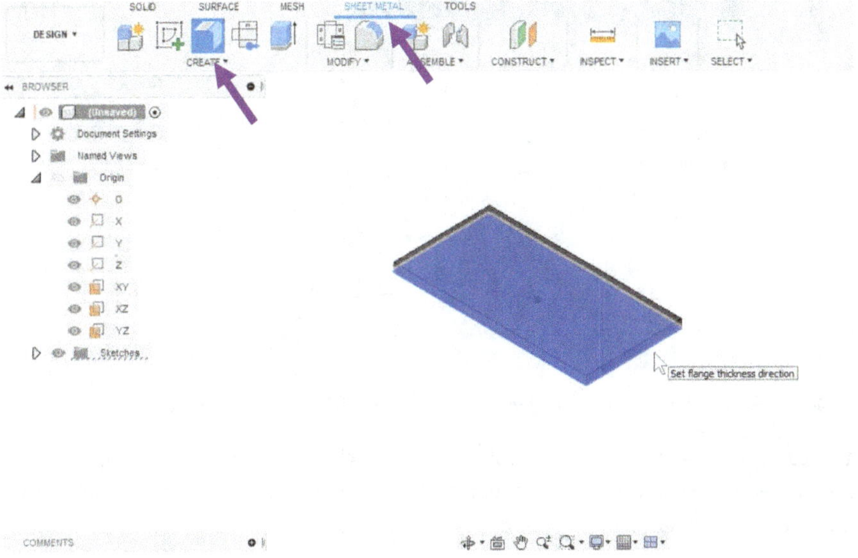

Figure 202: We use the "Flange" command in the "Sheet Metal" tab

On the left in the browser, you can see that the symbol has now changed to "Sheet metal" and the "Rule" element has been added. This contains the material and all important sheet metal specific parameters for sheet metal constructions such as the "K-Factor" or bending conditions. If necessary, you can switch to a different material here.

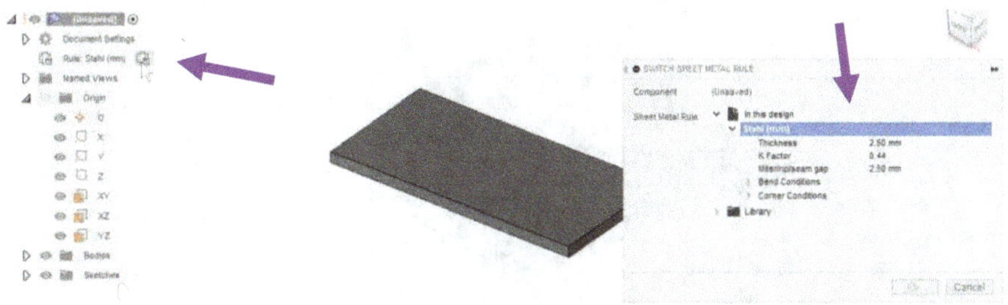

Figure 203: Calling up sheet-specific parameters via "Rule" in the browser

To edit the "Sheet Metal Rules" you need to look for this element in the "Modify" section.

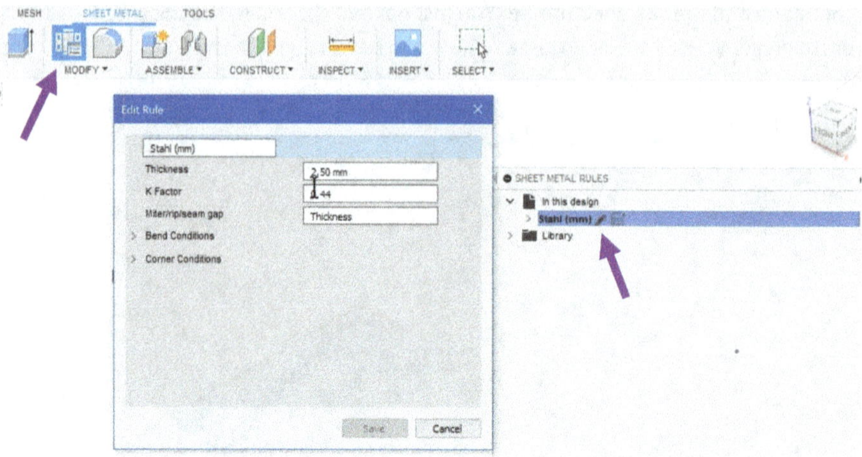

Figure 204: Call up the "Sheet Metal Rules" from the "Modify" section and change them if necessary

You can now change all relevant values with a click on the small pencil icon, but it is recommended to only adjust the sheet thickness and to ask your sheet supplier for the parameters or to leave them with the default values.

What's next? In order to complete the sheet metal example, we use the "Flange" command for the further steps. In the following we always select edges or sketches. Since our sheet metal is relatively simple, we simply select the lateral edge of the basic element and pull it up by grabbing the displayed arrow.

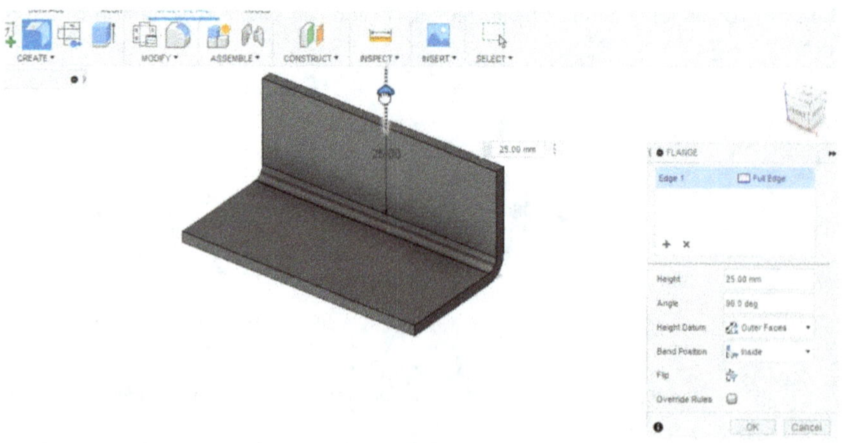

Figure 205: Complete the sample with another "Flange"

As you can see, the program now immediately creates the material with the correct bend. In the options window on the right side you can change all important parameters, e.g. the bending angle or the bending position.

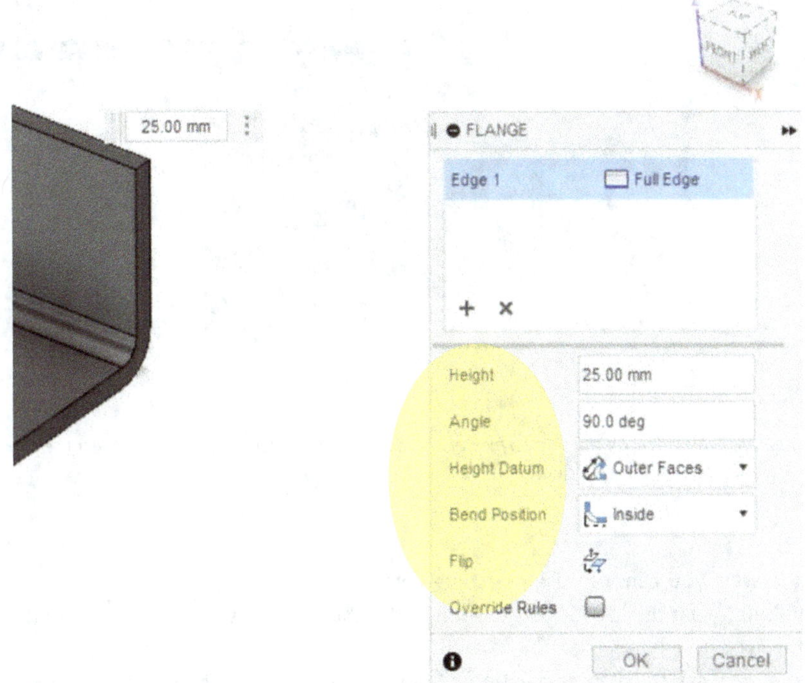

Figure 206: The possible options for the "Flange" command

Let's also construct the other missing elements of our example sheet.

Figure 207: The missing elements of the sample (angles / lengths freely selectable)

Instead of edges, we can also select a sketched profile with "Flange" if we want to add a smaller element of a desired length, for example. A line is already sufficient for this purpose.

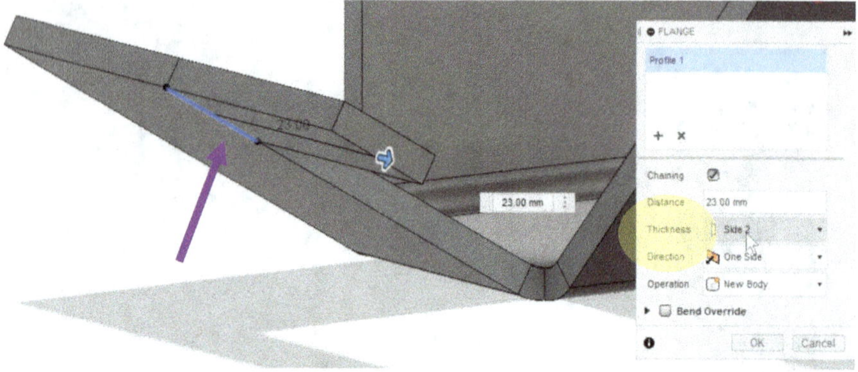

Figure 208: Draw a line on the side surface of a flange and extrude it with "Flange"; select the correct orientation (here e.g. Side 2) at "Thickness"

By the way, you can also use matching commands from the other sections, such as "Combine" from the "Solid" tab, to reunite the sheet metal sections into one body.

Further processing, such as creating a hole or chamfers or edge fillets, would in turn proceed as usual.

In the "Sheet Metal" area, there are three more important functions that we would like to take a look at. The first is the "Bend" command, the second is the "Unfold" command and the third is the "Create Flat Pattern" command.

The "Bend" command can be used to create a bend. This is as simple as it sounds. For example, if you want to bend an element of the sheet body at a specific line, simply draw a bend line where you want to bend the body in a 2D sketch on the face of the element.

Then select the "Bend" command (from "Create" in "Sheet Metal"), as well as the surface to be bent, and the bend line. Now you can bend the sheet metal along this line in the desired orientation.

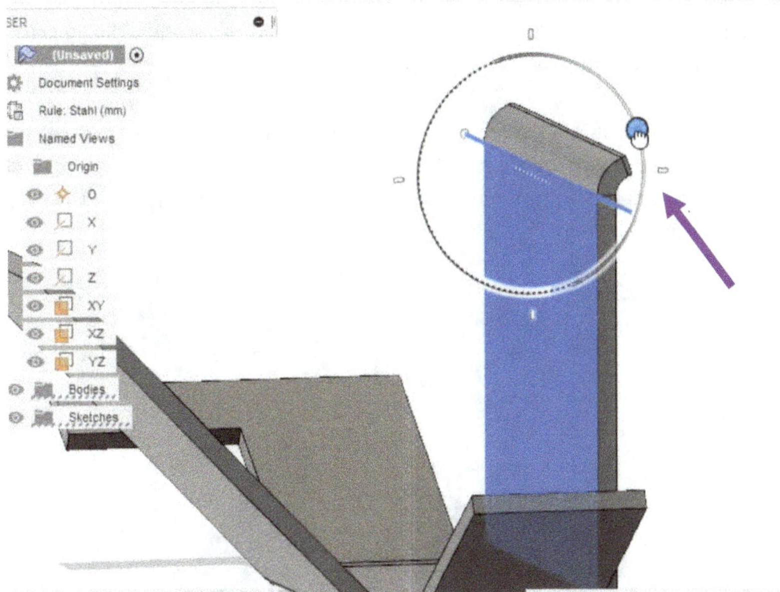

Figure 209: Select a line created on a surface in a 2D sketch as a bend line using the "Bend" command

In order to create an flat pattern from our sheet metal for the manufacturing documents, we can on the one hand use the "Unfold" command from the "Modify" section (Sheet Metal tab). To do this, first select the sheet metal section that should remain stationary, i.e. around which part of the sheet metal should be unfolded, e.g. this one:

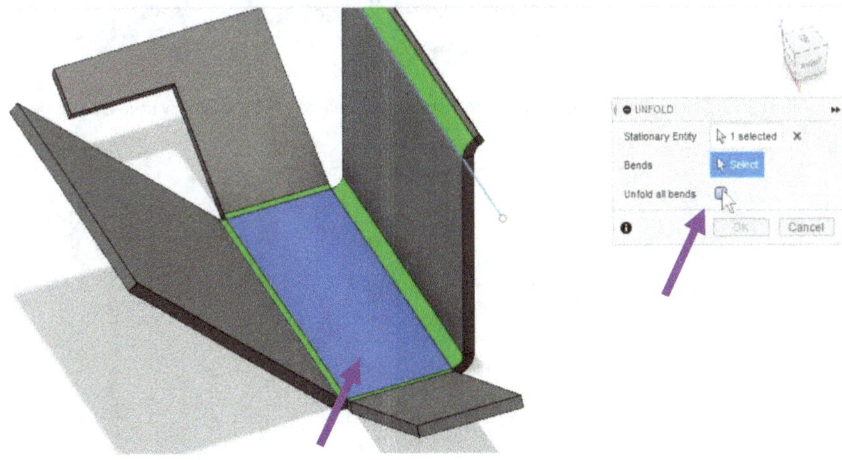

Figure 210: "Unfold" command; stationary part is the blue area

In the options bar, select "Unfold all bends" to select all bends, or individually select any bends you want to unfold.

For the actual production documents, however, you should use the "Create Flat Pattern" command from the "Create" section.
To do this, you again select a stationary section and are then transferred to the "Flat Pattern" workspace.

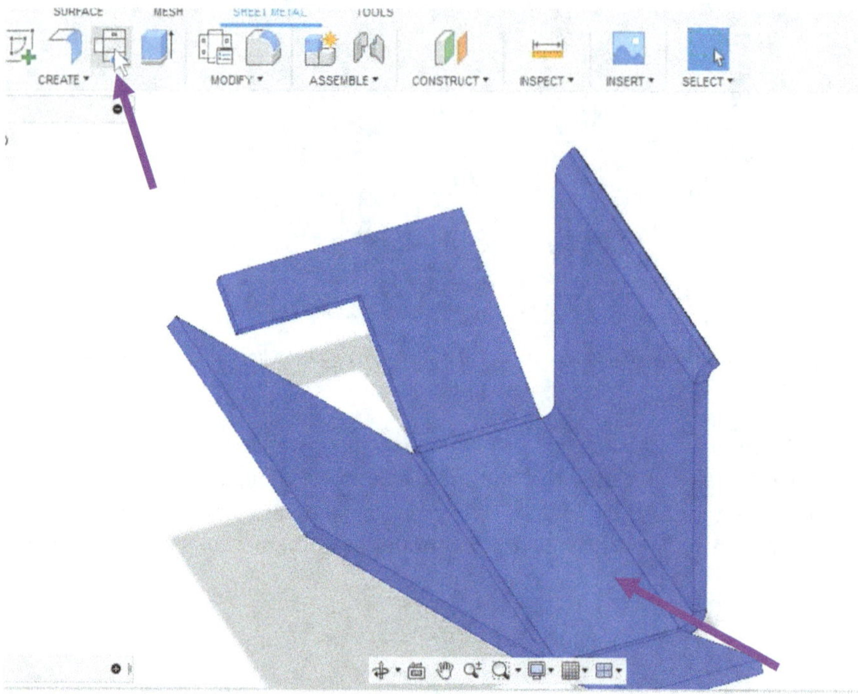

Figure 211: Select the "Create Flat Pattern" command and define a stationary area (see arrows)

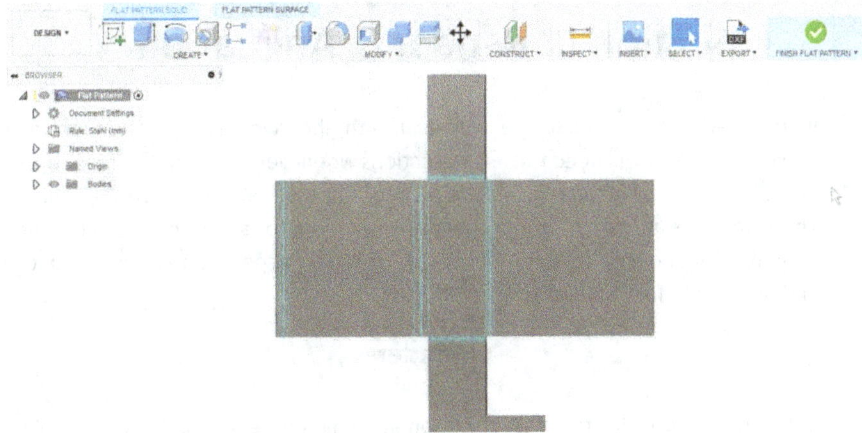

Figure 212: "Flat Pattern" workspace with further editing options

If everything fits, click on "Finish" and you will see the generated "Flat pattern" in the browser on the left. You can then export the flat pattern for production or create a technical drawing from it.

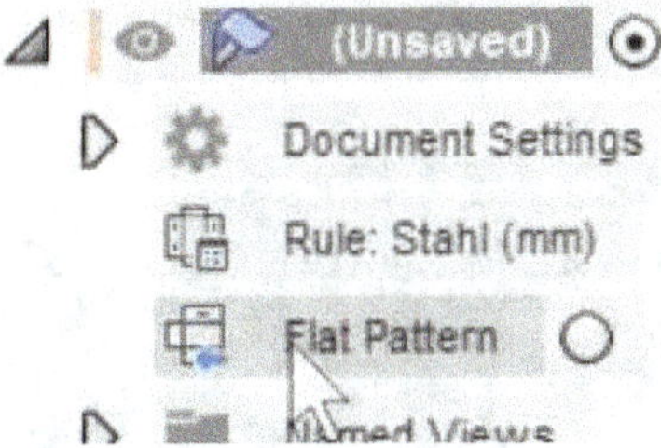

Figure 213: The generated "Flat Pattern" in the browser

That's it for the "Design" section and CAD design! Great job so far!

Be sure to keep going to learn to take full advantage of Fusion 360. In the next section, we'll first look at "Render" and "Animation" before moving on to "Simulation" and the other sections.

Section II: Render & Animation

In this part of the course we will deal with the two sections "Render" and "Animation". You will need these two sections whenever you want to present your individual parts or assemblies in the form of photos , or in the form of a video. These sections are good for a product presentation, for a website, for a meeting or simply for showing to family & friends. It is, so to speak, an integrated photo and film studio for your designs.

6 Render

In this lesson we will start with the "Render" environment, which you can select from the main menu at the top left. We will use one of our design projects, for example, the cup with handle.

Figure 214: Switch to the "Render" workspace of the program

As you can see, the program environment is once more very identical to what we already know. On the left is the browser and at the top the "Render" tab with the individual functions or commands.

New is the "Rendering Gallery" in the lower area, where we can access the rendered graphics.

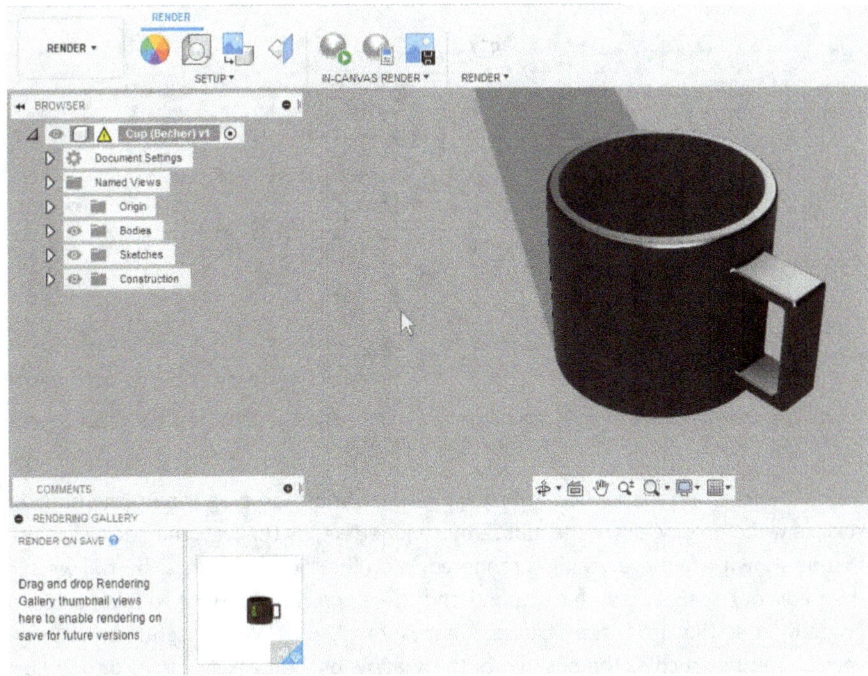

Figure 215: The program environment in the "Render" workspace

By the way, rendering simply means that a graphic or image is generated from the geometric information of the CAD component. Of course, you could also just take a screenshot if you are in a hurry. However, a rendered graphic will be quite different in resolution and realism, but will also take more time to create.

Let's just try it step by step. First, of course, you can hide all the elements you don't want by clicking on the little "eye" icons in the browser, but this is not necessary in our case because we only have a single part. In the second step we can change the appearance of our object.

We can use this to apply a certain texture or materials to our entire design object or just to individual surfaces. A variety of materials are available to choose from. For example, we could simply have the cup represented in bronze.

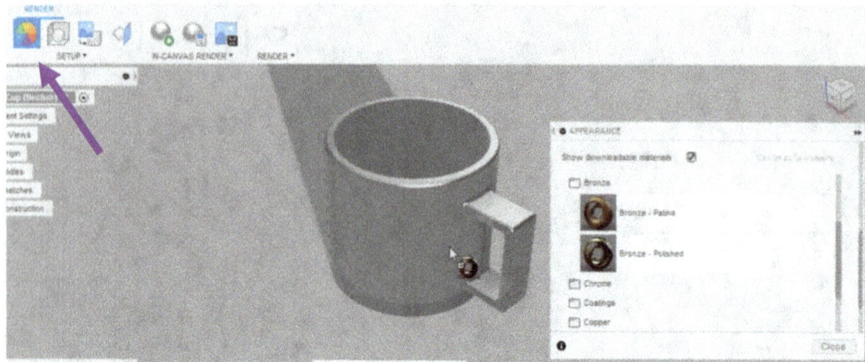

Figure 216: Change the Appearance of our object. Select the desired material and drag it onto the cup with the mouse button hold

Simply select the material or another appearance and then drag it onto the body or surface while holding down the mouse button. Perfect, by the way, the final result will first be shown when everything is rendered. With the "Scene Settings" button we can then edit our scenery, the background and the environment. Here you can select a predefined setting from the "Environment Library", e.g. "Warm Light" and change specific settings such as the position of the shadow or the background color or adjust the camera perspective in "Settings". It is best to try out many different settings by yourself so that you can find something that suits you best.

Figure 217: Change the "Scene Settings" (background) . Select the desired preset or create it from scratch and drag it over while holding down the mouse button

With the command "Decal" we could put an image, for example a label, on our cup. Simply select a suitable image from your own collection, select a surface on which it should be placed on and then use the options or the arrows and cursors to adjust its size and position.

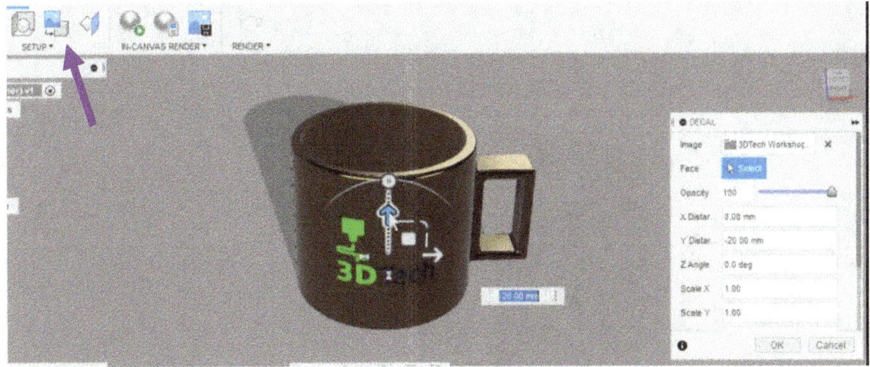

Figure 218: Put a label or sticker with "decal" on the object

With the command "In-Canvas Render" we can create a quick preview of the rendering in the program environment and with "Capture Image" we can create a screenshot.

Figure 219: For a quick preview you can use "In-Canvas Render"

However, the actual rendering is started with the "Render" command. Simply click on the teapot and enter the desired settings. Before that, you need to save the project. You can choose between several preset resolutions or specify your own at "Custom". The higher the resolution and render quality, the longer it will take. At "Render with" we can simply choose "local", so that our own PC provides the computing power.

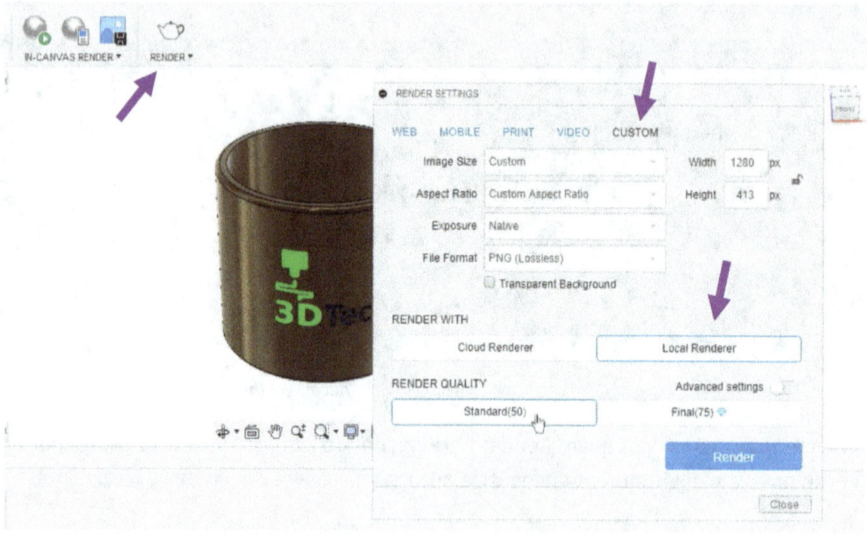

Figure 220: The actual "render" function of the workspace

Then simply start the rendering and wait. The file and progress will be shown at the bottom of the "Rendering Gallery". By clicking on it, you can open the rendered graphic and save or delete it. As you can see, the position also plays a big role, i.e. how you rotate and move the design object is how it will eventually be rendered.

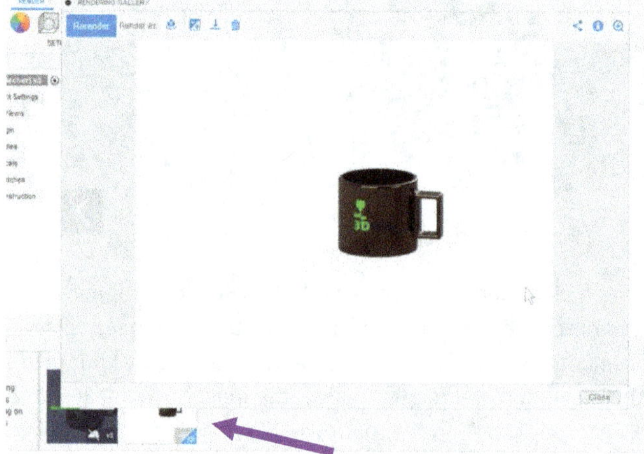

Figure 221: Open the rendered image with a double click in the Rendering Gallery

That's it for rendering, there's not much more to talk about for this part of the software. We'll continue with the "Animation" environment and then move on to a more exciting topic.

7 Animation

We use the model of our 4-cylinder engine to discuss the possibilities of the "Animation" part of the program. As you can see, the environment is structured as we are already familiar with it, the only difference being that the "Animation Timeline" is located in the lower area.

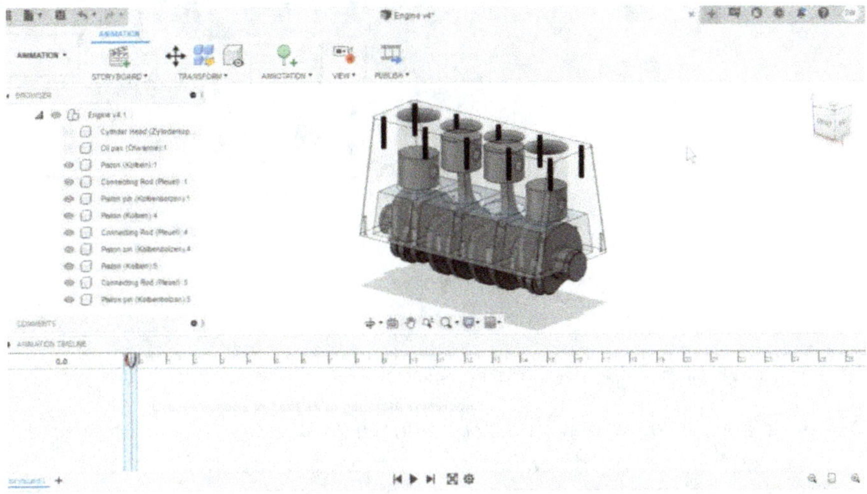

Figure 222: The "Animation" program environment with the "Animation Timeline" (below)

We would now like to create a kind of video in which the pistons move up and down and is zoomed into a few different positions. Unfortunately, we can't make it as easy as in the design environment and just animate the joint of the crankshaft, because joints are unfortunately not shown to us in "Animation", but only components. That's also the reason why we only want to animate the pistons. If you want to capture the whole engine running in a video, the easiest way is to animate the crankshaft joint in the "Design" environment, as we had already done. And then to create a screen casting video from it, i.e. a screen recording, with external software. Otherwise, the animation is very complex, as you will see in a moment.

Back to "Animation". For the animation, we have to give each individual component a movement. By the way, we are joint independent in the direction of movement. To make a movement, we use the command "Transform Components" from the section "Transform". The first step is to hide all other components so that only the crankcase and piston remain displayed.

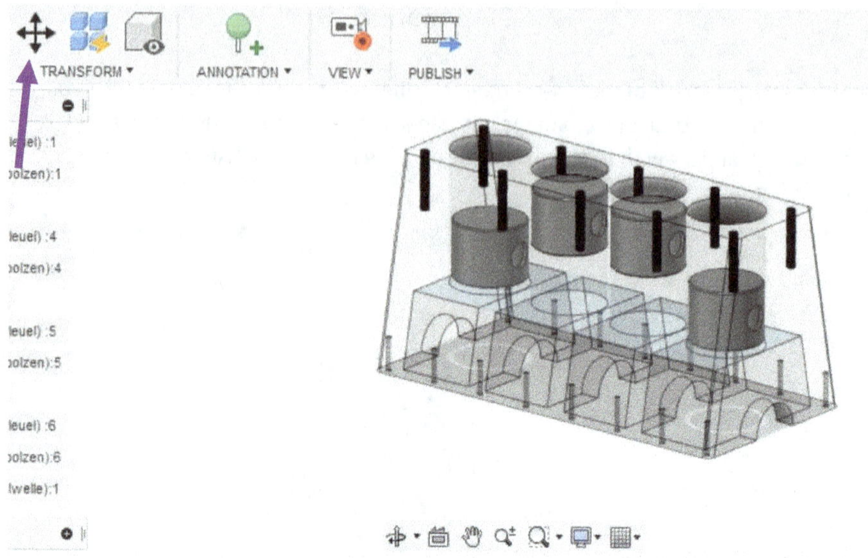

Figure 223: All unnecessary elements are hidden; pistons and crankcase remain displayed

Before we start, we must then set the cursor in the timeline to a duration, for example to 2 seconds, because that is how long the first scene should last. If we zoom into the model after setting a duration, we will notice that a recording feature will be created automatically. This always happens when we have selected a time duration and make a movement in the program environment or a component shift or another action to the scene.

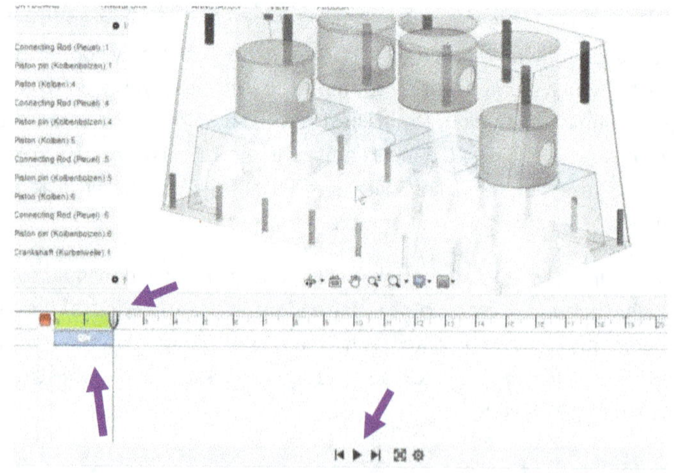

Figure 224: A camera feature (light blue) is automatically created after we set the timeline to 2 sec. and make a movement with the mouse in the drawing environment; playable with Play

This feature already reflects for example a zooming in. We can play it with a click on Play. If you don't want this, use the "View" button, this will suppress the recording function.

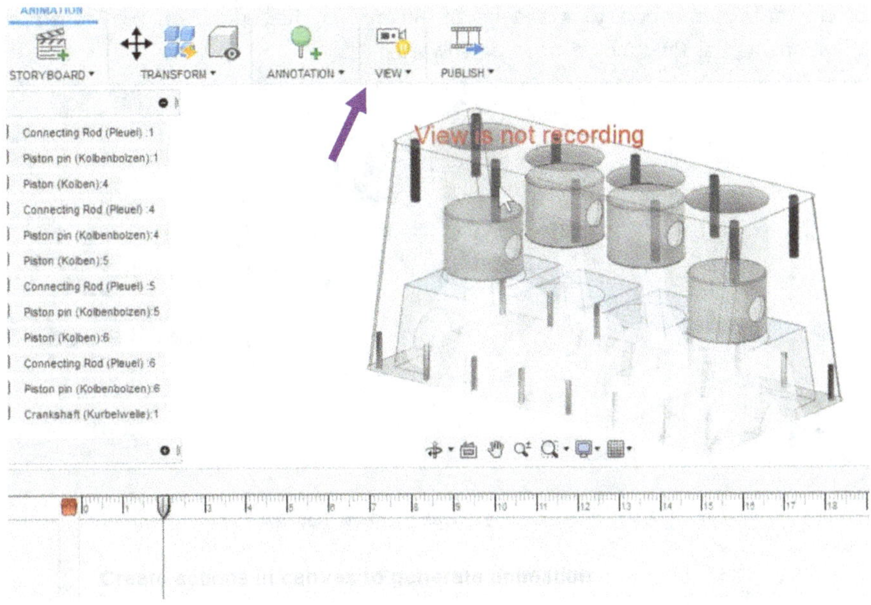

Figure 225: Suppress the automatic recording function of the view with "View"

But first to the initial movement of the pistons. For the first movement we select the command "Transform Components" and two of the pistons, each at the same height. We either trace the movement with our mouse or enter a value with the keyboard, in this case +80 mm in z-direction for the first two pistons, as they should move upwards.

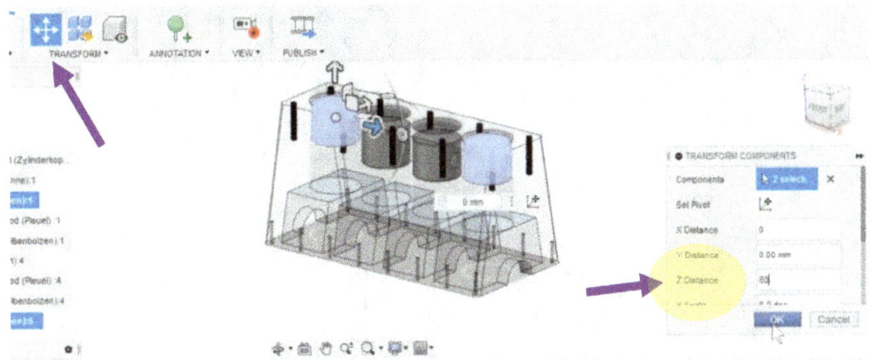

Figure 226: Select the outer two pistons and enter +80 mm

This movement takes 2 seconds, since we are at 2 seconds in the timeline. For the movement of the other two pistons, we must now remain at this 2 sec. mark in the timeline for the time being, since all components must move at the same time. We select the other two pistons and enter -80 mm in the z-direction at "Transform Components", as they should move downwards.

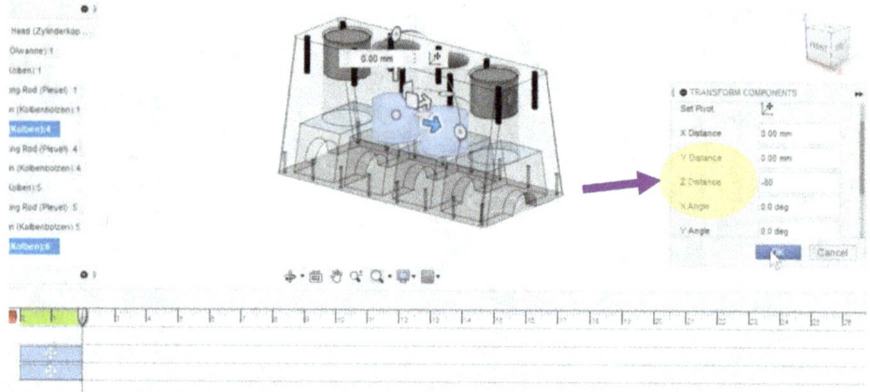

Figure 227: The two middle pistons should move downwards by - 80 mm

If we then press "Play" we can watch the first scene.

For the second scene we need the exact opposite movements. That means for the first two pistons: - 80 mm and for the other two: + 80 mm. To do this, we first set the timeline to 4 sec, since this movement should again last 2 sec, exactly following the first movement.

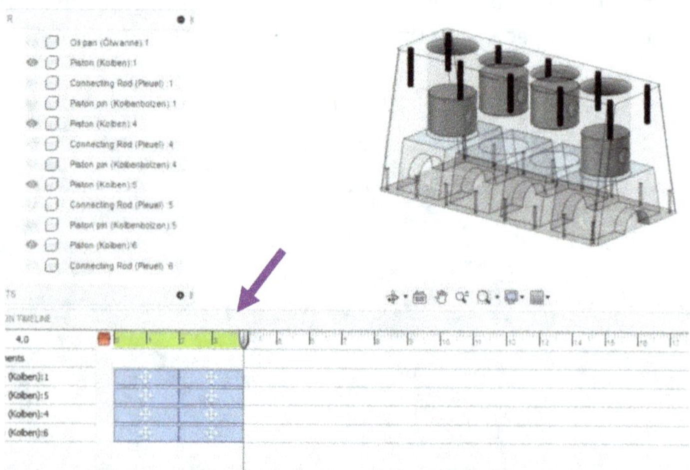

Figure 228: In the end, there must be eight recording features for one rotation in the timeline, two each per piston or four each per 2 sec.

We have to repeat the whole thing for as long as the video is supposed to last. Quite complex, isn't it?

In these 4 seconds we would like to finally add a zoom or a change in view. For this we stay with the 4 sec. on the timeline and simply execute the zoom or view movement we want to have.

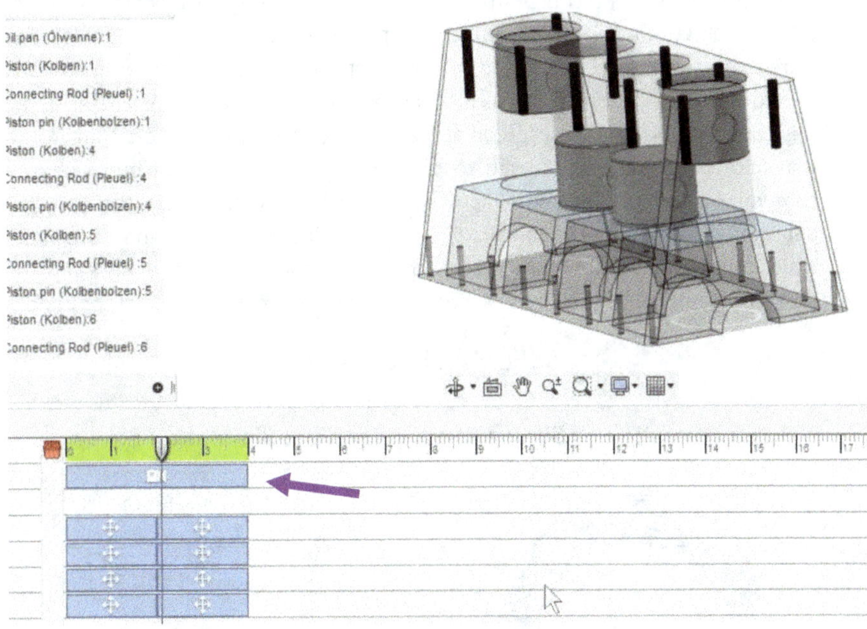

Figure 229: Execute view movement (rotate, move or other) and press "Play".

Done is the short animation! With a click on "Publish" we could save our video with the desired settings.

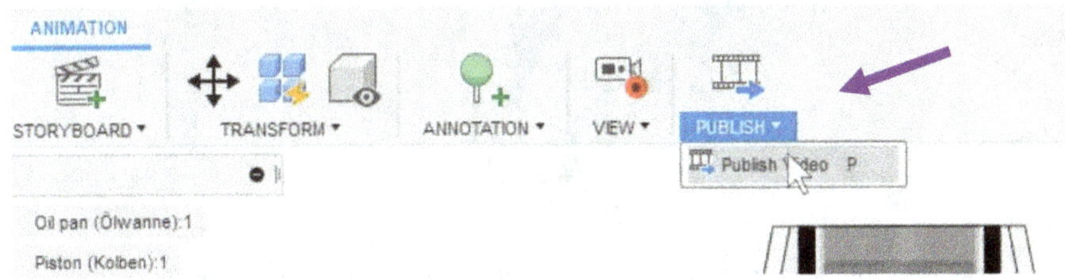

Figure 230: Publish the animation with "Publish" or save it in a desired format

Section III: Simulation, Manufacture & Drawing

In this final part of the course, things get really interesting once again, as we will take a look at Simulation, Manufacture and Drawing. The "Simulation" section allows you to simulate loads and material behavior. Perhaps the term FEM, i.e. "Finite Element Method", sounds familiar to you. Without going into detail about this complex principle, you should at least have heard the name once and know that FEM software can be used to simulate loads and material behavior of a component. In this hands-on course, we exclusively focus on the practical application of the methodology. The sections "Manufacture" and "Drawing", which follow, are needed for direct machine manufacturing on the one hand and for creating technical drawings as manufacturing documents on the other hand.

8 (FEM-) Simulation

8.1 Introduction to Simulation and the First Simulation Study

Figure 231: The aim of this chapter: The simulation of a load to the snap hook CAD model

We would like to use the carabiner - created in one of the previous design projects - as a sample to get to know the "Simulation" environment of Fusion 360. With "Simulation" we can simulate loads and will get values, such as: resulting stresses or displacements as a result. That means in simple terms, for example, the bending of a component under an applied load.

To do this, we open the file and then switch to the "Simulation" menu in Fusion's selection option at the top left. The first window that appears is "New Study", where we can select which simulation we want to run. For example, we can choose to simulate static stress, thermal stress or nonlinear static stress.

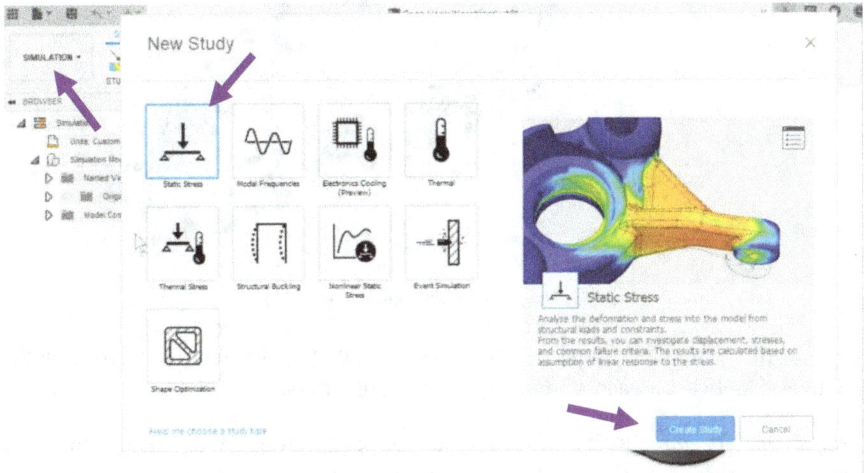

Figure 232: Open the file of the carabiner and switch to the "Simulation" area

In this beginner's course, we will only focus on what is probably the most common application: static loading. Therefore, we select this one. With a click on "Create Study" we start a new so-called load study. This study is then displayed with all relevant options and settings on the left in the browser under the folders of the object.

In the "Simulation" area, there is only the "Setup" menu tab in the upper menu bar, where we make all the settings we need for the simulation. If we want to have different loading situations calculated, e.g. if we want to simulate two different forces, we can also create several studies. For this we would simply click on "New Study".

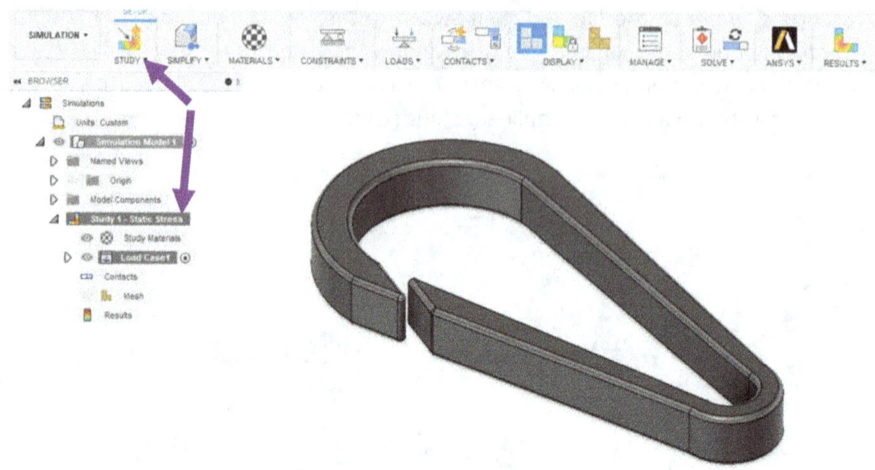

Figure 233: The program environment of "Simulation"

We now proceed in five steps, for the simulation of a component. This procedure is relatively identical for each study, only the content differs.

Before we start with a load study, we first consider whether it makes sense for us to simplify our component somewhat. This makes sense if we had a geometrically very complex component or a large assembly with many components that would not contribute to the computation. The more complex the analysis, the longer the computation time. In our case, however, we can leave the geometry as it is.

Figure 234: If we click on the "Simplify" command in the menu bar (top image), the menu bar for the "Simplify" area opens (bottom image), in which we could make simplifications to solids and surfaces; close the area with "Finish Simplify"

The second step is to check if the correct material is assigned to our part. To do this, we use the "Materials" menu. Clicking on "Study Materials" opens a window that shows us the respective materials for all components.

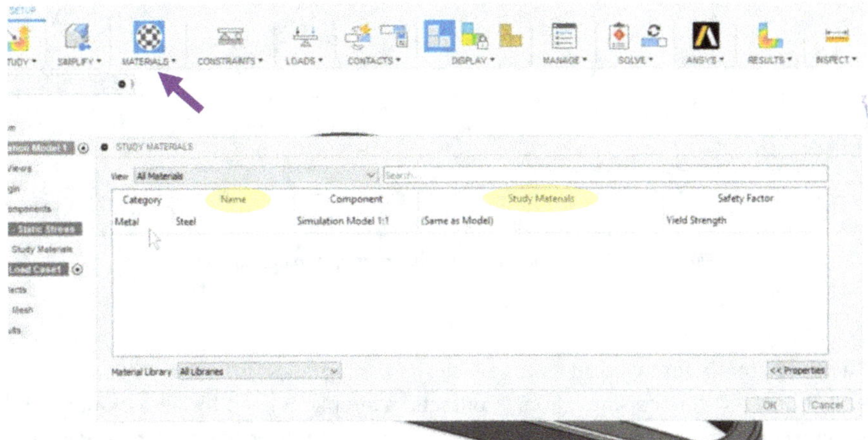

Figure 235: Clicking on "Study Materials" in the "Materials" menu opens a window

In this case we have only one material, because it is a single part. Depending on what we selected as the material during the design process, we will see the material displayed at "Name" - steel is selected by default. At "Study Materials" we can now select the material of the part for this study. Currently it is set to "Same as model", so the actual material of the object will be used for our load study, i.e. steel. If we want to select a different material for, say, a different loading study, we simply select it from the drop-down menu. Alternatively, we could also change the material in the design environment, but this will be more cumbersome for multiple studies. For this simple snap hook, we select "aluminum" as the material for the analysis, since steel would have a far too high Young's modulus, for the snap hook to open, i.e. it would offer too much resistance to deformation.

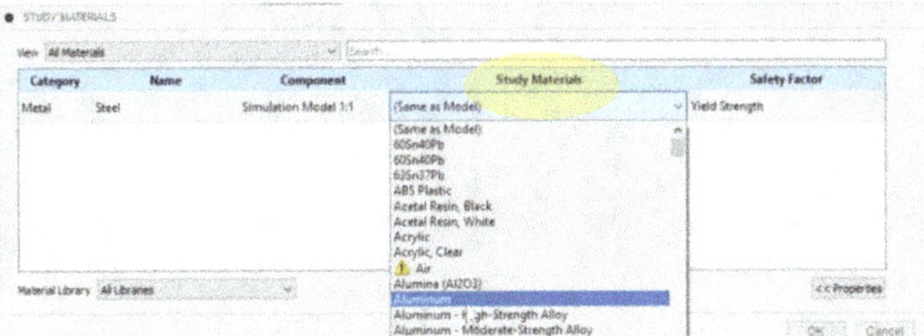

Figure 236: Select aluminum in the drop-down menu at "Study Materials"

With a click on "Properties" we can also display the preset material properties such as density, Young's modulus, etc.

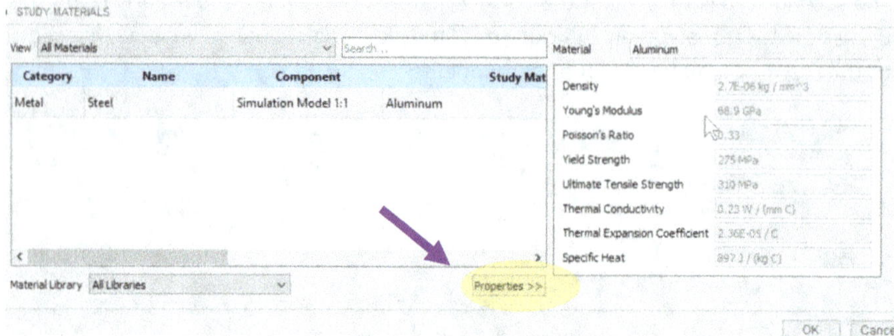

Figure 237: Display the material properties after material selection

The third step before we can start solving the computation is to select "Constraints" and "Contacts" for the simulation. "Contacts" are only needed for an assembly with several components, because with "Contacts" we define the load transfer between the individual components, i.e. the connection between the components. But we'll look at that in more detail in the second simulation example.

At this point, we only need to define "Constraints". "Constraints" simply represent bounding conditions in the "Simulation" section. It means, at which points or surfaces our component is fixed in space, or how or where it is mounted.

Imagine it in a very practical way: You would take the carabiner in one hand and press its back against the palm of your hand, therefore we select the back surface of the carabiner as the support.

For this we create a constraint with the command "Structural Constraints".

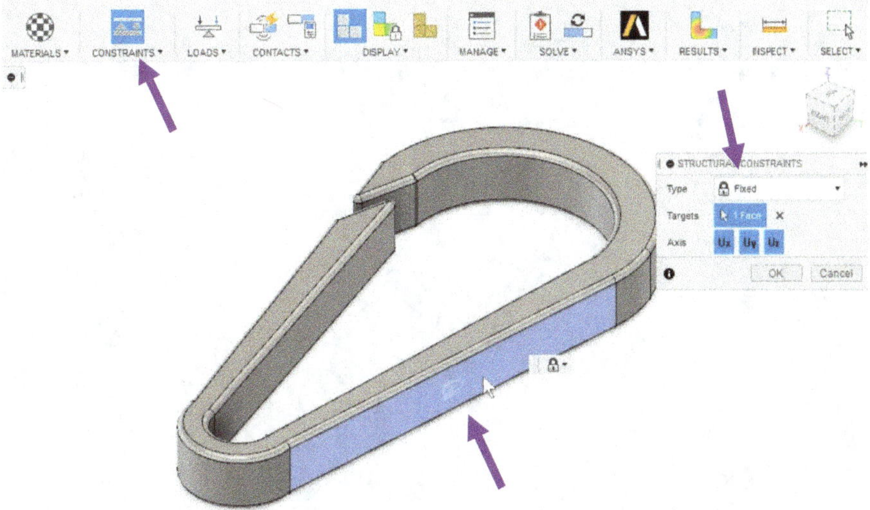

Figure 238: Fix the back of the carabiner with the "Constraint": "Fixed"

We can choose between "Fixed", "Pin", "Frictionless", and so on. For the carabiner, we choose "Fixed" as the simplest constraint and assume as a simplification that it applies in all directions, so the carabiner does not move a bit in the palm of the hand.

Then, in the fourth step, we need a load, of course. We consider how the carabiner is actually loaded.

In the present geometry, the front element of the carabiner is loaded by pushing, so as to widen the opening of the carabiner, for example, to insert a rope.

For example, one will press with the index and or middle finger against the upper edge of the carabiner, i.e. just before the opening.

For the simulation of this load we select the command "Loads" or "Structural Loads" and as type: "Force".

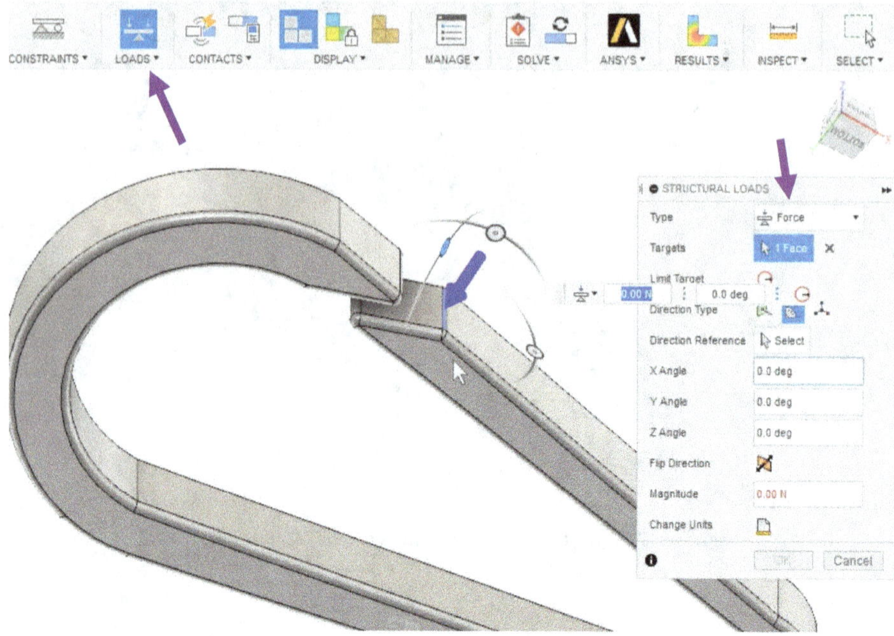

Figure 239: Select the load direction, the point of application and the force at "Structural Loads"

We could also apply a "pressure", a "moment" or other load, depending on the situation.

Then we select the front upper rounding of the carabiner, just before the opening, and enter a value of 100 N as force, for example. This corresponds to a load of about 10 kg. By the way, a man can apply up to 500 N of grip force, i.e. approx. 50 kg. Let´s assume a perpendicular direction of force on the surface. But we could also change the direction of the force vector if needed.

Then we have almost everything complete. In the last, fifth step, have to have a mesh generated, before we can start the computation and get the results displayed. With the FEM method, the computation is performed using a mesh with nodes, which is placed over the solid body. We do this by right-clicking on "Mesh" in the structure tree and selecting "Generate Mesh" on the left side. The generated mesh will then be displayed to us. You could actually skip this step, because the software will automatically generate the mesh during a calculation anyway.

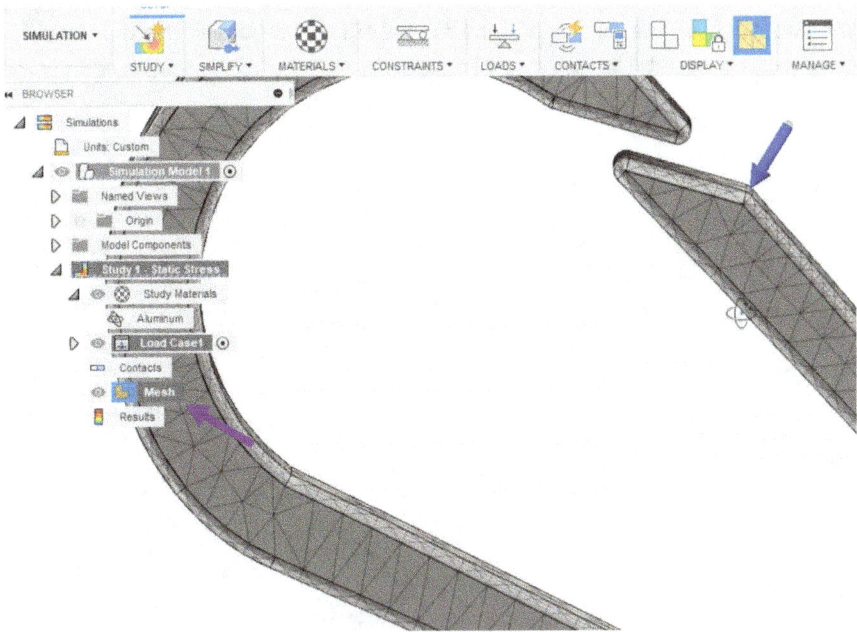

Figure 240: Generate the mesh shown with "Generate Mesh"

Afterwards, we can start the computation and will get the results by pressing the "Solve" button at the top. By the way, with the "Pre-Check" we could check beforehand if all relevant data for the computation have been defined, e.g. constraints and loads have been set.

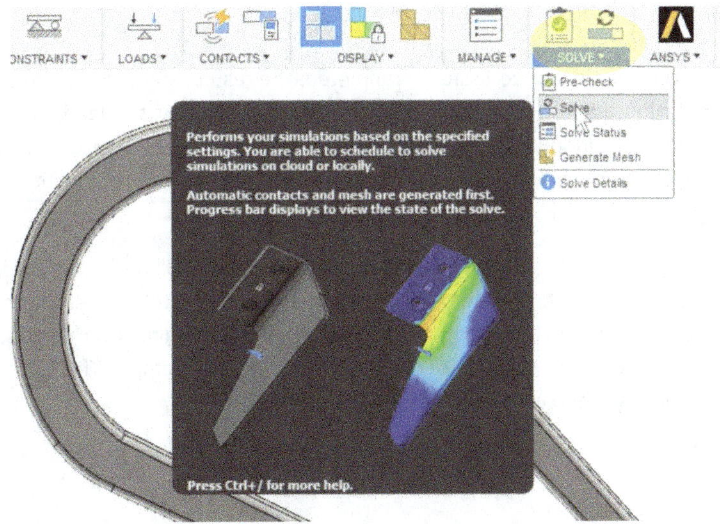

Figure 241: "Solve" for the computation and "Pre-check" for the verification beforehand

Then we can have the calculation solved in the "Cloud" or locally. Use the "Cloud" in case "local" does not work.

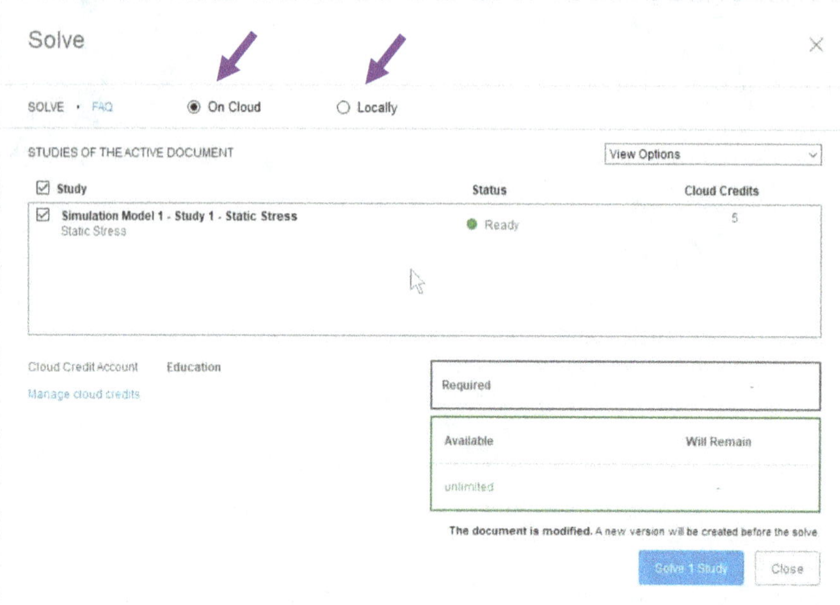

Figure 242: Have the calculation done in the "cloud" or locally

When the computation is successfully completed, the results are displayed to us. After the computation, we are first given general information about the load study in the "Result Details" window. The minimum safety factor is displayed, as well as recommendations on how we can improve the safety factor or weaken it if it is too low or too high.

A safety factor of less than one means that the material will fail under the load, and a safety factor of more than one means that the material will safely withstand the load. If the safety factor is much too high, we can speak of "over-engineering" and may save unnecessary material by making the component thinner, for example. This factor is also shown graphically when we close the "Job Status" window.

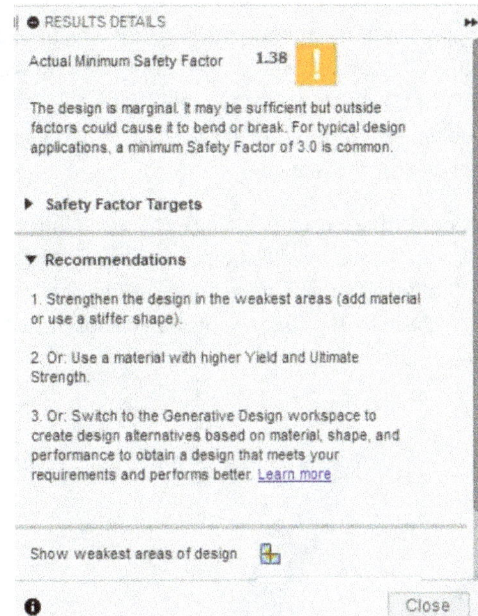

Figure 243: After the computation, the "Result Details" window opens with an initial overview and initial recommendations for improving the model

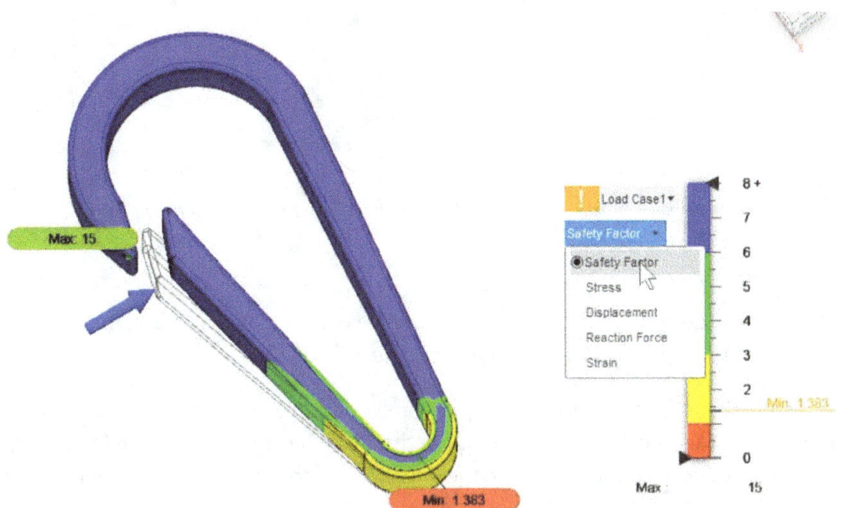

Figure 244: The graphical representation after we have closed the "Result Details" window and computation; in the drop-down menu it is possible to choose between several display options (Safety Factor, Stress, Displacement, Reaction Forces, Strain)

The color gradient displayed on the component indicates which safety factor is present in which area. The safety factor is lowest in the area of the lower curvature of the component. This was to be expected with this application of load; the stress in the component will also be highest at this area. If the snap hook breaks when it is opened, it will first break somewhere in this area.

To display the stresses or displacements, we open the small drop-down menu in the color scale area below "Load Case". We can display "Stress", "Strain", "Displacement" and "Reaction Forces", as well as make other options and change units. If we look at the "von Mises Stresses", we see that there is probably about 198 MPa of stress in the inner curvature of the carabiner.

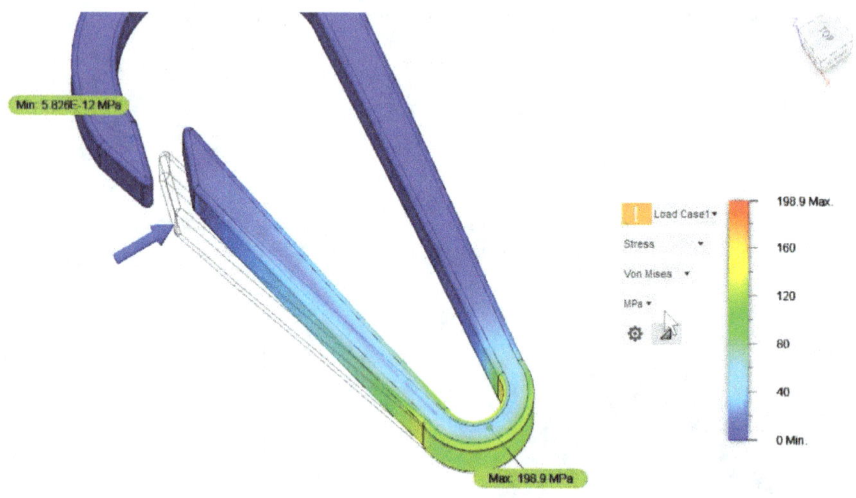

Figure 245: The maximum stress in the area of the lower rounding of the carabiner

When showing the displacement, we see that we could open the carabiner by approx. 2.2 mm in the y-direction with the applied force.

On the one hand, this is graphically exaggerated, andon the other hand, it is of course too little to open the carabiner. We would therefore have to apply more force and, if necessary, reinforce our carabiner in the lower area if the safety factor were no longer sufficient.

Figure 246: The maximum displacement in the area of the opening of the carabiner

Perfect! That was the first part of "Simulation".

With this knowledge we can already simulate a simple component with a defined load situation. In the second part, we'll take a look at simulating our engine model. Stay tuned and proceed, it will be exciting!

8.2 Perform a Simulation Study with an Assembly

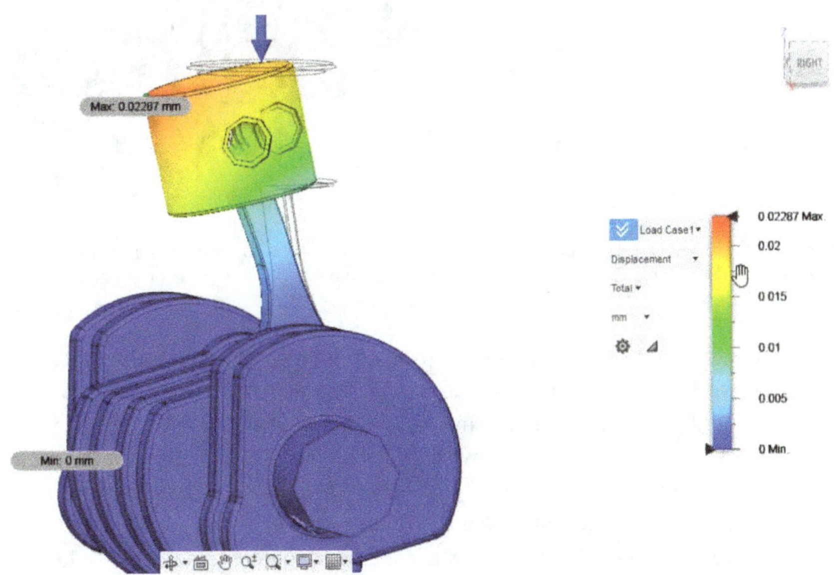

Figure 247: The goal of this chapter is to simulate our engine model

In this chapter we want to deepen our knowledge and skills in simulation by means of doing an assembly simulation. There are a few small differences to consider in comparsion to individual parts. We will choose the 4-cylinder engine to get to know them. For this we start a new "Static stress" study to the engine.

Before we start, we will first simplify the model for our purposes. We want to simulate the forces acting on a piston, and for this we consider only one piston, with a single piston pin, connecting rod and the crankshaft. Therefore, we will remove all other components. I have already prepared this. You can do it easily with the command "Simplify" from the menu bar. To do this, we select the command and then select one or more redundant components in the browser and, after right-clicking, select the "Remove" command. Finally, we close the area with "Finish Simplify".

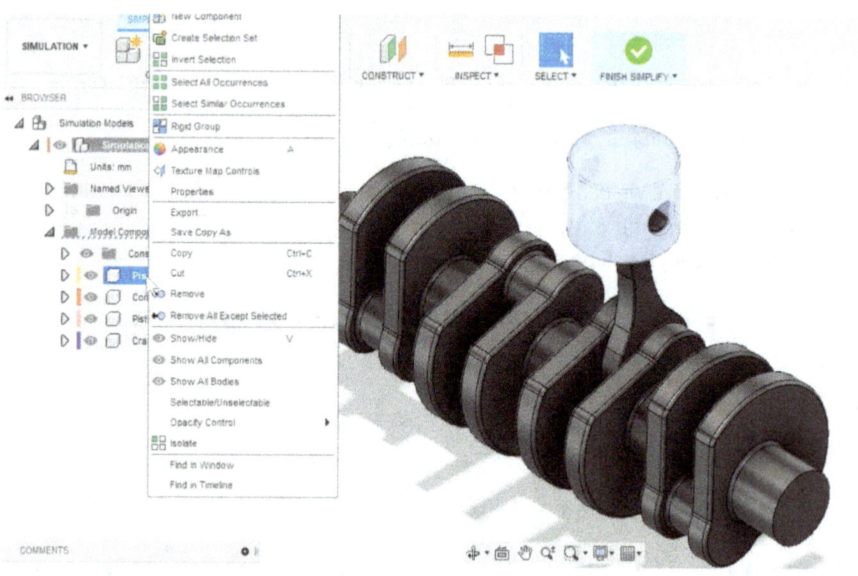

Figure 248: We are in the "Simplify" area in this image; right click on the component in the structure tree and select "Remove"; crankshaft with one connecting rod, piston and piston pin each should remain as shown

The simulation of an assembly runs relatively identically to the simulation of single parts, i.e. we first have to think about simplifying the model again, which we have already done. Then choose the right material. In our case we leave the material for all components being steel, that's what we chose by default in the design. In the next step we need to define the "Constraints" and "Contacts". We had already covered what "Constraints" are and how we define them in the previous chapter. In this chapter, however, we also need "Contacts" because we need to determine how the load that we later want to apply vertically from above to the piston surface is transferred via the components. So "Contacts" is used to define the load transfer between the individual components, i.e. the connection between the components.

There are two possibilities for this. We can have "automatic contacts" generated by the program itself, or we can use "manual contacts", i.e. generate all "contacts" by ourselves. In general, it has proven to use "automatic contacts" first and to subsequently check them manually and, if necessary, modify them.

Figure 249: Choice between "Automatic contacts" and "Manual contacts

Once we have created "Automatic contacts", we can see the created connections, by clicking on "Manage Contacts". In our case we need: connections between piston and piston pin, between piston pin and connecting rod, and between connecting rod and crankshaft.

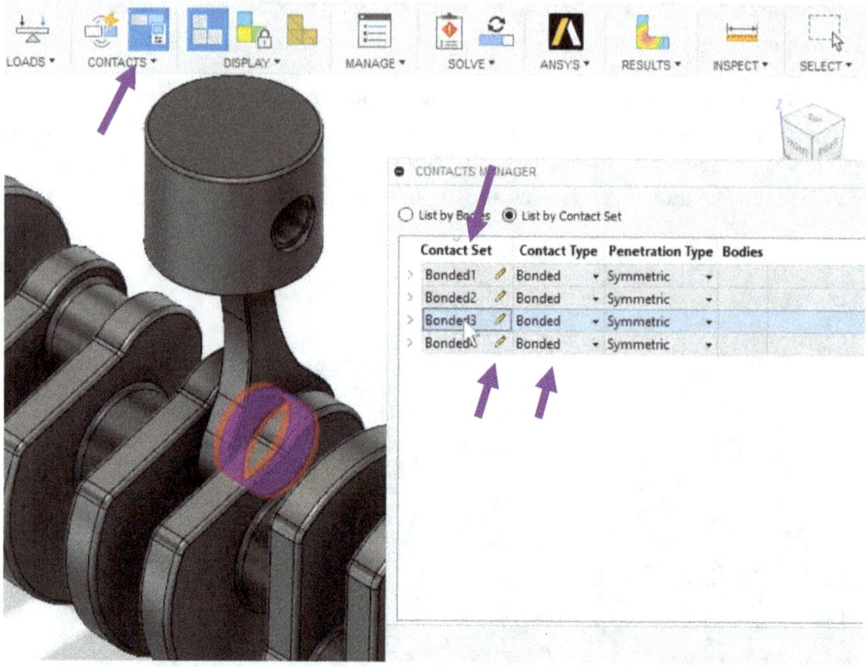

Figure 250: After clicking on "Automatic Contacts" and "Manage Contacts" (menu bar) we will see the contacts created

If we click on the small pencil icon of a created "Contact", we can edit it.

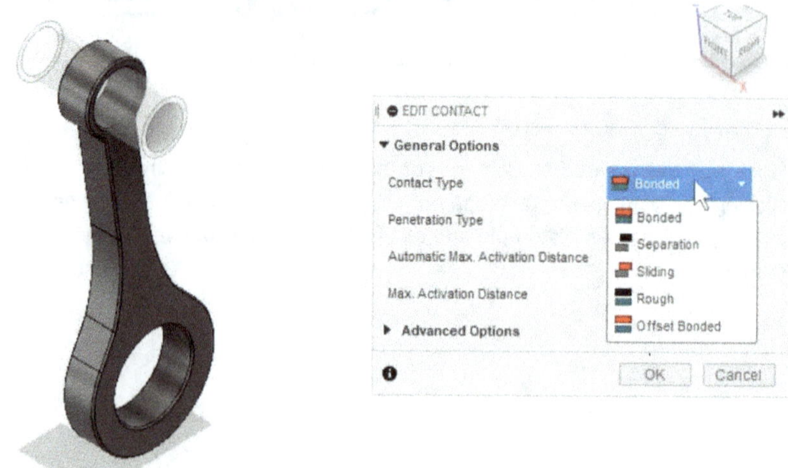

Figure 251: Edit an automatically created contact (click on the "pencil icon" of a contact; see previous figure) and then select "Contact Type"

We can select the "Contact Type" in the general settings. There are six basic "Contact Types" available. "Automatic contacts" has the type "Bonded" selected by default, which corresponds to a fixed or bonded connection state. In our case, we will leave all "Contact Types" set to "Bonded" to perform a simplified analysis on our anyway simplified model.

However, we will briefly look a little more closely at how we would select the correct "Contact Type" for a more detailed computation. To do this, it is important to know the motion sequences of a model. In our case, for example, we know that the connecting rod is mounted rotationally in the two connecting rod eyes, which means that rotary motion must be possible here. It is also important to know the individual "contact types". You can choose between "Bonded", "Separation", "Sliding", "Rough" and "Offset Bonded".

"Bonded", as already mentioned, reflects a fixed connection, it is like being glued together, with "Offset Bonded" it is nearly the same, with the difference that you can set an "offset" between the two components for preventing the bodies from touching each other. "Separation" allows bodies to move away from each other during loading. "Sliding" allows components to not move away from each other, but the surfaces can move tangentially to or from each other, i.e. slide on each other. "Rough" ultimately allows full or even partial movement apart from each other and in reality approximates a joint with very high static friction. In our model, however, we only use "Automatic Contacts" with the type "Bonded" in this beginner's course.

What are we still missing for a calculation? Exactly! "Constraints", i.e. the fixation in space, as well as a load that is applied. As "Constraints" we select all crankshaft surfaces, with which the crankshaft is mounted in the crankcase. We fix them in all directions and select as "Type": "Fixed", that means we simulate in this case that the crankshaft does not move, normally it would rotate. However, we only want to simulate a static and not a dynamic case.

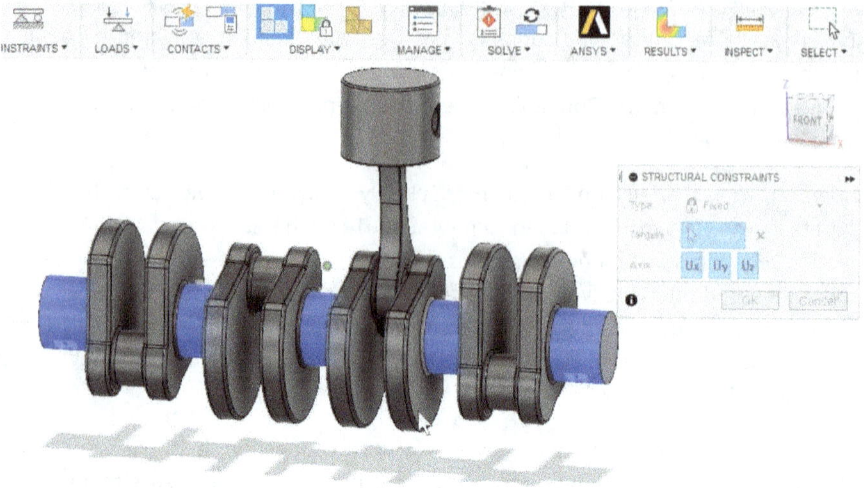

Figure 252: Use the main bearings of the crankshaft as supports ("Structural Constraints")

Finally, we define a load, perpendicular to the piston surface, e.g. 1000 N.

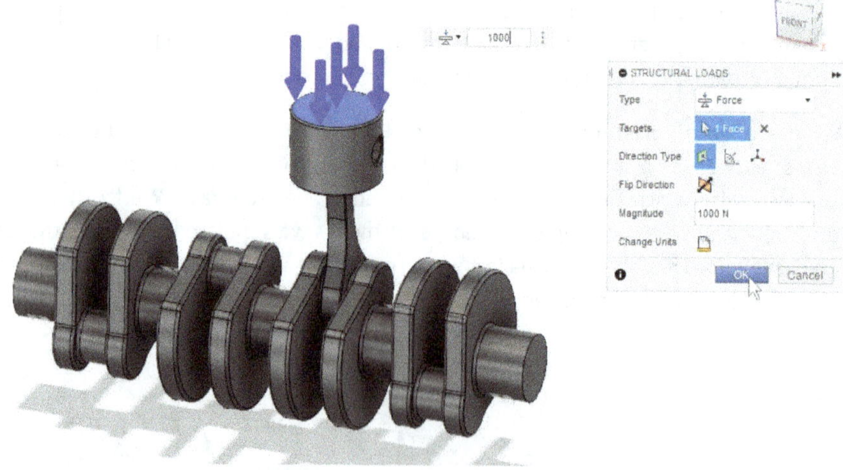

Figure 253: 1000 N should be applied to the piston surface

Now we could generate the mesh, but with a click on "Solve", the program will do it automatically.

After the model has been successfully solved, we can once more display the desired results such as "stress", "strain" or the safety factor. In our case, we can see how the connecting rod would deform under the load. Of course, this is very exaggerated.

Figure 254: The deformation of the connecting rod shaft under the load can be easily seen

By the way, with the help of the scale on the right side, we can also limit the display range, and thus, for example, only display the areas of very high stress.

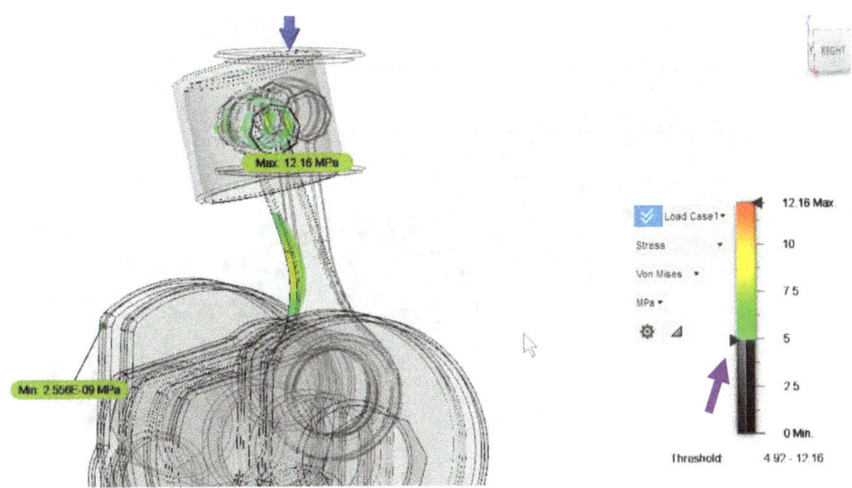

Figure 255: Limit the scale with the cursor to display only a certain range of values

Very good! That should be enough to get us started in the world of FEM simulation with Fusion 360. You have learned how to perform a load study on a single part and on an assembly.

More advanced case studies and other applications are beyond the scope of this beginner's course. Look forward to a continuation in the advanced course!

But don't worry, the course doesn't end here, in fact in the next lesson we'll get into another exciting feature of Fusion 360. We'll now look at the "Manufacture" section, which allows you to optimally plan the production of parts!

9 Manufacture

Welcome back! In this penultimate lesson of the course we will deal with CAM. CAM is the abbreviation for "Computer Aided Manufacturing" and describes the computer aided planning of the production of a component, which is manufactured e.g. with the help of a CNC machine. One of the main functions of the "Manufacture" area is to create "toolpaths" for tools. We can then export these, for example as a "gcode", and send them to the tool, e.g. the CNC. Let's have a look at it in this lesson with an example. To do this, we will first build a very simple part and then take a look at the menu bars and functions of the "Manufacture" area. Make the very simple example part using the following dimensions and as shown below.

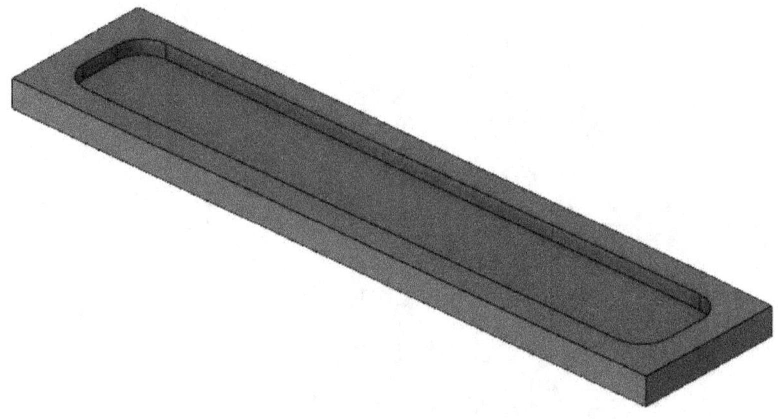

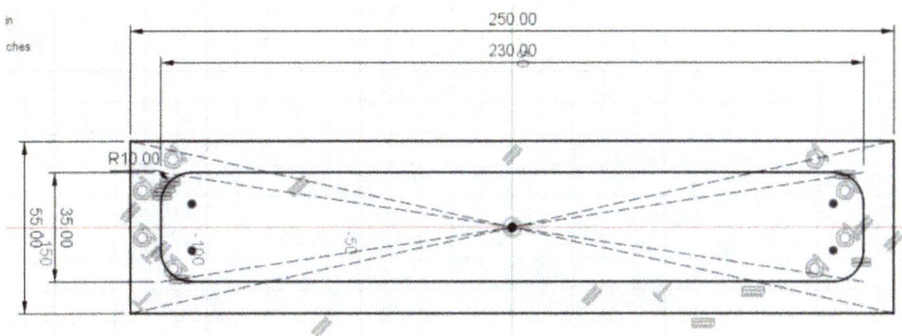

Figure 256: Design the part with the dimensions shown (10 mm extrusion, 5 mm depth for the cutout)

Then we switch to the "Manufacture" area and first take a look at the menu bar in the upper area. There are the menu tabs "Milling", "Turning", "Additive", "Inspection", "Fabrication" and "Utilities". In the areas "Milling" to "Additive", you will always find the command or function "Setup", as well as important commands for the respective manufacturing type.

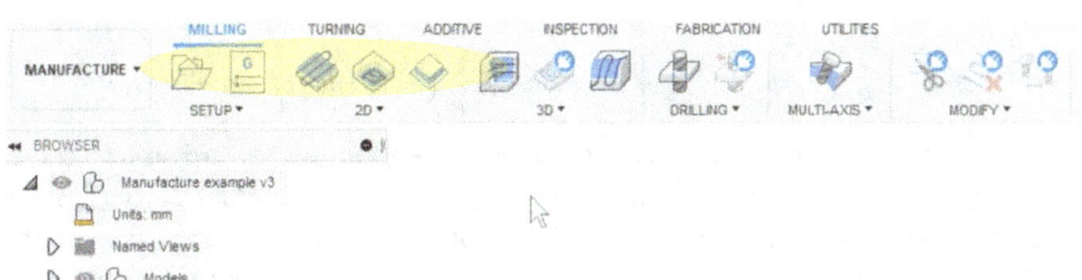

Figure 257: The "Milling", "Turning" and "Additive" production methods

In the following, we will deal with production planning for our example. To do this, we need to switch to the "Milling" tab, since we want to mill a pocket into the component. First we have to create a "Setup", i.e. make general specifications, as well as select our semi-finished product, i.e. the initial material.

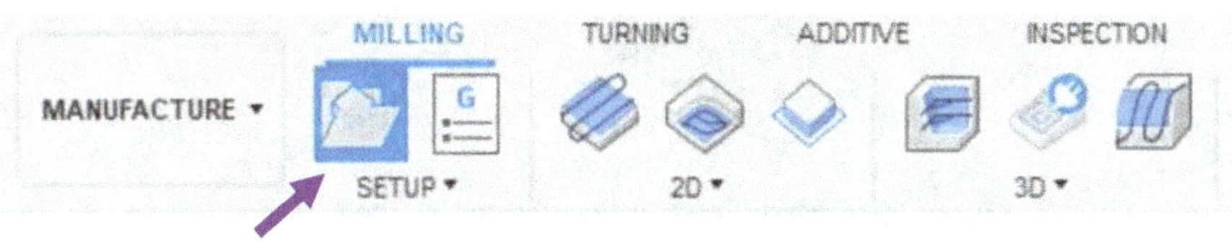

Figure 258: Select "Setup" in the "Milling" area; a window opens

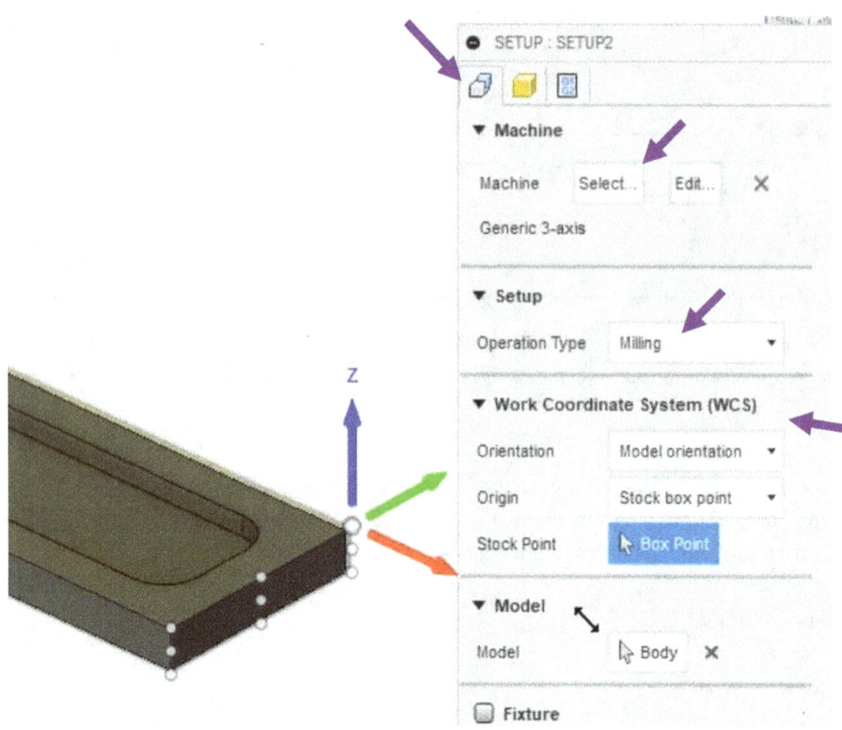

Figure 259: Place the WCS (work coordinate system) on a corner of the component

In the "Setup" area, we first select our machine, here as an example a 3-axis machine. Then the "Operation Type". We need "Milling". Another important setting, is the placement and orientation of the workpiece coordinate system "WCS". Orient the coordinate system so that it makes sense for the particular operation or machine. For "Milling", for example, the z-axis should point upwards, and the x and y-axes should define the milling plane. In our case, the orientation is already correct. For the origin we choose a point at the edge of the part.

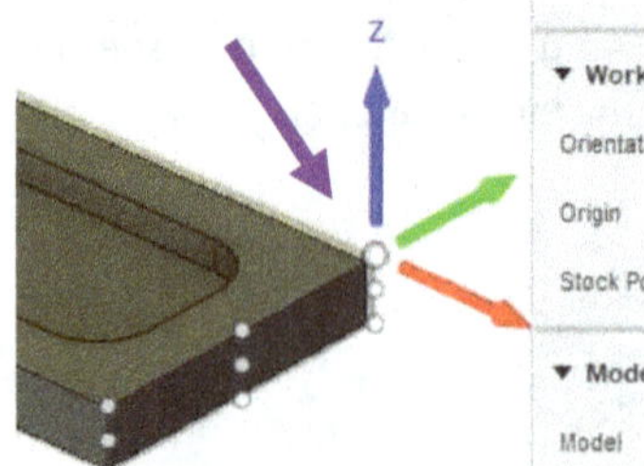

Figure 260: Set "WCS" coordinate system to a point on the edge

Then we switch to the "Stock" area in the "Setup" command menu and enter some data about our semi-finished material. Here, depending on the selected "Mode", we can make specifications for the size of the semi-finished part. For example, we can use "Fixed size box" to enter defined dimensions and specify where the model should be located within the semi-finished material. Since we do not want to edit the outer surfaces of our material and assume that we have already cut the correct dimensions, we select "from solid" and the part.

Figure 261: "Select "From Solid" in "Mode" under "Stock""

Our virtual CAD model for the milling is now identical to the outer dimensions of our semi-finished material. We can then exit the Setup menu. We select a suitable command in the 2D area, in order to determine the working path of the milling tool for the creation of the 2D pocket. As we can see, there are a wide variety of commands here, and it's best to take a closer look at them one by one. In our case, we need the "2D Pocket" command, with which we will create the path of the milling tool for the pocket.

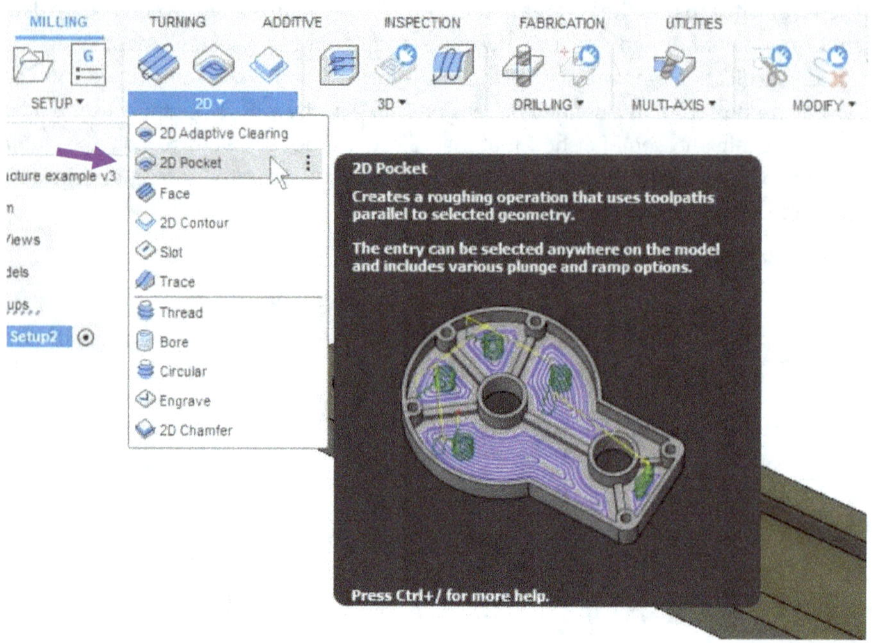

Figure 262: The 2D command "2D Pocket", which we will use to mill the cavity

A menu opens in which we have to make a few settings. First, we select a suitable milling tool in the "Tool" area.

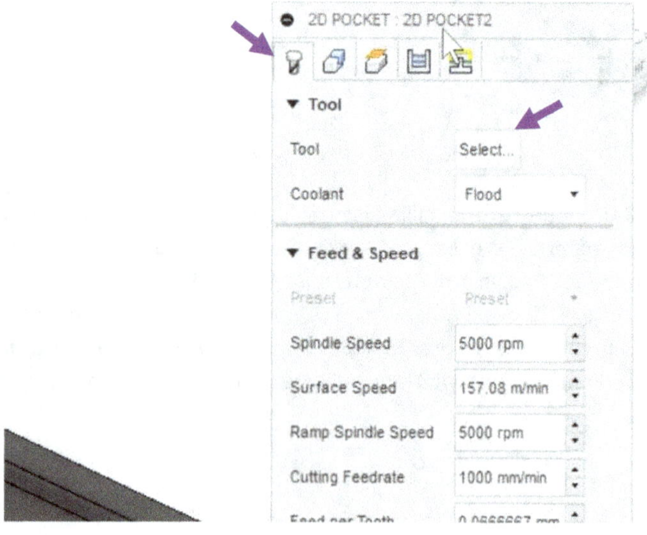

Figure 263: Select "Tool" in the menu box, a new window opens

You can either choose one in the Fusion 360 library or create your own. In this case, I'll select a 5 mm flat end mill as an example. Then, in the lower section "Cutting data", the most suitable process parameters are suggested to us, depending on the material and the type of machining. For example, we want to mill aluminum.

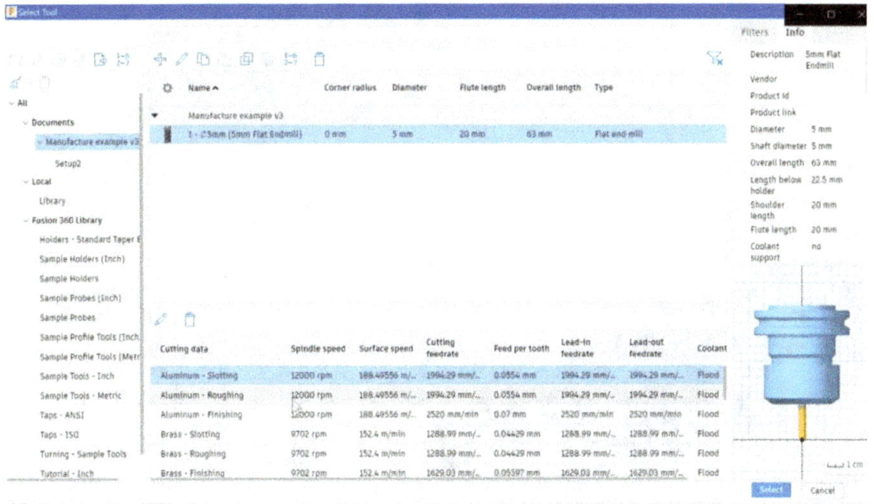

Figure 264: Select a tool in the new window and view the cutting data (below)

The cutter head displayed in transparent hovering over our workpiece coordinate system origin. In addition, the parameters for the tool settings have also been applied.

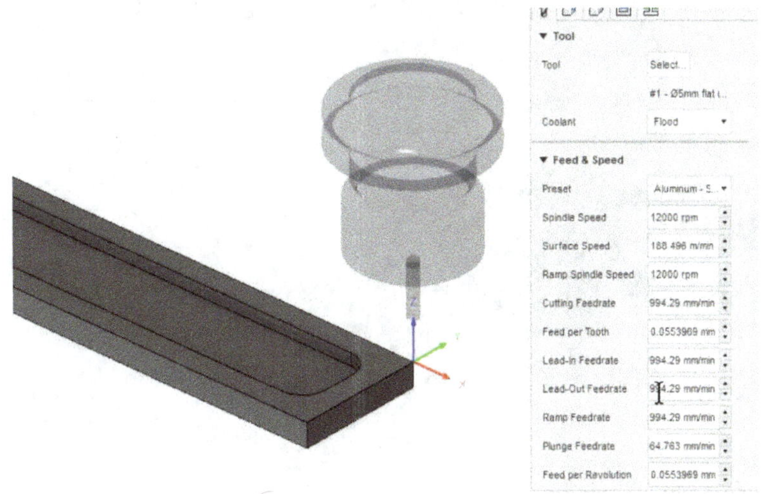

Figure 265: The simulated tool head is displayed transparently

If desired, these can of course also be modified individually. Then we have to determine which cavity we want to mill out at "Geometry".

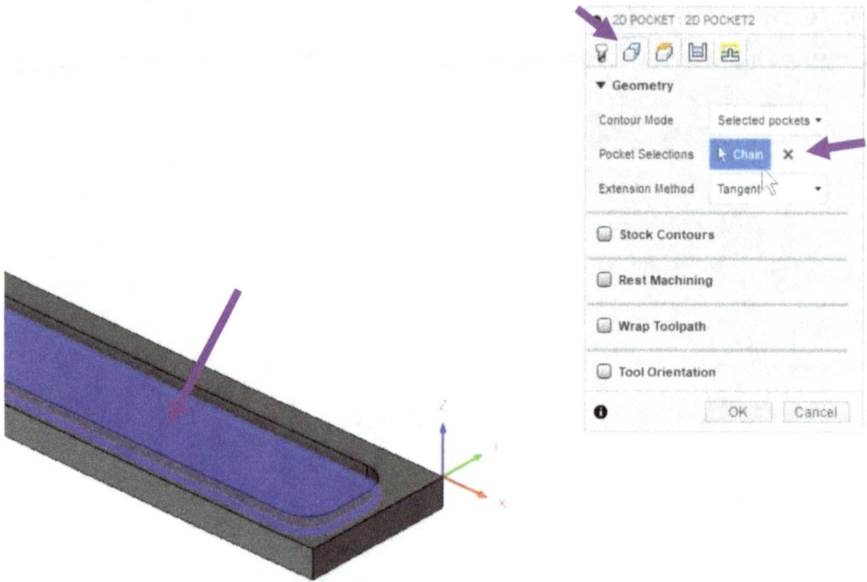

Figure 266: Switch to "Geometry" and select the cavity (click on the surface)

In the next tab "Heights" we have to define the heights in which the tool is to move for the operations "Clearance", "Retract" and "Feed", during manufacturing of the part.

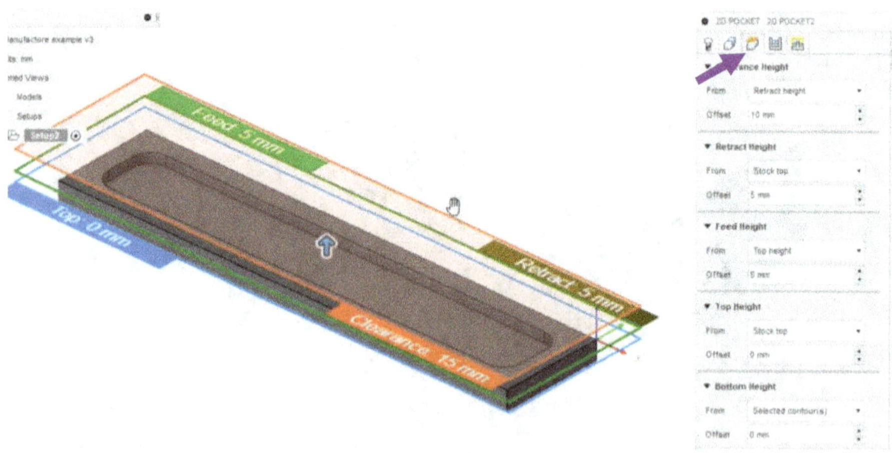

Figure 267: Determine the correct heights for the respective tool operations

Depending on the milling machine, you should adjust these values. In our case, we can leave the default values. In the next two sections, further special settings can be made. Each field shows a short explanation when you hove over it or when you select an option. Search for further important settings for your individual project as required. If you don't have any background knowledge in milling, turning or CNC machining, you should leave the "Manufacture" area alone for the time being anyway, but first enroll in a basic course for these manufacturing technologies. In our case we leave the other settings as they are. Then, we can display the tool and its working path by first selecting the created "2D Pocket" operation in the browser. With a right click and the selection of "Simulate" - which you can also find in the top menu - we can also view an animation of the manufacturing process.

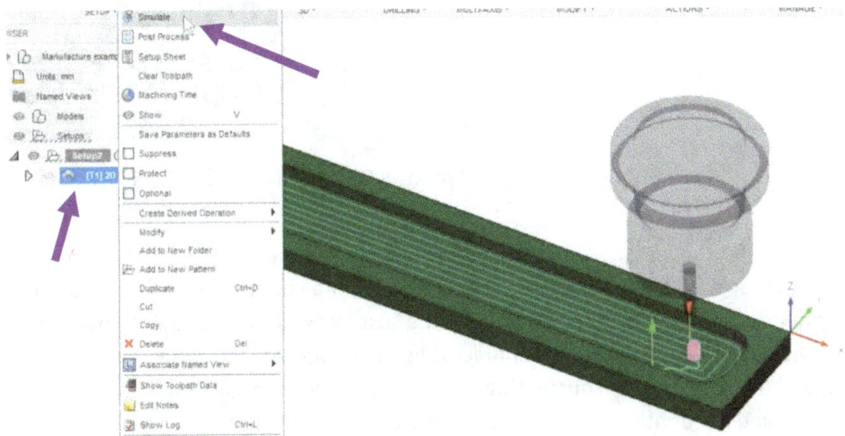

Figure 268: With a right click on the created "2D-Pocket" in the browser and the selection of "Simulate" the working path of the tool will get animated (press "Play")

Very good! We could machine the first component. For this we only have to create the "gcode", i.e. the code for the machine.

We do this with the command "Post Process" in the top menu bar. In this window, we first select the correct configuration for production type and machine and assign a name.

Then we can specify a location and create the "gcode" for machining.

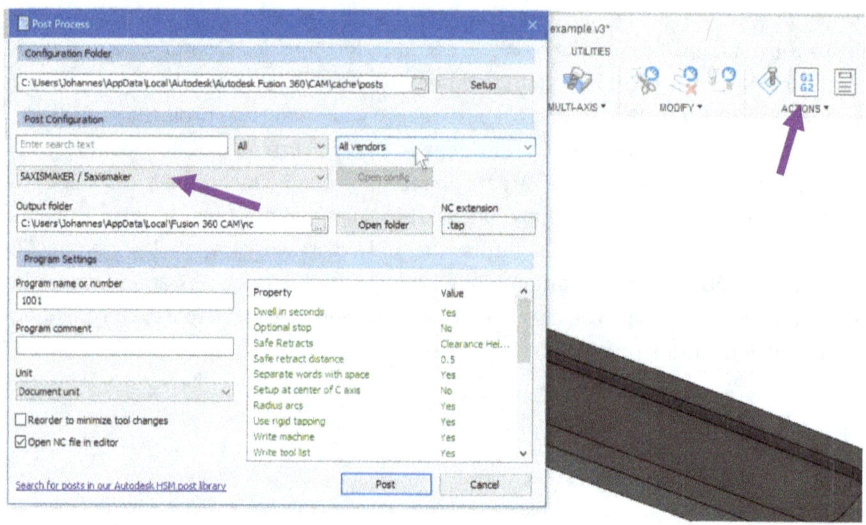

Figure 269: Create the ".gcode" for manufacturing using "Post Process"

The other options of the "Manufacture" area will not be discussed in more detail in this beginner's course, as this would not be useful without adequate background knowledge of the individual manufacturing technologies and types and would go beyond the scope of the course. However, it should be mentioned that operations for turning and 3D printing as well as for 5-axis CNC machines can also be created here. Fusion 360 offers numerous and very helpful functions for these purposes.

For the very exciting topic of 3D printing, I recommend that you take a closer look at my book "3D Printing | 101", in which you will learn in detail and step by step all the necessary hard- and software for 3D printing. If we don't manufacture a part in-house, Fusion 360 also gives us the option of creating technical drawings that we can then pass on to a manufacturing company. We'll see how that works in the next and also final chapter before we finish the course. Now we're almost done, let's move on to the last chapter!

10 Drawing

Welcome back to the last chapter of this Fusion 360 course! As mentioned in the previous chapter, if we don't want to or can't manufacture a part by ourself, e.g. because we don't have the machines to do so, we can create a technical drawing for a manufacturing company. To do this, we first add two 10 mm holes to our simple model, which are supposed to go through the component.

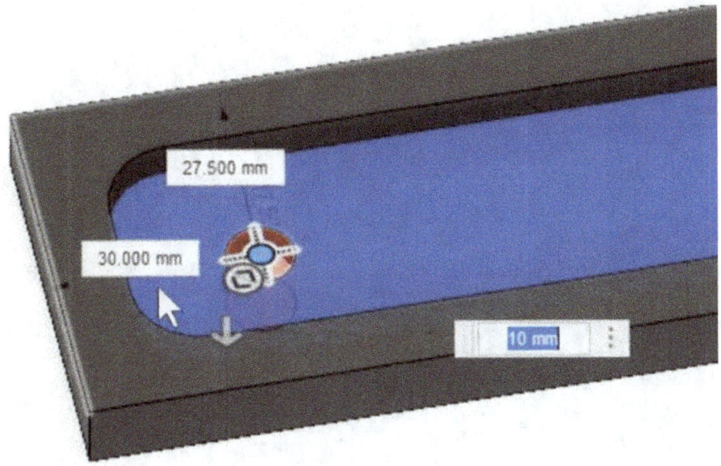

Figure 270: Create two holes (left and right 1x each) with the dimensions shown

In order to create a technical drawing from this CAD model, we switch to the tab "Drawing" -> "From Design" in the main menu.

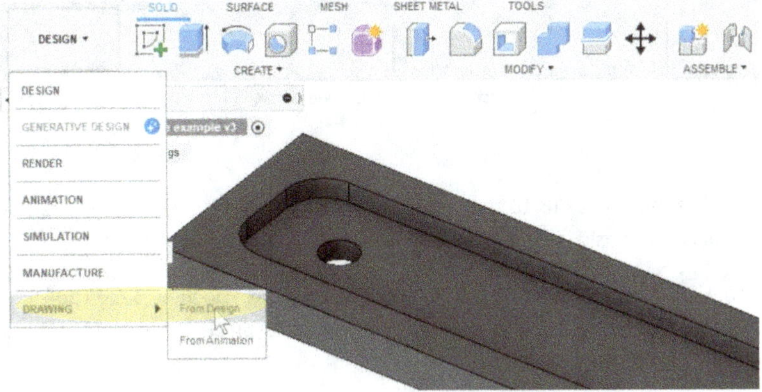

Figure 271: Switch to the "Drawing" - "From Design" tab

First we select the general drawing settings, i.e. we may use a template or we start with an empty template. It is also important to set the units and the paper size.

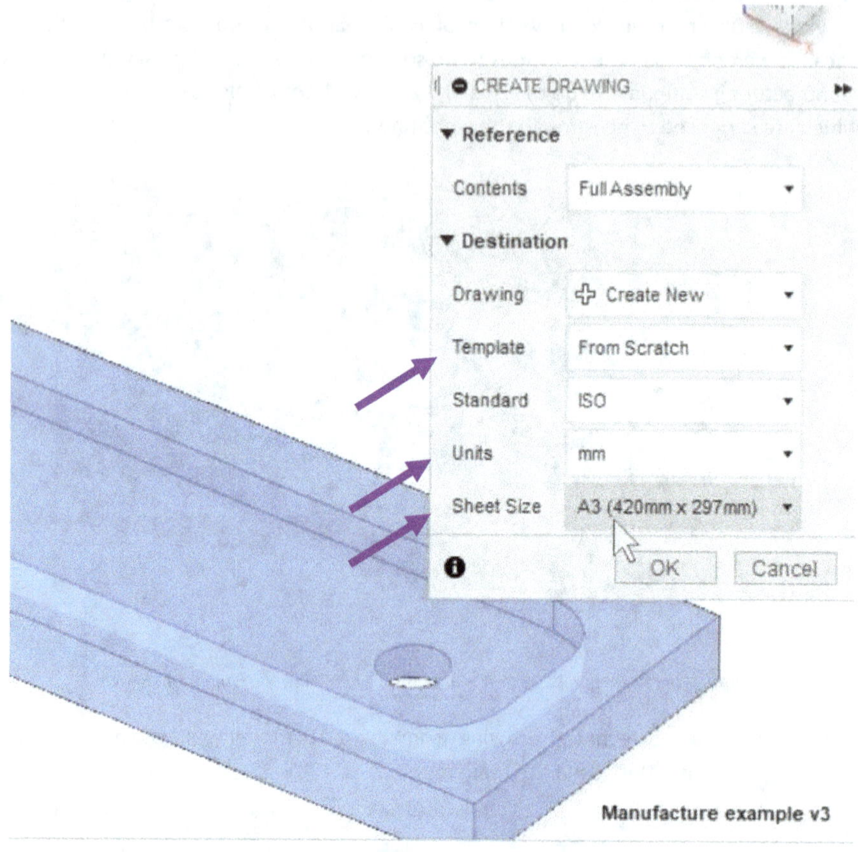

Figure 272: Before the program automatically switches to the drawing environment, we need to specify paper size and units

The program then takes us to the technical drawing environment. In the first step we have to place the basic view of the component on the drawing.

To do this, we select the orientation of the view, e.g. the top view, i.e. "Top" and scale the drawing view as desired, e.g. slightly larger. We place the first view by simply clicking anywhere on the sheet.

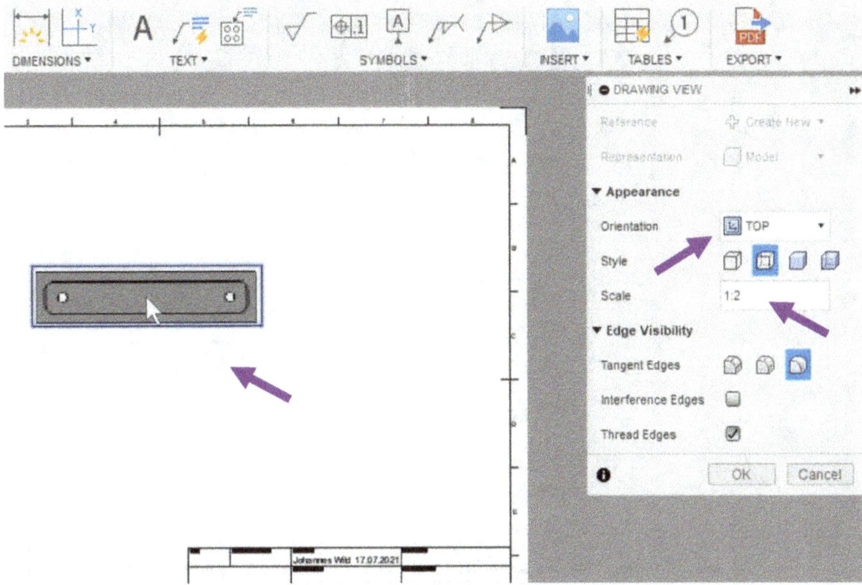

Figure 273: First select the orientation and scale, then click on the drawing sheet to set the first view of the part

A technical drawing is created in the form of a three-sided view, depending on the folding method. In simple terms, this means that the component is shown from above, from the side and, if necessary, from the front in order to be able to place all the necessary dimensions and other annotations. In addition, an isometric view is usually added to help with spatial imagination.

To place a new view, in this case a derived or projected view on the sheet, we use the "Projected view" command and create a second view by clicking on the component from which we want to derive a view.

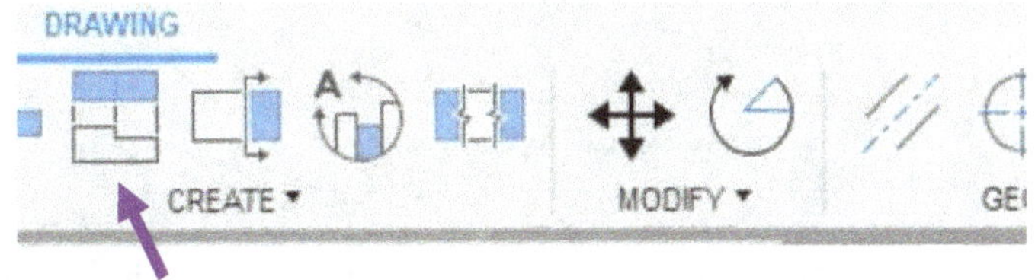

Figure 274: Select "Projected View" for one or more new views of the same component

Depending on where we move our mouse cursor, the referenced view is generated. For example, if we move up or down, the view from the front or back of the component is displayed, and the same applies to the sides. If we move diagonally, we are shown an isometric view.

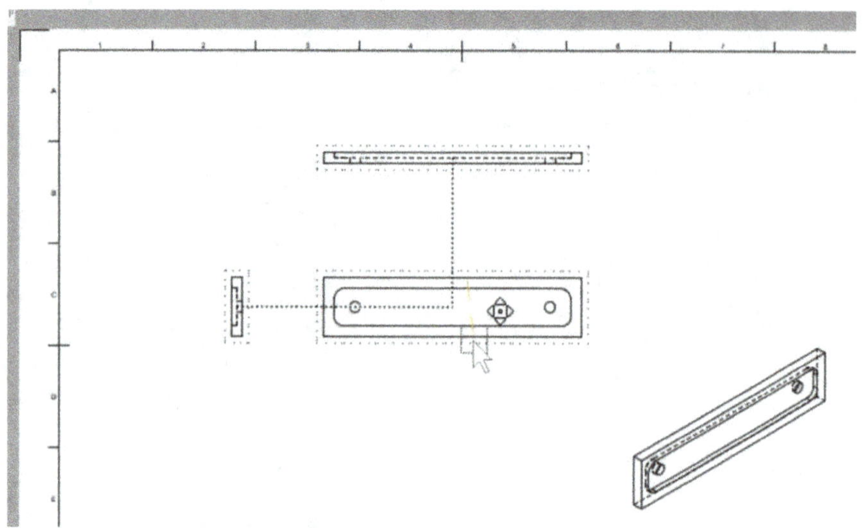

Figure 275: We would like to create the shown views using "Projected View"

In the top left menu, we can also create a section view: "section view", a detail view: "detail view" or break the view: "break view".

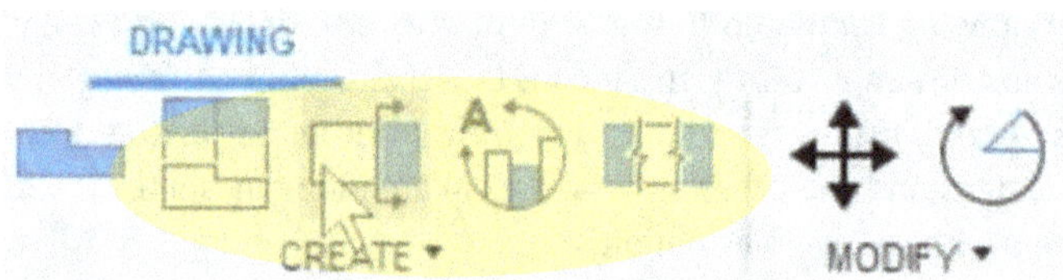

Figure 276: Create several views

The main dimensioning function is located at the top in the middle area and is called "Dimension" as usual. Using this function, we can create dimensions for our part.

Figure 277: Dimension the geometric elements with "Dimension"

It is almost the same as creating a 2D sketch, except that in this case we provide our finished part with dimensions that are already defined and serve as information for manufacturing.

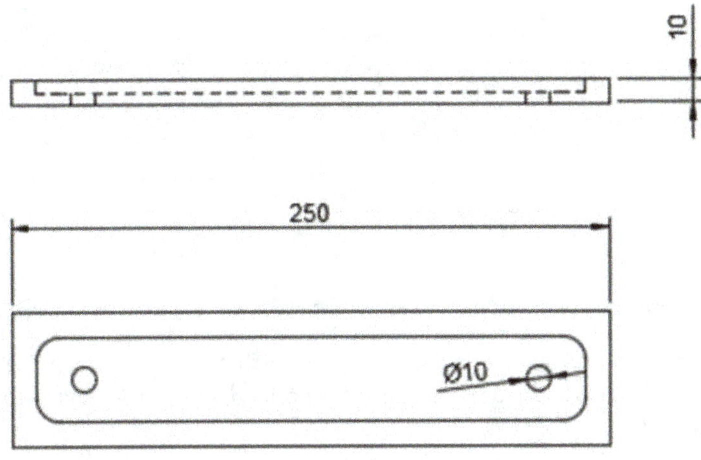

Figure 278: Place different measurements with "Dimension"

With the elements of "Geometry", we can furthermore draw some geometric information, such as a center line or, in this case, symmetry lines and circle centers.

Figure 279: Tools for center / symmetry lines or circle centers

For the symmetry line we simply select two parallel lines of the component and for the circle centers we simply select the desired holes or circles. By the way, by clicking on the dimensions we can also edit them or add more data, such as a quantity.

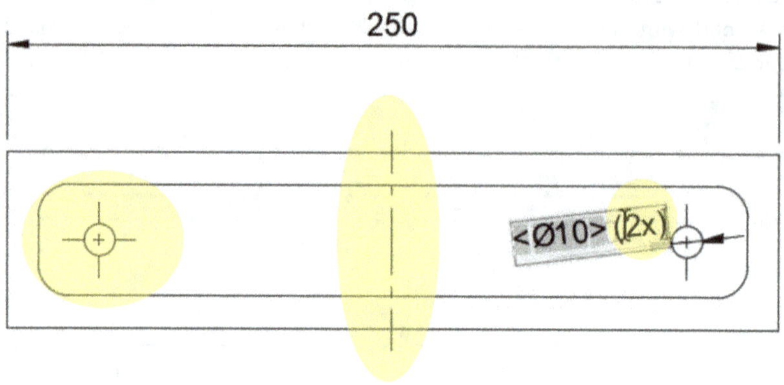

Figure 280: A view with symmetry line, circle centers and added dimension info

Perfect, now all information that a company would need for manufacturing is on the drawing. All lengths and widths, as well as the positions of the holes and deepening are dimensioned.

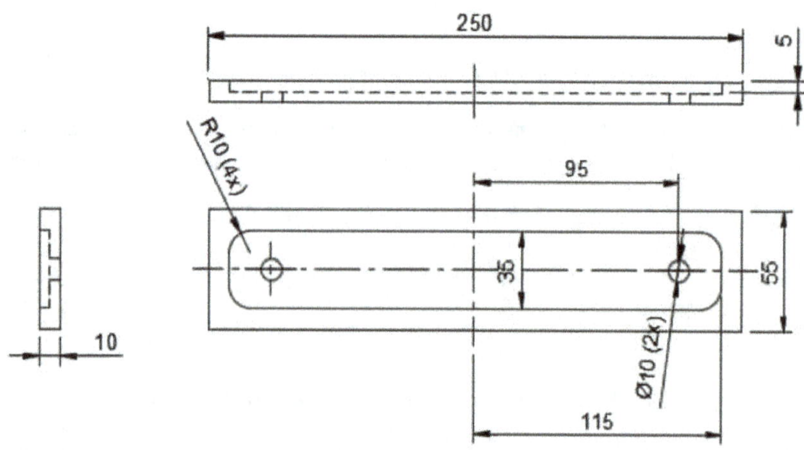

Figure 281: Fully dimensioned drawing of our part; isometric view not shown

If special characters are required to specify form and position tolerances, surface finishes or texts, these can be found in the upper right area of the menu bar.

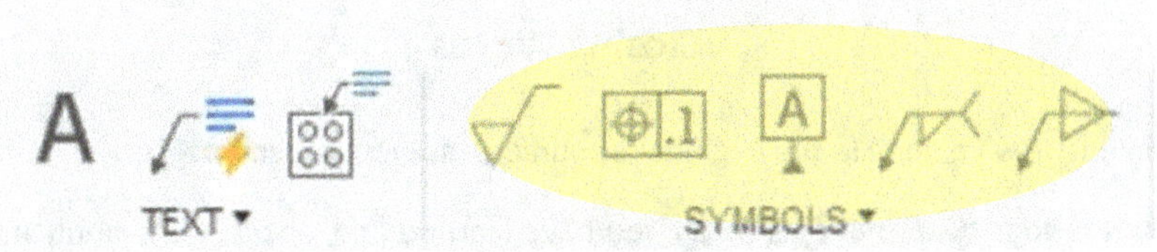

Figure 282: Special characters for dimensioning surface properties, tolerances and more

By the way, additional sheets can be added in the bar in the lower area, depending on the space required for drawing. After the title block has been filled with title, drawing number, material and other information, the drawing can be saved e.g. as ".pdf" and printed!

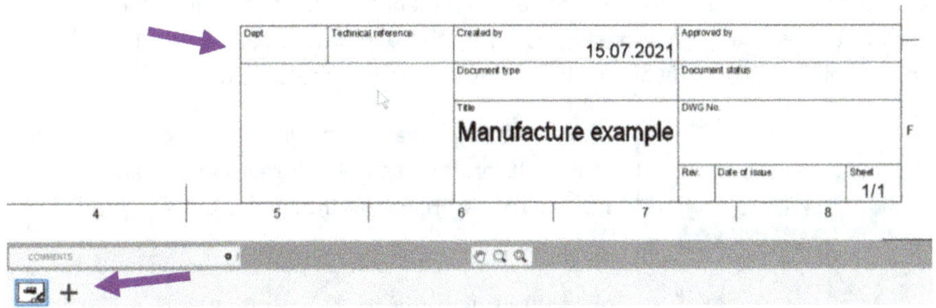

Figure 283: Add a new sheet (bottom; "+" symbol) and fill in title block

Closing Words

Excellent! You've done it, the beginner's course ends with this chapter!

Now it is your turn to deepen what you have learned and, above all, to apply it. You should now have a firm understanding of the most important functions of Fusion 360, and you can approach new projects, CAD designs, simulations and everything that goes with them on your own!

Congratulations!

You have learned all the relevant operations and features in this course. This enables you to design, simulate, render, animate and manufacture or have manufactured your own CAD files in a quick and easy way. Together we have accomplished quite a bit in this course! Be proud of yourself if you have made it to this lesson!

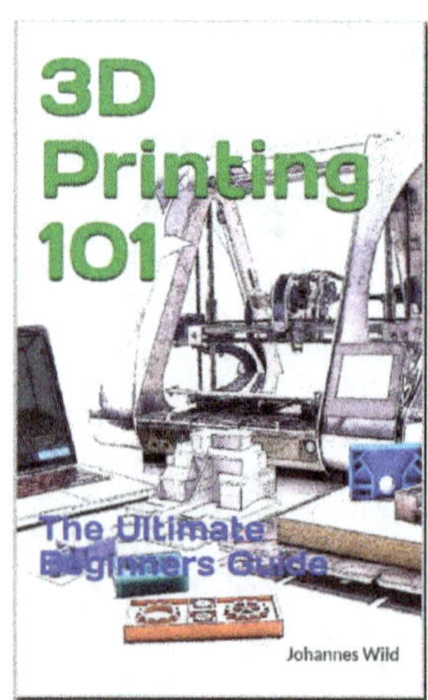

And as mentioned at the beginning of the course, take a look at 3D printing as well. It's really greate and useful to be able to materialize your own designs.

This way you can create parts in-home and have a solution at hand for all sorts of no longer available but urgently needed spare parts or anything else. The best way to do learn is to use my book: "3D Printing | 101" and get your copy rightaway.

If you enjoyed this Fusion 360 course, it would mean a lot to me and other interested persons if you leave me a rating and a short feedback, as well as recommend the book! Thank you very much!

Books you might also like

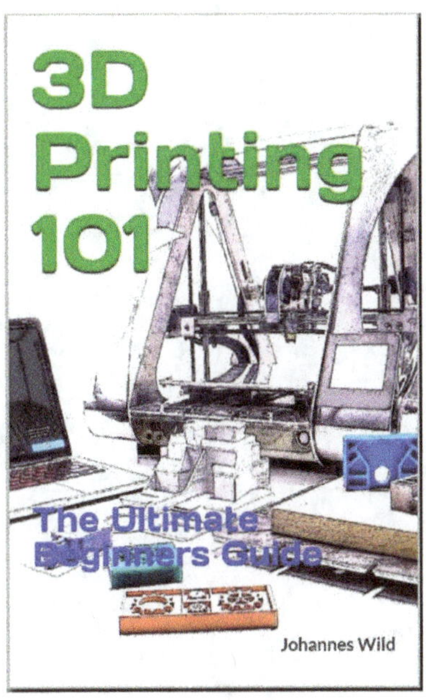

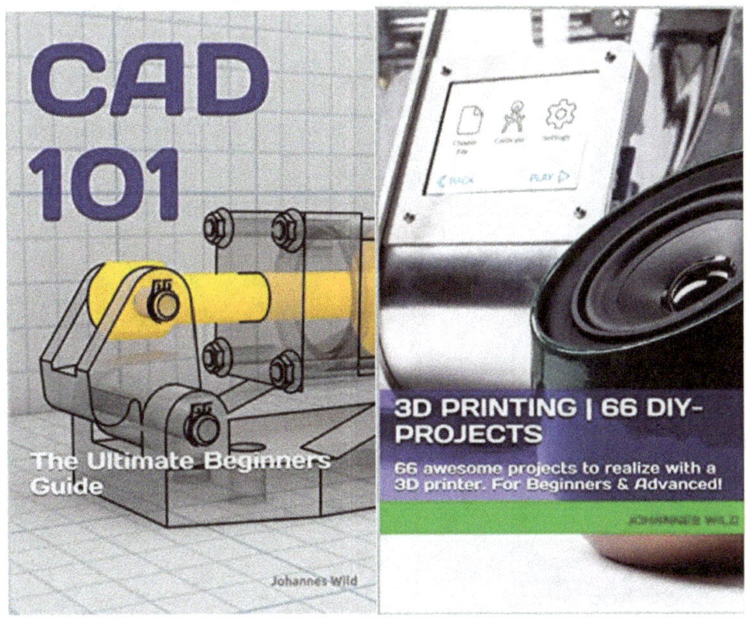

www.ingramcontent.com/pod-product-compliance
Lightning Source LLC
LaVergne TN
LVHW021317200726
843509LV00002B/66